PSYCHODYNAMIC CHILD AND ADOLESCENT PSYCHOTHERAPY

PSYCHODYNAMIC CHILD AND ADOLESCENT PSYCHOTHERAPY

Theories and Methods

Liselotte Grünbaum and
Karen Vibeke Mortensen

KARNAC

First published in Danish as *Psykodynamisk Psykoterapi med Børn og Unge – En Grundbog om Teorier og Arbejdsmetoder* in 2016
by Hans Reitzels Forlag

This expanded and updated version in English first published in 2018 by
Karnac Books Ltd
118 Finchley Road, London NW3 5HT

British Library Cataloguing in Publication Data

A C.I.P. for this book is available from the British Library

ISBN 978 1 78220 522 7

Edited, designed and produced by The Studio Publishing Services Ltd
www.publishingservicesuk.co.uk
email: studio@publishingservicesuk.co.uk

Printed in Great Britain

www.karnacbooks.com

CONTENTS

PART II
THERAPEUTIC SETTINGS AND THE THERAPEUTIC RELATIONSHIP

PART III
THE EXPERIENCE OF TIME IN THE PERSPECTIVE OF OBJECT RELATIONSHIPS

PART IV
PSYCHOTHERAPY WITH CHILDREN WHO HAVE SUFFERED MALTREATMENT AND COMPLEX TRAUMA

ACKNOWLEDGEMENTS

We are deeply grateful to the children and young people and their parents who have taught us so much, not only about how to conduct child and adolescent psychotherapy, but also about human generosity by forgiving our mistakes. They taught us the importance of observing and listening with empathy in order to take a gentle approach and avoid rushing headlong into painful areas while also not shying away from painful topics that it is helpful to share with another human being.

We also thank our copy-editor, Dorte H. Silver, for her invaluable help in the preparation of this manuscript, not only for her patience in correcting and enriching our English, but also for picking up on ambiguities and inconsistencies that needed to be addressed.

The book contains a number of case descriptions and brief clinical examples from child and adolescent psychotherapies. The majority of these originate from our own psychotherapeutic practice, but we also wish to thank psychologists Anna Julie Højsgaard and Lisbeth Vagn Søgaard for their permission to reproduce material that was originally brought in for supervision purposes.

Finally, we thank our Danish publishers, Hans Reitzels, for their permission to publish the book in English.

ABOUT THE AUTHORS

Liselotte Grünbaum (MSc in psychology, PhD) is a registered psychologist, specialist practitioner, and supervisor of clinical child psychology and psychotherapy. Her PhD work, concluded with the dissertation *Breaks as a Window to Core Object Relationship Themes* (2014), was carried out at the University of East London and the Tavistock and Portman NHS Foundation Trust. She is a member of the Tavistock Society of Psychotherapists (TSP). Drawing on her extensive work experience with children, adolescents, and their families in various public settings, she is currently in private practice in Copenhagen, a part-time associate professor at Aalborg University, and a teacher and supervisor in the Danish training programme for psychoanalytic child and adolescent psychotherapists. She is a former co-ordinator of the Child and Adolescent Section of the European Federation of Psychoanalytic Psychotherapy. She has published several articles in English on child and adolescent psychotherapy and clinical child psychology with children suffering the after-effects of early neglect and complex traumatisation. Together with Karen Vibeke Mortensen, she co-edited *Play and Power* (2010) in the EFFP book series.

Karen Vibeke Mortensen (MSc in Psychology, DEd) is a registered psychologist and group analyst, and a specialist practitioner and supervisor of psychotherapy and child psychology. She is an honorary professor of clinical child psychology at Aalborg University and is in private practice in Copenhagen. She has extensive teaching and supervision experience, including teaching and providing supervision in the Danish training programme for psychoanalytic child and adolescent psychotherapists. She has edited books and articles on various clinical and theoretical subjects, including group analysis with children and adolescents, theories of psychopathology, assessment, research, psychodynamic psychotherapy with adults, and supervision. Her doctoral thesis, *Form and Content in Children's Human Figure Drawings*, was published by NYU Press in 1991. Together with Liselotte Grünbaum, she has edited *Play and Power* (2010) in the EFFP book series.

FOREWORD

Margaret Rustin

It is a great pleasure for me to write with admiration and enthusiasm about this book. It is an impressive and most welcome addition to the growing international literature of psychoanalytic child psychotherapy. The establishment of the profession of child psychotherapy in many European countries over the past fifty years has been a remarkable story, and it is exciting that two senior Danish child psychotherapists have had the courage to write the kind of knowledgeable, interesting, and readable introduction to the whole field that is needed.

Readers will welcome the clarity of exposition, the breadth of focus, the sensitivity of the presentation of the clinical material used in illustration, and the intelligence with which the authors have integrated their experience in describing the rationale and methods of their work. The professional community has reason to be very grateful that such a coherent and wide-ranging volume has been written at a time when the need for accessible and scholarly accounts of psychoanalytic approaches to mental distress in children is so pressing.

The book begins with a historical account of the intellectual origins of psychoanalytic work with children, and offers a careful definition of what constitutes a psychoanalytic or, more inclusively framed, psychodynamic approach to child psychotherapy. The major ideas informing clinical practice are outlined and the scene is set for chapters that discuss referral and assessment, the nature of the clinical setting, the relationship between child and therapist, the function of play, and the complexity of how to relate to parents.

These two first sections contain a distillation of what must have been a remarkable collaboration between long-term colleagues. The writing flows naturally and there are many memorable sentences that seem to express with economy the essence of child psychotherapy thinking. Many are quotable and it is easy to imagine that indeed they will be in the years to come. I will pick out a few of the insights that particularly struck me to give a taste of their way of going about things.

Particularly outstanding is the way that the "two-way relationship" between child and therapist is described. The transference of child to therapist and the therapist's countertransference, much of it inevitably not conscious, are presented as the core of the matter, while, at the same time, the therapist's task of observation of child and herself means that she has a dual-track engagement with what takes place. There is no avoidance here of the necessary subjective involvement of the therapist, with all its potential for disturbance. Yet, simultaneously, we are given a beautifully clear picture of the cognitive resources psychoanalytic theory now provides. The line of theoretical development running from Freud to Klein and Bion, with, of course, many other significant contributions, is the backbone of their understanding of the development of mind.

The authors make evident their commitment to established psychoanalytic technique in which the therapist's scrutiny of her own feelings belongs in private reflection or in supervision. They distinguish between the special demands of the therapeutic relationship created by child and therapist in the therapy room and more "goal-directed" thinking, which is a discourse the therapist must engage in externally with parents or institutions, or both. Reasonably enough, the adults supporting a child's therapy will want to know what is being achieved within it. All this challenges those of us working in publicly funded clinics to think hard about the pressures to predefine goals and to privilege conscious feedback and behavioural outcome.

However, the classical rigour of their technique turns out to include space for humour, the value of surprise, and a great deal of flexibility in ways of working. While child and therapist are indeed in an asymmetric relationship, it is the therapist's task to find a way for the child to communicate his worries. The balance evident in their discussion of technical problems, as, indeed, also in their assessment of the different contributions of the various schools of child psychotherapy, is admirable. While their own position is close to contemporary Kleinian child psychotherapy, their range of reference and interest is impressively wide and this will make their book of great value to a broad spectrum of clinicians.

When they explore initial steps in work with a case, their practicality and openness to doing things differently, depending on the case, is what I appreciated. Cases are described, for example, in which family consultations are what are needed, or joint work with a child and parent, or considerable initial work with parents before seeing a child. One topic not discussed is work with siblings, which perhaps deserves a larger place in clinical thinking and practice. The emphasis in work with parents on the combination of shame and guilt that many parents are burdened by is most helpful. They define the locus of the therapeutic alliance in work with children not so much as what we find between child and therapist, but, rather, what is needed between therapist and parents. This is a really interesting and original way of bringing together the language of child psychotherapy with the concepts of psychotherapy as a broad field. The difference in working with children is a big and important topic, particularly in the context of so much cognitively based work being provided for adults. The authors make a powerful case for therapy for children based on an emotional relationship as what is best suited to facilitate their development, and that development is what we should be aiming for.

Both the framework of public clinic and of private practice are in their minds and their recommendations, therefore, attend to these very different contexts. The chapter on work with parents is helpful in thinking about what is possible and necessary to support ongoing therapy with a child. Limitations in what is now provided for parents in clinics is, I think, quite a serious difficulty and this book's way of demonstrating the difference between giving a child a psychiatric diagnosis and understanding the basis for the symptomatic difficulties takes us straight back to the question of family context and parental functioning.

Variation in the level of provision of child psychotherapy and in psychoanalytic cultures between countries is, of course, a fact of life, but the authors' wide reading has ensured that some of these are taken into account. In the later sections of the book, there are chapters that resonate strongly with the current clinical experience of therapists across Europe. Deprivation, neglect, loss, and maltreatment and trauma are addressed at length. These chapters bring alive the children, their families, and their therapists in painful detail and give a proper sense of the necessity for longer-term and more intensive work with such children.

There are two sections that draw on current research in child psychotherapy, one a most useful overview, and one making use of the work of one of the authors on breaks (interruptions in the regular rhythm of therapy sessions) in child psychotherapy, seen as "a window to fundamental relationship themes". This makes available extremely interesting material from a meticulous doctoral study of a long-term psychotherapy case in which the child's response to breaks, both planned and unplanned, was investigated, and the results linked to an understanding of fundamental processes in development. Other recent work on the importance of the experience of time, of beginnings and endings in life and therapy, links naturally with this theme.

I believe the authors hope to publish a second volume based on case histories. On the basis of the quality of the thinking they have demonstrated in this book, we must certainly hope that they go ahead with that project. There might not be a very large group of child psychotherapists in Denmark, but these two have certainly written a book we have needed and done it outstandingly well.

Introduction

This book is a translation of the first volume of a previous Danish publication: *Psykodynamisk Psykoterapi med Børn og Unge—En Grundbog om Teorier og Arbejdsmetoder* (2016). Strictly speaking, however, this book is not quite like the original in all respects, but, rather, an extended version. As we struggled to articulate our ideas in a language that is not our native tongue, some of our previous thinking seemed to take on new dimensions, sometimes adding new depths, sometimes bringing forth previously undetected ambiguities, all in all inviting a second working through.

The book is intended as a textbook, describing the basic theories, principles, and methods relating to any psychodynamic child and adolescent psychotherapy; in addition, however, we have included discussions and illustrations of more complicated concepts and techniques that are relevant in work with severely disillusioned children and adolescents. Thus, the book targets both novice therapists, who are just beginning their professional training and who need a detailed account of psychotherapeutic theories, setting, and methods, and experienced psychotherapists wishing to enrich their work with an updated overview of established concepts and techniques as well as newer developments in the field.

Psychodynamic child and adolescent psychotherapy had its early beginning in classical psychoanalysis. Since then, myriad psychoanalytic and psychodynamic ways of working have developed. We have chosen the term psychodynamic rather than psychoanalytic child and adolescent psychotherapy because we feel a need to emphasise affinities and common methodical starting points between various psychodynamic child and adolescent psychotherapies. We contend that psychodynamic child and adolescent psychotherapies share at least two principal features which differentiate them from other psychotherapeutic traditions. The first is a firm conviction that therapeutic action primarily comes about through the therapeutic relationship, wherefore this should be the psychodynamic therapist's primary focus. The second is the continual inclusion of non-conscious and unconscious impressions, experiences, feelings, and phantasies in the therapist's thinking, whether her chosen way of working encourages verbalising these or not, based on the keen awareness that subjective phenomena originating in the minds of both participants contribute to the development of the relationship and process.

For simplicity's sake and in reflection of the fact that even today, most child and adolescent psychotherapists are female, throughout the book, the feminine "she" refers to the therapist, and the masculine "he" refers to the child, except in reference to specific cases.

The book is divided into five parts. Part I contains three chapters that all deal with the preconditions for the feasibility and effect of psychodynamic child and adolescent psychotherapy. The first is thorough knowledge of child development and the development of psychopathology; the second is knowledge of the theories and methods of psychodynamic child and adolescent psychotherapy; the third is familiarity with the procedures of referral and assessment.

Chapter One gives a short presentation of the most important psychodynamic theories of both normal and psychopathological development during childhood and adolescence. Child and adolescent psychotherapy has its origins in early psychoanalysis. The most important of the first pioneers were Anna Freud and Melanie Klein, who laid the theoretical and methodological foundation for child and adolescent psychotherapy. A number of later theorists and psychotherapists, particularly within object relation theory, have elaborated on, and expanded, our knowledge about both healthy and pathological development in children and adolescents and methods of treatment, among others, Donald Winnicott and Wilfred Bion. After the Second World War, John Bowlby and his colleagues developed their theories about the infant's early attachment to his carers, contributing with crucial new insight into children's early development. Later contributions from Daniel Stern and from neuropsychology are briefly mentioned. Development during adolescence calls for special attention and has been described by a number of theorists. The understanding of psychopathology in children has changed in line with the general theoretical shifts that have taken place in psychoanalysis, and the current understanding is very different from the early theories. The chapter is concluded with a discussion of the classification of psychopathology and complications in the use of the current diagnostic systems, which rest on theories that are fundamentally different from the psychodynamic theories and operate with a very different understanding of psychopathology.

In Chapter Two, we describe what psychodynamic child and adolescent psychotherapy is, the broadly defined principles that guide the practice of it, and the mental and interpersonal mechanisms through which it operates. This kind of therapy is driven mainly by the relationship between the child and the psychotherapist and their mutual communication. The balance of their relationship shapes the development of a transference–countertransference relationship between them and this focus on the transference relationship is the key factor distinguishing this kind of therapy from other approaches. A definition of psychodynamic child and adolescent psychotherapy, resting on modern Kleinian principles, is suggested. The therapeutic attitude and a number of different interventions are outlined. The concepts of projective identification and containment are central to the understanding of the therapeutic stance. These concepts are described along with the ability to form symbols and to adopt a relational way of thinking. The distinction between aims and methods is emphasised. In closing, some key differences between different traditions in psychodynamic psychotherapy are outlined.

Chapter Three contains a description of referral and assessment procedures and emphasises the importance of a sufficiently thorough assessment, not only of the child, but also of his parents and his environment. It is described how, for several reasons, assessment of a child or an adolescent differs from assessment of an adult. The necessity of building a good working alliance with the child's parents is emphasised. The individual steps of the assessment process are outlined, including early contact with the referring agency, gathering the child's history, and assessment of the child, including his personality functions and total personality structure. The most important outcome is not the formulation of a psychiatric diagnosis, but an understanding of the essential problems, how extensive they are, and where they lie. A potential intervention should be planned on the basis of the assessment and be communicated to the child's parents or other carers as well as to the child or young person. Finally, the chapter describes the conditions under which individual child psychotherapy is the method of choice, and what the process requires of the parents and of the treatment organisation.

Part II consists of five chapters that deal with the therapeutic setting and the therapeutic relationship. Chapter Four is about the setting, which may be defined in a narrow as well as a wider sense. The narrow setting consists of the therapy room and its furnishings, play materials, agreements, and time—that is, frequency and duration of the therapy. The importance of a stable setting is emphasised. However, both the therapist and the child will inevitably necessitate breaks and other breaches of the boundaries; how these can be handled is discussed. The wider setting is understood as the organisation in which the psychotherapy takes place. To enable individual psychotherapy, a good understanding of, and a structure for, safeguarding the unique requirements of this process must be in place in the organisation.

Chapter Five deals with the therapeutic relationship in child and adolescent psychotherapy, which is understood as a complex, composite concept, constituted on the basis of the following three dimensions: a transference relationship, a current, real-life object relationship, and a therapeutic alliance. In the development of the therapeutic relationship, these dimensions unfold as interrelated processes, which, in practice, cannot be observed independently of one another. The chapter describes the development from an initial, not yet personal, transference attitude to the development of highly personal and specific crises in the transference relationship. The therapeutic alliance in child psychotherapy is more difficult to define than in psychotherapy with an adult. We discuss how such an alliance might be facilitated, what characterises it, and how the therapist can test whether such an alliance is in the making.

Chapter Six concerns the child's spontaneous symbolic expressions, for instance, pictorial representations and symbolic play, as communication about his inner world. Creating a picture requires a suitable balance between an impulse to express oneself and a controlling or structuring force that might modify it. Through pictures and other forms of symbolic expression, the child can often express things that he is not yet conscious of. Consequently, the therapist needs to be careful with her interpretations. Play—and not talk—is the child's spontaneous form of expression and offers him the opportunity to explore and go over his experiences and feelings, test their reality, and learn from his experiences. The child, therefore, needs space and time to use his toys according to his inner processes. The young child's play can be characterised by psychic equivalence, with a lack of differentiation between object and symbol, and the same could be true of traumatised children. The chapter ends with reflections on pictorial production and symbolic play as a special kind of language, analogic or primary process communication, and on the difficulties of translating these kinds of language into our ordinary spoken language.

Work with parents is a central, but sometimes underestimated, element in any psychotherapy with a child or young person. This subject is discussed in Chapter Seven. Such work can be particularly complex if the parents are divorced, or if they are foster parents. Work with parents has some general characteristics; for example, the parents often experience feelings of guilt and shame about their child's problems, but, apart from this, the work develops in different and specific ways, depending on the parents' personalities and general situation. In the chapter, two models of parent work are described, with respective reference to Chethik (1989) and Rustin (2000). They both distinguish between four partially different forms, ranging from mostly supportive work on a relatively conscious level to work on increasingly deep and unconscious levels. A number of aims for the work with parents as well as the methodology of this special work is discussed. In closing, the chapter describes the co-operation with the network around the child that is commonly important.

The final chapter in Part II, Chapter Eight, is about psychotherapy with adolescents. Adolescents differ from children in a number of ways, including their physical development and sexual maturation. Furthermore, they are undergoing a process of separation from their parents, increasing independence, and a change in their position in society. All these factors inevitably influence psychotherapy with adolescents, and the methods in this work, therefore, differ from those in psychotherapy with both children and adults. Adolescents do not play the way children do, but neither can they express themselves verbally as well as adults can; thus, psychotherapy with adolescents might require both flexibility and creativity of the therapist. Psychotherapy with adolescents can trigger characteristic and often intense countertransference feelings in the therapist. As in work with children, co-operation and work with parents and the surrounding network is important.

Part III deals with time in relationship to child and adolescent psychotherapy and comprises two chapters. Chapter Nine addresses beginnings and endings of psychotherapy. The chapter begins with a presentation of the child's experience of space and time, which is closely interwoven with the emotional quality of his early object relations. Before the beginning of a psychotherapy, sufficient preparation of the parents should take place to ensure that they understand what child therapy is about, the purpose of their own sessions, their own role in the process, and how they can prepare their child for his first therapy session. The therapist's first meeting with the child and the importance of it in the future therapeutic relationship is discussed. The ending is a process that should be considered from the outset of therapy. The child's experience of the ending might be seen to reflect his general way of dealing with separation and absence. The chapter contains considerations about when it is appropriate to end psychotherapy and descriptions of emotional themes that often come up in that process. Finally, the arrangements and time structure of endings are discussed and what to do in case of unanticipated endings.

Breaks, whether planned or unplanned, are unavoidable. That is the main theme of Chapter Ten. We assume that every child has certain core object relationships, created early in life, which can also be recognised in his relationship with the therapist. Case studies by, among others, Grünbaum (2014) have shown that breaks could intensify and clarify such fundamental relational themes and the related defensive phantasies and reactions. Some characteristic reaction patterns are outlined. Different reactions might be found to occur before and after the breaks. It is important to remember that breaks are not only stressful, but also a precondition for development and growth.

In Part IV, we address the issue of psychotherapy for children and adolescents who have suffered maltreatment and complex traumatisation. Chapter Eleven reviews issues that might complicate psychotherapy with children who have suffered severe psychosocial deprivation, neglect, and/or abuse early in life. We begin with a historical outline of these concepts and a description of the current diagnostic systems in the field. Certain preconditions must be met for psychotherapy with this group of children and adolescents to be effective; among other things, the therapy must have sufficient duration and frequency, and certain modifications of the therapeutic setting and way of working might be necessary. This places great demands on the therapist's abilities and skills, and qualified supervision is necessary unless the therapist is very experienced. She will often encounter strong opposition in the shape of rejection and distrust as well as explosive rage and chaotic dissociation. Specific strategies might, therefore, be necessary when working with these children. Towards the end of the chapter, a number of relevant strategies are outlined.

In Chapter Twelve, we describe psychotherapy with children who have suffered complex trauma. The chapter offers a definition of the concept and describes the relevant diagnostic categories. Next, the concept is addressed from a psychodynamic perspective, and a distinction is made between acute shock trauma and complex trauma. A developmental adaption to complex trauma often takes place, which is important to know and understand for therapists working in this field. The work confronts the therapist with major challenges; for example, the children might be inhibited in their play and capacity for symbolisation and might prefer not to deal with traumatic feelings and memories, which will make it difficult for them to accept emotional understanding. We describe how a working through of the traumatic memories can be facilitated, and a number of important psychotherapeutic strategies are outlined that could be useful in working with complex trauma.

Part V deals with research in child and adolescent psychotherapy and comprises only one chapter, Chapter Thirteen, describing the current state of the field. There are special complications in doing research with children; for example, meaningful research requires the researcher to have both research and clinical training. Outcome research in child and adolescent psychotherapy is further complicated by the complexity of the treatment: for example, the requirement of always including the parents. In the beginning, research in child and adolescent psychotherapy mostly consisted of single-case studies. The growing pressure to document the effectiveness of psychotherapy led to considerable growth in outcome research in the form of randomised control trials (RCTs), which, however, were not easily generalised to ordinary practice. Over the past twenty years, however, there has been considerable development, and a number of systematic reviews of outcome research are now available. They demonstrate that psychodynamic child and adolescent psychotherapy has a positive and lasting effect on a number of mental disorders in children and adolescents, including some of the most severe. Process research is important in order not only to illustrate what works, but also how and why it works. Process research calls for systematic qualitative research, a field that has been lagging, but which now seems to be receiving growing attention.

PART I

FOUNDATIONS OF PSYCHODYNAMIC CHILD AND ADOLESCENT PSYCHOTHERAPY

CHAPTER ONE

Psychodynamic theories of development and psychopathology

Psychotherapeutic work with children was introduced in the early days of psychoanalysis. In 1912, the Austrian teacher Hermine Hug-Hellmuth published a monograph about child psychotherapy, which was later followed up with an article (1921). These works have been described as "the invention of child analysis" (Geissman & Geissman, 1998), and they influenced both Anna Freud's work and that of Melanie Klein.

At the beginning of the twentieth century, the so-called child guidance movement arose in the USA. In child guidance clinics, psychiatric social workers, psychiatrists, and psychologists worked together to help children with mental problems. The movement came to Britain in the early 1920s where it aroused great interest. In 1928, Margaret Lowenfeld established the Children's Clinic for the Treatment and Study of Nervous and Delicate Children, and in 1935, in connection with this clinic, the three-year training programme "Psychopathology and Psychotherapy with Children"—the world's first training course in psychodynamic child psychotherapy.

Without any doubt, however, the best-known early child analysts are Freud's daughter, Anna Freud, and Melanie Klein.

Anna Freud

Anna Freud was born in 1895 as the sixth and last child of Sigmund and Martha Freud. She soon took an interest in psychoanalysis and joined the psychoanalytic meetings held by Freud, who acted as her psychoanalyst. She was a teacher by profession. She began working as a child analyst in Vienna, where, among other initiatives, she co-founded an experimental day care institution for one- to two-year-old children, a novel innovation at the time. Child guidance clinics were established for young and older children as well as for young offenders, and teachers were offered courses in psychoanalytic child psychology. The periodical *Zeitschrift für Psychoanalytische Pädagogik* (Journal for Psychoanalytical Pedagogy), was launched, but closed down shortly before the outbreak of the Second World War, in 1938. After the war, however, it was relaunched in an Anglo-American edition as the highly esteemed periodical, *The Psychoanalytic Study of the Child*. This rich developmental work was disrupted in 1938, when Anna Freud and the rest of the Freud family had to seek refuge in London, but she soon resumed her work in England.

During the war, she established an evacuation centre for toddlers from London, the Hampstead War Nurseries. After the war, in 1947, it turned into the Hampstead Child Therapy Course and Clinic as a centre for training in psychoanalysis, and, in 1951, a treatment clinic with a nursery and a nursery school was added. These institutions served both observational and training purposes. The clinic, which now is called the Anna Freud Centre, also became the centre of a comprehensive research effort, which continues to this day.

Besides being a clinician and a researcher, Anna Freud took an active part in the development of psychoanalytic theory and methodology and published widely on both child analysis and child development. Together with Dorothy Burlingham, she described the work at the Hampstead War Nurseries in the book *Infants without Families* (1944). Her best-known books are *The Ego and the Mechanisms of Defence* (1937) and *Normality and Pathology in Childhood* (1966b).

Anna Freud developed and expanded on Freud's theories, particularly with regard to normal child development, a subject that received little attention in Freud's own works. She extended the description of ego functions and delineated a number of so-called developmental lines in the child's transition from dependence to independence.

Moreover, she described new defence mechanisms, including "identification with the aggressor", a defence mechanism that is often seen in children who have been subjected to violence and abuse. As mentioned later in this chapter, she was also among the first to describe development in adolescence. She became aware of other forms of developmental disturbances than neuroses, including borderline states in children and the consequences of deprivation. In connection with this development, she emphasised the necessity of sufficient care for children. She was always concerned that analysis should not only be for the children of the wealthy, but should be available for all children.

Anna Freud combined fine observations of children with very thorough records of the clinical work at the centre. The high quality of these records made them an invaluable source for research, and it has even been possible to use them in recent research (Fonagy & Target, 1996). In addition to its significance for child analysis, her work has also played an important role in the development of ego psychology and early child psychiatry.

Melanie Klein

Melanie Klein was born into a Jewish family in Vienna in 1882. She wanted to become a doctor, but married relatively early and, consequently, never attained an academic degree. She moved with her family to Budapest, where she took an interest in psychoanalysis and went into analysis with Sándor Ferenczi, who recognised her abilities for child analysis and encouraged her to continue along that path. In 1921, she moved to Berlin, where she established a psychoanalytic practice with both children and adults. Here, she went into analysis with Karl Abraham, but the process ended abruptly when he passed away in 1925. For other reasons, too, life in Berlin was difficult for her; among other issues, she was criticised for not being a doctor. Hence, she gladly accepted an invitation in 1925 from Ernest Jones to come to London and give lectures. In London, she gave six lectures, which later formed the basis of her book, *The Psychoanalysis of Children* (1932). She was very positively received in Britain, where there was already an interest in child analysis, and she stayed there for the rest of her life.

Melanie Klein experienced many losses throughout her life. As a child, she lost two of her elder siblings, in 1925, as mentioned, her analyst Karl Abraham died, and, in 1934, her elder son died in a climbing accident. These significant losses undoubtedly contributed to her preoccupation with depression and grief. In 1935, for example, she published "A contribution to the psychogenesis of manic-depressive states", which was followed up in 1940 by her article, "Mourning and its relation to manic-depressive states".

In 1938, when Anna Freud arrived in London, serious disagreements about child analysis arose between her and Melanie Klein that almost led to a split of the British Psychoanalytic Society. The discussion was interrupted during the first years of the war, when Klein spent a year in Scotland. Here, she carried out a four-month analysis of a ten-year-old boy, as described in her book, *Narrative of a Child Analysis* (1961), where the therapy is detailed hour by hour.

After her return to London, a number of meetings were held at the British Psychoanalytic Society with the goal of reaching an agreement between the two wings, but the attempts were unsuccessful. Eventually, the conflict resulted in a three-way split. One branch consisted of Anna Freud and her followers, another of Melanie Klein and her followers, while a third, more neutral, school included Winnicott, Balint, and Fairbairn, among others. Once again, Klein became a central figure, and her theories were widely used, for example, at the Tavistock Clinic and Institute, which established a training course in psychoanalytic child psychotherapy in 1948. Today, these divisions are of less importance, and, in contemporary training courses on psychoanalytic child and adolescent psychotherapy, contributions from the different schools are included in the curricula.

Klein is regarded as one of the founders of object relation theory. In contrast to Sigmund Freud, she argued that children relate to other persons from the very beginning of life, and that an ego—albeit rudimentary and undeveloped—exists from the infant's very first days of life. An important point in Klein's theories is the concept of unconscious phantasies, which she regarded as the primary unconscious content. These phantasies contain both the child's drives and inner impulses and his subjective processing of his early relations to his closest carers. She assumed such unconscious phantasies to be active throughout the lifespan of all human beings as constant concomitant phenomena to everything that the child (and, later, the adult person) experiences. The earliest phantasies are bodily and visual; only later do they become verbal. The personality structure is mainly determined by the more permanent of the child's phantasies about himself and his inner objects. This connection between the structure of personality and unconscious phantasy is a central point in object relation theory.

While Klein initially described the development of the child using Freud's libidinal phases (oral, anal, and phallic), she gradually changed her theory and began describing a development that encompasses two positions: the paranoid–schizoid and the depressive. When a position is developed, it is a permanent mental structure, unlike Freud's phases, which are transient. A position consists of (1) a certain way of experiencing other people (objects), (2) a characteristic kind of anxiety, and (3) specific defence mechanisms.

Klein held a conviction that, from the start of life, the infant tries to organise his impressions. Klein regarded the paranoid–schizoid structure as the earliest organisation, developing as early as the very first months of life. The infant tries to keep good and bad experiences separated from each other and rid himself of the bad ones. At that age, he still cannot organise his impressions of other persons into a unified whole, but experiences other persons as what Klein referred to as part objects. Klein made an important distinction between the child's relations to, on the one hand, the real (external) persons around him and, on the other hand, his (internal) object relations made up of his (unconscious) phantasies and conceptions about his relations to other people.

The child attempts to rid himself of his negative feelings, for example, anger, by projecting them into other persons; consequently, he begins to see these persons as potential persecutors. The anxiety that characterises this position is paranoid anxiety (hence, the "paranoid" aspect of the position). The defences in this position are primitive and, besides projection, they include introjection, splitting, and denial. Splitting is a schizoid mechanism, the purpose of which is to keep positive and negative parts of the psyche separated. The mechanism is the source of the other half of the designation of the paranoid–schizoid position.

If the child's development is positive, which, among other things, presupposes that he receives sufficient parental care and love, he proceeds to the depressive position, in which—also as a consequence of his improved cognitive abilities—he is now capable of experiencing other persons as whole objects—that is, as persons with both positive and negative qualities. The child begins to understand that his own acts have consequences, and he begins to fear that he might harm the persons he loves through his anger. Therefore, he develops the capacity to feel guilt and the desire to repair the parents, whom he has attacked in his phantasies. As mentioned, Klein named this position the depressive position, which Winnicott (1955), among others, was critical of. He pointed out that what the child feels is not depression; rather, he develops the capacity for concern for others, which causes both his anxieties and his defences to change. The primitive defence mechanisms are replaced by more mature forms, such as repression, and, through so-called reparation, the child attempts to repair what he fears he has destroyed: his good parental figures and his own inner goodness.

The understanding of children's sexuality and the development of the superego are other important points of difference from early psychoanalysis. Freud was of the opinion that even young children have sexual feelings, although they are different from adult genital sexuality. He used the boy's development as a prototype and argued that his development culminates during the oedipal phase at the age of three to five years, when the child falls in love with the parent of the opposite sex and feels jealousy towards the same-sex parent. Freud assumed that the superego is created as a consequence of this conflict, as the child resolves the conflict through identification with the parent of the same sex as himself.

Klein, on the other hand, believed that girls go through a development based on a primarily feminine identity, and that both sexes wish to possess the qualities not only of their own sex, but of both sexes. She placed the beginning of the oedipal conflict in the first year of life and believed that, even at this time, an early superego has begun to take form. This superego is strict and cruel, in accordance with the child's phantasies at that age. As mentioned, Freud believed that the superego (the human conscience) is created as a consequence of the resolution of the oedipal conflict, whereas Klein maintained that the early oedipal conflict and the early superego are two sides of the same coin. She described that they both tone down and are integrated during the following years as a consequence of the child's love for both parents and a consequent wish to repair the parental couple, which, in his oedipal phantasies, he tried to break up. Klein regarded the Freudian Oedipus complex as the final culmination of this process.

Klein was a prolific writer, and her writings are partly collected in the books *Love, Guilt, and Reparation and Other Works 1921–1945* (1975a) and *Envy and Gratitude* (1975b). It is impossible to mention all Klein's important theoretical innovations; interested readers are referred to, for example, Segal (1979, 1992), Petot (1990–1991), or Bronstein (2001).

Discussions between Anna Freud and Melanie Klein

Anna Freud and Melanie Klein both regarded themselves as faithful followers of Freud's psychoanalysis; none the less, however, they both modified his theories, each in her own way. One of the most important reasons for these changes, undoubtedly, was that they both worked with children in psychotherapy and psychoanalysis, something Freud only did indirectly, in a single case where he relieved Little Hans of a horse phobia through consultations with his father (1909b).

Although Anna Freud and Melanie Klein worked in the same field (psychopathology in children), they arrived at very different models of the mental development of the child. Their psychotherapeutic methods also differed in a number of respects, as did their points of departure, although they both had children in psychotherapy. Anna Freud saw many children who were temporarily separated from their parents, as well as many neglected children. Besides, her work was initially restricted to older children and to neurotic or neglected children. From the outset, on the other hand, Melanie Klein analysed children as young as two years of age, and she saw children with psychosis and autism for psychotherapy, which, at that time, was something new. The efforts to try to understand and describe what happens in the development of children with such serious pathology require other theories than those that are suited for describing the consequences of neglect and less serious developmental disorders.

Although the two schools initially had many theoretical and methodological differences, they have since gradually approached each other (see Chapter Two for an outline of the most important differences).

Other object relation theorists

Other analysts later built on Klein's work, both theoretically and methodologically. Among the most important are Donald Winnicott and Wilfred Bion. While Klein mainly described the infant's phantasies and inner life, Winnicott was also occupied with the actual interaction between the infant and his mother. As a paediatrician, he saw many mothers with their babies. He emphasised the importance of the mother's "holding" of the child, by which he referred to both the physical and the mental care she provided for the child. He coined the term "the good-enough-mother": a mother who cares sufficiently for her infant's needs, without being perfect. He further underlined the importance of play and creativity. Another influential concept of Winnicott's is "the transitional object", soft objects such as, for example, blankets and teddy bears that function as a defence, especially against depressive anxiety and, thus, help the child manage separations from his mother. These concepts are described in his book, *Playing and Reality* (1971a), among other sources.

Among other things, Bion described the development of thinking and elaborated the understanding of the defence mechanism of projective identification, which Klein had already described. He also described the concept of containment (see Chapter Two for a more thorough treatment of these concepts).

It is impossible, in this limited space, to give a satisfactory description of the object relation theories; a good presentation can be found, for example, in Bronstein (2001).

Attachment theory

Attachment theory, which evolved from the middle of the twentieth century, supplements object relations theory in important areas. It was mainly the work of the British child psychiatrist and psychoanalyst, John Bowlby (1907–1990), who was the director of Tavistock's Child Department, and his co-workers, including the Canadian psychologist, Mary Ainsworth.

During the 1950s, some psychologists and physicians were becoming interested in the strong reactions of infants and young children when separated from their mothers; at first, the children react with crying and protest, later with grief, and, finally, with apparent indifference, but at the expense of their attachment to their carers. After the Second World War, Bowlby was asked by the World Health Organization to draw up a report on the many homeless children in Europe, which resulted in the book, *Maternal Care and Mental Health* (1951). In the book, he described how children who had become separated from their parents either developed extreme dependence on others or lost their ability to form close attachments. He was of the opinion that these reactions were due to early lack of sufficiently tender, personalised parental care and loss of their parents, but he lacked evidence in support for this hypothesis (see Chapter Eleven for an expansion on this point).

Bowlby was influenced by ethology (the theory of animal behaviour) and, throughout his life, he maintained a biological and empirical approach to his work. He maintained that infants have an instinct-based urge to attach to their parents, and that the need for security is the strongest drive in human beings. He described a number of so-called attachment behaviours in infants and young children: for example, smiling, crying, and following the carer; these were also considered to be instinct-based. During the first couple of years, the child develops an emotional bond to his closest carer, so-called attachment. The development of this bond begins from birth, but it takes time; in the second half of the first year of life, however, the child's attachment is evident, and the child reacts with reservation towards strangers. During the following years, the bond is further consolidated—the child is said to develop "a secure base". The first years seem to be a critical period, during which attachment must take place. This is supported by neurological research, which has shown that the brain is particularly plastic during the first years of life and apparently adapted to go through exactly this development. It was also found that the appropriate time for attachment might be missed if the child does not have the opportunity to establish an early attachment to one or a few carers. Bowlby named the inner structures formed during attachment "internal working models". They contain images of the self and other important persons and the emotions that are connected to them. They shape the child's later experience of other people and himself as well as his fundamental experience of the world in general.

Attachment is closely linked with exploration, which is another main element in child development. Security has a higher priority than exploration, however, which means that an anxious child expends a great deal of energy on trying to find security and, consequently, has less energy and interest available for exploration of the world, play, and learning. As a consequence, in many cases, the child's cognitive functions might suffer. Ainsworth and her co-workers (Ainsworth et al., 1978) performed a number of experiments that demonstrated how attachment can assume different patterns: (1) secure, (2) anxious–ambivalent, and (3) anxious–avoidant. Main (Main & Hesse, 1990; Main & Solomon, 1986) later demonstrated an additional pattern: (4) the disorganised pattern, which often appears in combination with one of the anxious patterns. The way in which the child is treated is the most decisive factor for the kind of attachment he will form. Attachment behaviour is activated when the child becomes anxious or needs help; in such situations, it is crucial how the child is treated by his carers. A child with a secure attachment has mainly been met with care and understanding and has had his needs met. A child with an anxious–ambivalent attachment feels insecure with his carers, who, in many cases, will react to the child's needs on the basis of their own needs rather than the child's. A child with an anxious–avoidant pattern is not used to having his needs met and is afraid of awakening the carer's anger through his desire for help. Children with a disorganised attachment are frightened of their parents, either because their parents show violent or threatening behaviour, or because the parents, themselves, are frightened: for example, as a result of traumatisation. Children with an avoidant or ambivalent attachment have developed strategies that, over time, are not always appropriate, but they are well organised; however, parents who react very unpredictably make it impossible for their child to find a consistent attachment strategy.

Thus, Bowlby and his co-workers focused their attention on the child's early-life conditions, and, more thoroughly than anyone before them, they described the conditions that are necessary to establish a secure foundation for the child's development. They showed, empirically and in detail, how the carer's reactions to the child's attachment behaviour shapes the child's personality development. The subsequent consequences of the attachment patterns have also been the object of thorough empirical studies, and it has been demonstrated how the anxious patterns might lay the foundation for later problems and, at worst, for psychopathology.

Bowlby also dealt with the issue of grief in both children and adults. He was concerned with the fact that children who suffered early losses and received insufficient help ran the risk of developing pathological grief, also later in life. He described his work with attachment, grief, and loss in the trilogy *Attachment* (Volume 1, 1969) *Separation: Anxiety and Anger* (Volume 2, 1973), and *Loss: Sadness and Depression* (Volume 3, 1980). A shorter presentation of attachment theory may be found in the book, *A Secure Base. Clinical Applications of Attachment Theory* (1988).

Fonagy and his co-workers (Fonagy et al., 2002a) have expanded attachment theory with a theory on mentalization. Mentalization is—very briefly put—the capacity to understand one's own and other persons' feelings, to be able to react empathically, and to master reflection and symbolic thinking. According to these authors, however, to develop a capacity for mentalization, the child has to receive help with affect regulation from the people around him. The child needs what Fonagy and co-authors (2002a) describe as the congruent and marked mirroring of his feelings, which helps him to identify and name his feelings and establish clear boundaries between himself and other persons. With sufficient help, the child gradually learns to regulate his own feelings and manage them in socially acceptable ways. There is a connection between incongruent mirroring of feelings and difficulties with identifying and recognising one's own and other people's feelings; ultimately, it might even give rise to a false self.

Other contributions

Over time, a still growing number of researchers and psychotherapists have contributed to the development of theories and methods in psychodynamic child and adolescent psychotherapy. Unfortunately, it is impossible to do them justice in this restricted space, and we shall, therefore, only mention a few of the most important contributors.

Daniel Stern

The late American psychoanalyst, Daniel Stern, has developed his own theory of child development, in which the changing subjective senses of self are regarded as the organising principle of development. In his book, *The Interpersonal World of the Infant* (1985), he has described four senses of the self: (1) the emergent self, (2) the core self, (3) the subjective self, and (4) the verbal self. Each sense of self defines a domain of self-experience and a corresponding way of relating to others, so-called domains of relatedness.

Stern also described the condition of motherhood in his book, *The Motherhood Constellation* (1995) and the minute interactions between infant and carers. In that connection, he coined the concept of "affective attunement", which is related to the concept of "mirroring" and describes how the carer responds to the child's approaches. Stern's own psychotherapeutic work also focused mainly on the very early interactions between mothers and their infants.

Neuropsychology

At an early time, Sigmund Freud attempted, with little success, to base his psychological theory on neurophysiology (1895); since then, however, neurophysiology and neuropsychology have developed enormously, and they now contribute to a better understanding of the connection between brain processes and psychological phenomena.

Today, for example, there is considerable knowledge about how emotions might be located at different levels in the brain, and it could be helpful for a therapist to be aware of the level at which her client functions at a given moment. It is also recognised that we have different kinds of memory, which it is similarly important for a psychotherapist to know.

The plasticity of the brain during the first years of life is well documented, and it has been shown how positive and negative experiences leave different traces in the brain. Once formed, however, the synaptic links are fairly solid, and these early structures, therefore, often have long-lasting consequences, affecting not only the structures of the brain, but also the hormonal systems. Psychologist Susan Hart calls this field "neuroaffective development" (Bentzen & Hart, 2015; Hart, 2008). To a great extent, this new knowledge aligns with existing theories: for example, attachment theory.

Regardless of the importance of this knowledge, however, it is essential to remember that we are dealing with human beings, and what we can observe directly are acts, statements, and emotional reactions. Our hypotheses about what is going on in the brain while these outer representations occur are just that—hypotheses. It might be worth remembering professor in neuropsychology Jesper Mogensen's statement that neuropsychology should complement psychology, not take it over. He emphasises the risk of misperceiving the results of neuroscience as more scientific than those of psychology (Nordbo, 2004).

Theories on adolescence

Puberty and adolescence have received less theoretical interest within the field of psychoanalysis than child development. A few theorists, however, have written about adolescence, focusing on different aspects of this period in life.

The first author to write more in depth about adolescence was Anna Freud, who, in 1958, published the article "Adolescence", and who also addressed the subject, for example, in her book, *The Ego and the Mechanisms of Defence* (1937). Adolescence is the designation of the mental development during the teenage years, but it is also used as a joint term for the physical and the mental development. In particular, Anna Freud emphasised the importance of drive development and described how increased sexuality and aggression disturbed the equilibrium between id and ego that was established during childhood. She was of the opinion that puberty would necessarily create so much turbulence that it might be difficult to distinguish between normality and pathology in this age group, and that a normal adolescent state might be difficult to distinguish, for instance, from borderline states.

Erikson, who was the next author to treat adolescence in detail wrote the book, *Identity. Youth and Crisis* (1968), among other works. As is evident from the title, identity problems were at the centre of his interest, and he delineated different models to describe how identity may be more or less successfully formed. In particular, he stressed the importance of giving adolescents the opportunity of a moratorium, that is, a space in the transition from child to adult where, as yet, no demands are made of the adolescent to take on actual responsibilities in society, and where he may try to determine what he wants to make of his life. Erikson also emphasised the need for developing an ideology during adolescence.

A third theorist was Blos, who, in his book, *On Adolescence* (1962), took Mahler's theory on separation–individuation (Mahler et al., 1975) as his starting point and described adolescence as the second separation–individuation period. His focus was especially on the separation from the parents and the difficulties it might cause.

For many years, Anna Freud's ideas about the extent and the characteristics of problems in adolescence had great significance for the clinical work with adolescents, and there was a tendency, also in psychiatry, to regard even considerable difficulties as "puberty problems" rather than manifestations of pathology. This was also due to the fact that personality disturbances were much less well described and understood than they are now. This view of adolescence seems now to have been abandoned, however.

The theories of Anna Freud and Erik Erikson seem to have a close connection with difficulties they encountered in their own lives. Anna Freud had a problematic adolescence, including developing anorexia nervosa. She suffered from the conflict between her wish to be a psychoanalyst and the lesson she had incorporated from her father: that the fulfilment of this wish was incompatible with being a woman (Young-Bruehl, 1989). Thus, it was not surprising that she would perceive the experience of sexuality as a threat. As the course of Erikson's life shows, it was difficult for him to find a professional identity; he wavered between wanting an artistic and a scientific career, and, although he ended up a recognised scientist and psychotherapist, he never completed any formal education.

Marcia (1980) elaborated further on Erikson's concept of identity and suggested four different outcomes of the identity crisis. They rest on the combination of two independent variables: commitment and exploration. An established identity implies that the adolescent has examined different possibilities before making his choices; this kind of identity offers good opportunities of commitment. A forced identity rests on premature choices, which have not been sufficiently examined, and this prevents a strong commitment. A moratorium implies that the adolescent is still exploring different possibilities, but often with considerable anxiety and difficulties in committing himself. Finally, Marcia mentions identity diffusion, where the adolescent has not resolved his identity crisis but is left in a state of confusion and anxiety. Wrangsjö and Salomonsson (2007) add yet another possibility: a negative identity—that is, an identity that is defined by being in opposition to society's general norms, and which might, for example, result in violence, criminality, or other forms of protest.

Understanding of psychopathology

In psychoanalysis, the understanding of psychopathology has changed in line with the general theoretical shifts that have taken place. Freud's interest in psychopathology centred particularly on the neuroses, which he regarded as the result of an intrapsychic conflict between drives and conscience. Although aggression might play a part, too, it was, first and foremost, sexuality that was considered a threat to the psychic equilibrium of the individual. Freud ascribed a considerable part of the development of the neuroses to the child's own drives, although seduction from other persons might also contribute. He regarded the neuroses as fixations in, or regressions to, earlier normal states in the child—a way of thinking that was maintained for a long time, but has now been abandoned.

An important innovation was Anna Freud's drawing attention to the fact that defect-based pathology differs from conflict-based pathology, partly because other functions are affected than in a neurotic state, and partly because the environment plays a crucial role in the development of it. She maintained that defect pathology might be at least as serious as neurotic disturbances and could result in, for example, borderline states or antisocial behaviour.

Klein expanded the psychopathological spectrum further by also having very young children in psychotherapy as well as psychotic and autistic children. She had a deep understanding of even the most serious mental disorders and described, for example, how such children's anxiety might be unidentified by being regarded as insensibility or retardation. In Klein's view, the main threat to mental health was not sexuality but, rather, an excess of aggression. This viewpoint receives support from the Canadian psychiatrist, Susan Bradley, who, in her book, *Affect Regulation and the Development of Psychopathology* (2003), based on both empirical evidence and theory, describes difficulties with affect regulation as one of the main causes of psychopathology. In this book, she maintains that anger is exactly the affect that causes the greatest suffering and most serious mental disorder in human beings.

Freud regarded drive development as key to personality development; in object relation theory, however, the child's relationships with the primary carers are seen as crucial to the formation of personality. The greater the predominance of aggression and the more primitive the defences, the more the inner object and self-representations will deviate from reality, and the more pathological the state will be. Klein's two positions are excellent points of reference for determining the degree of developmental disturbance. In successful psychotherapies, it is often possible to see how primitive defences, such as splitting and projection, dominate at first, but are gradually replaced by more mature defences, such as intellectualisation, rationalisation, and regression, and how an angry child, full of hate, will change and begin to be able to express empathy and concern for others, including the therapist (see, e.g., Philps, 2009).

In attachment theory, pathology is mostly seen as being caused either by early losses and trauma or by problems in the relationship with the carers, resulting in attachment disturbances and deficient development of attachment. Bowlby also described internal conflicts as possible causes of psychopathology, but he did not see them as a result of a disturbed psychosexual development, but, rather, as a result of conflicts between the child's personal experiences (episodic information) and what he has been told, usually by his parents (semantic information). Bowlby also understood that, in many cases, depression is anger turned inward against oneself instead of outward against other persons. His differentiated understanding of the various forms of normal and pathological grief and the many transitions in between is also worth noticing.

For each sense of self, Stern described a number of patterns in the relationship between child and carer that could cause later developmental disturbances. In general, the earlier a disturbance occurs, the more serious the consequences might be; here, he is in agreement with most other theorists.

Common to all the theories mentioned above is the understanding that there are gradual transitions between normality and pathology, and that they are not categorically separated. However, as mentioned, over the more than 100 years that have passed since Freud published his first works, there have been many decisive changes in our understanding of psychopathology. Generally, the weight has shifted from attributing the main cause of psychopathology to factors in the child himself to seeing it as a consequence of difficulties in the interaction between the child and his environment. It must, of course, be emphasised that inborn problems might also play a part, such as birth trauma and physiological issues.

This overall understanding of a number of different pathological states, however, does not create an actual classification of child mental disorders. A rudimentary approach to such a classification can be found in the description of the various attachment disturbances; Klein's two positions can also be seen as a very simple form of classification. For a long time, unfortunately, classifications have not been taken seriously in psychoanalysis, something that Anna Freud also noticed. To address this issue, she developed a diagnostic meta-profile for children (1966b), which contains information about, among other things, personality structure, patterns of defence mechanisms, reality testing, progressive and regressive tendencies, and the ego's ability to deal with anxiety. By now, of course, this profile is outdated.

If a more detailed classification is needed today, it is necessary to use either the American *DSM* system (*Diagnostic and Statistical Manual*) or the World Health Organization's *ICD* system (*International Classification of Diseases*). In both these systems, diagnoses are based solely on the presence of symptoms. It is explicitly stated in *ICD-10* (World Health Organization, 1992) that no implications should be drawn about inner states in the person. In this way, these systems distance themselves from a dynamic way of thinking where the understanding explicitly builds on the theoretical assumption of mental processes. There must necessarily be coherence between the theories underlying the classification and those underlying the treatment, and it is, therefore, obvious that these diagnostic systems are not suitable as the basis of a treatment according to psychodynamic principles.

Anna Freud's criticism of the problem of basing diagnoses exclusively on symptoms is as relevant today as it was when it was written, not least in regard to children whose symptoms may often fluctuate and, in the course of development, change in appearance. In spite of the simplicity of these systems, it quickly became clear that they are neither sufficiently reliable nor valid (Cantwell & Rutter, 1994). As mentioned, a classification that only rests on symptomatology is particularly problematic in regard to children. As described, children's problems are very often closely interwoven with their overall life situation and environmental circumstances. Therefore, if one only looks at the child's symptoms, it is easy to fail to see the importance of these factors. This leads to a considerable risk of misjudging a child as mentally ill when he or she is, in fact, suffering from insufficient care and, perhaps, maltreatment.

However, the current diagnostic systems are also met with criticism. The authors of the *Psychodynamic Diagnostic Manual* (Psychodynamic Diagnostic Manual Task Force, 2006) maintain that a clinically useful classification of mental health disorders must begin with an understanding of healthy mental processes, something that is completely missing in the existing classification systems. They further emphasise that any attempt at developing a description and classification of mental health problems must include many more features of human function than the observable symptoms; the essential problems are often found in functions and patterns of the personality that are more fundamental and not as directly visible as symptoms are. Moreover, especially in childhood and adolescence, apparently identical symptoms can reflect vastly different mental problems. The *PDM* has tried to meet the need for a more comprehensive diagnostic system by including both an overall personality profile and a number of personality functions as the basis of a diagnosis that goes beyond the symptoms (see Chapter Three for an outline of these functions). Besides the adult classification system, there are separate systems for children and adolescents and for infants.

Concerning infants, it is absolutely necessary to include an assessment of the child's carers in any attempt at a diagnostic classification. Therefore, a diagnostic system of mental health disorders has been worked out for infants, *Diagnostic Classification: 0–3R* (ZERO TO THREE, 2005), which also contains an assessment of the relation between the infant and his carers. This system also includes a number of other mental disorders than the official systems, including traumatic stress disorder, which is regarded as especially important. This system is under current revision and is planned to be expanded to include children who are up to five years old.

CHAPTER TWO

What is psychodynamic child and adolescent psychotherapy?

In this chapter, we bring forward a conception of psychodynamic child and adolescent psychotherapy as a broadly defined term, including all such approaches that explicitly or implicitly take into consideration the unconscious phantasies and feelings of child and therapist as a continuous undercurrent influencing the therapeutic relationship and process. From this perspective, the chapter elucidates what psychodynamic child and adolescent psychotherapy is, according to which broadly defined principles it may be carried out, and through which mental and interpersonal mechanisms the action of therapy might work. In this connection, the fundamental concepts of projective identification, containment, and the ability for symbolisation, thinking, and relational thought (mentalization) are presented and their implications in child and adolescent psychotherapy are discussed.

As described in the preceding chapter, during the past century, several psychoanalytic traditions developed and, correspondingly, from the early days of child psychoanalysis, certain differences of opinion also developed concerning the basic principles of how to work with children. In this chapter, the main differences are summarised; however, the principal focus of this chapter (and the book) is on the common perspectives and methods that differentiate psychodynamic child and adolescent psychotherapy from other (non-dynamic) therapeutic approaches. In conclusion, possible interpretational perspectives are summarised that might, in combination, enrich the therapist's understanding of the dynamic processes enacted in the professional and personal network involved in the care of the child or young person.

A definition

Psychodynamic psychotherapy primarily works through human contact, that is, through the relationship between the child and the therapist and, within this, through the communication that unfolds between them. Thus, it is a relational approach to psychotherapy, and the relationship between child and therapist is the prime mover of the therapeutic process as well as the mainspring of the therapeutic effect. A fundamental commonality of the psychodynamic strategies is that therapists tend to focus their attention on the interaction between the child and themselves. Continually keeping in mind this focus, psychodynamic therapists thus facilitate the development of an especially intense, emotionally invested, two-way relationship between the child and themselves; in psychodynamic psychotherapy, this is designated the transference relationship. This relationship comprises two perspectives: the child's transference to the therapist and the therapist's countertransference to the child. The child's transference comes into being in the here-and-now of the therapeutic session, in which the child, in a process of projective identification (see below), unconsciously projects to the therapist such attributes (e.g., personality traits, expectations, feelings, phantasies, ways of behaving, and sometimes even specific aspects of appearance) that might flow from his subjective inner world of object relationships. Naturally, this explanation is only part of a much more complex story, the therapeutic relationship comprising several other aspects than the transference. Not least, because children and adolescents are often quite accurate in their perceptions of their therapist's personal distinctiveness (see Chapter Five).

The central vehicle of development in psychodynamic child and adolescent psychotherapy is the communication that grows out of the child's experience of his relationship with the therapist. Children and adolescents might, in any case, express their therapy-related experiences in a wide variety of ways, verbally or non-verbally, symbolically or literally, directly and deliberately, or subtly, perhaps unconscious of the experiences they communicate. Hence, the single most important factor that differentiates the psychodynamic therapies from other approaches is the therapist's attention to the transference relationship. The definition below of psychodynamic psychotherapy with children and adolescents represents our own point of view, inspired by the work of Meltzer and premised on modern Kleinian thinking (Grünbaum, 1999–2000; Meltzer, 1967; Spillius, 2001).

The term "psychodynamic child and adolescent psychotherapy" refers to the particular communication or dialogue between child and psychotherapist, which is shaped by:

1. *The therapist's creation of a therapeutic setting*, that is, the establishment of certain boundaries which together form a framework that delimits and anchors the relationship within a geographical, temporal, and mental space. This demarcation of the therapeutic space is a precondition for the relationship to develop into an embedded transference relationship. The planning of the setting is described in more detail in Chapter Four.
2. *The therapeutic interventions*, that is, the therapist's way of imparting his or her understanding of the subjective meaning of the child's ideas, experiences, feelings, and phantasies to the child, whether these are verbalised, manifest in the narrative themes of symbolic play, or implicitly expressed in the child's attitude or behaviour. The therapist's interventions must be timely and based on careful, continuous observation of the child's movements and expressions in the therapeutic session. Thus, a fundamental stance for child and adolescent therapists must be to perceive all the child's expressions and movements inside the therapeutic space, whether verbal or non-verbal, noisy, quiet, or listless, loving, hateful, or impassive, intelligible, secretive, confused, or violent, as subjectively meaningful communication of important statements relating to the child's experience of the present relationship and his inner world. Therapeutic interventions, thus, have their starting point in observations of the child, but this is not their sole source, since they are also derived from,

and enriched by, the therapist's scrutiny (in private) of her own countertransference and, thus, her own contribution to the state of the transference relationship. Sometimes, the first inkling of a valuable understanding might even appear in the countertransference of the therapist; however, before openly introducing this idea or feeling into the therapy process, a wise therapist could choose to wait and observe, looking for contradictory or corroborating evidence.

Therapeutic attitude and interventions

Therapeutic interventions include everything therapists might say or do in order to communicate to children in therapy their understanding of how the child (consciously and unconsciously) experiences the present state of the therapeutic relationship and the inner world of object relations. However, because psychodynamic child and adolescent psychotherapy is a relational endeavour, as described above, therapists will do their best to divide their attentional focus, listening impartially, with an open ear and mind, to impressions gained from both without and within by observing the child as well as their own countertransference feelings. Fundamentally, the therapist aims to maintain an open, non-focused, reflective mental state that allows all possible kinds of perceptions, sensations, inner images, memories, feelings, and phantasies (whether welcome or not) to emerge and become available for thinking. This mental state is akin to what Bion (1962b) called reverie, referring to an especially unfocused state of mind, in which the therapist consciously steps out of goal-directed thinking. Instead, he keeps his mind open to whatever might appear, whether it is related to the child's communication or to his own inner process of countertransference feelings and phantasies, broadly including such unfocused, dreamy states in which vague thoughts about the child, the therapy, and oneself can come and go. Hence, this kind of therapy requires therapists to continually pay attention not only to the child, but also to their own subjective, never-ending stream of countertransference-related thoughts, feelings, sensations, images, and dreaming states, as well as any sudden disturbances and blocks occurring in this inner stream of consciousness. In this tradition, therapists usually do not share their countertransference feelings with the child, but are aware of their own state of mind and sensitively reflect about possible connections between their own countertransference and the child's behaviour and communication.

A distinctive feature of psychotherapy with children and, in part, adolescents, is their tendency to communicate through enactment and play rather than by coherent verbal narratives. Accordingly, the psychotherapeutic process takes on a more agile character, fluctuating between play, talk, silence, and movement and between levels of functioning that are appropriate to the child's biological age and more immature or disturbed behaviour. Thus, narrations and symbolic play might give way to regressive or aggressive behaviour where the child communicates her feelings and memories through omnipotent behaviour, splitting, and projective identification.

Hence, in therapy with children and adolescents, the vast majority of therapist interventions are aimed at clarifying the child's intentions, hopes, feelings, anxieties, phantasies, and defensive gambits by means of interpretations that relate these to the transference relationship and (more sparingly) trace how they relate to the child's past or present life experience, especially in primary relationships.

Along with interpretations of the symbolic dimensions of play, dreams, drawings, and verbal narratives, it is also important to seek to understand the object-related, emotional meaning implied by the child's actions and ways of relating to the therapist. This pre-symbolic level of communication is often conspicuous during the initial phase of the therapy. In this phase, it is important—especially when working with young children, children who have suffered complex traumatisation and/or severe early neglect and abuse, and mentally ill children—for the therapist to be able to contain and translate, for instance, mute, confused, defiant states, mindless repetitions, and embittered attacks on the setting or the therapeutic relationship into simple, digestible statements. In such translations, which address how the child might view and feel about the therapy and the present relationship with the therapist, an element of surprise or humour could pave the way for mutual understanding.

The life experience of five-year-old Clive, from birth to his present age, included early traumatisation related to witnessing violence between his parents, his mother's depression, repeated loss, and moves. He was referred to child psychotherapy by the pre-school counsellor because of relationship difficulties and challenging behaviour: his teacher described him as defiant, controlling, and omnipotent, constantly in opposition, provocatively testing the limits of both children and adults. Further, when the teachers tried to regulate his behaviour, he would respond with manic giggling, aping their actions, hitting, and spitting. Conversely, at other times, the teachers saw a fragile and depressed Clive, who hit himself over and over again, repeating that he hated himself. He was an only child, but his mother was pregnant and due to give birth soon. Clive was seen once weekly for time-limited play psychotherapy (a total of thirty-five sessions) with concurrent, fortnightly parent consultations.

> (Excerpt from session 1). Clive investigates his box of toys and the playroom while asking a lot of questions, including whether other children are allowed to play with the doll's house and the doctor's kit. (I say, "You wonder if you're allowed to do the same here as other children?") Clive points at some boxes on a high shelf and says, "These are other children's boxes . . . anyway, I am not allowed to play with them." Later in the session, he finds the plasticine in his box, presses a pink lump down on the table and makes a protruding tip in the centre. (I think to myself that most of all, this looks like a breast with a nipple. I ask Clive, "What are you making?") Clive says, "Pancake and pizza, mmm-mmm, this will taste yummy." He raises his voice to a higher and higher pitch and adds, "This pancake will be giant, that's my favourite", and "I prefer giant-sized." Excitedly, he begins to toss the plasticine pancake/pizza high up into the air, saying that now he will try to catch it, even if it is so hugely enormous. (I suggest that this might be just like his worries; that he might find them so huge that he is not sure whether I can help him deal with them.) Clive says, "Yes," and adds, "but I like it best if I'm the only one to catch it; better than if others do it. It's just hard when the plasticine is so big." (I wonder why I suddenly find the atmosphere to be heavy and depressed.)

As seen in this short vignette, a child's behaviour in the therapeutic space will offer several possible interpretational perspectives. First, as mentioned above, one virtually invariable perspective is the more or less clear-cut relationship between the child's present behaviour and certain highly subjective—conscious or unconscious—phantasies of relationships with objects, which were fuelled in and by the present transference relationship. Second, the child's contribution to the interaction can also be understood from a historical perspective relating to subjectively processed memory traces of formerly important real-life relationships and other aspects of the child's past personal history: for example, losses, traumatic experiences, and other specific events leading to mental injuries, or, conversely, subjective memories of enriching and comforting aspects of past real-life experiences and relationships. Third, the child may have a concurrent or even future, external reality in mind: for example, what happened this morning in the family or at school, or what is going to happen after the session. Keeping this in mind is important, since therapists need to reflect on the relative impact on the child's experience and behaviour of these different interpretational perspectives as well as their own countertransference.

In addition to interpretation, other common interventions aim at preserving and safeguarding the therapeutic setting, protecting it from behaviour that might undermine the therapy and/or endanger the safety of the child or the therapist. Usually, the therapist achieves this by offering verbal interpretations of the underlying feelings that motivated the child's attack, sometimes supplemented by a contribution to the child's play activity: for example, by introducing caring or protective figures. Occasionally, however, with some children and adolescents, especially if they have suffered abuse or are prone to violent outbursts, it might be necessary to stage an intervention in the form of a resolute, energetic imperative intended to put an immediate stop to risky or vicious acts that endanger the child's or the therapist's safety. The effect of such interventions depends on the authoritative conviction with which they are put forward; for example, it is helpful if the therapist does not remain seated but literally demonstrates her grown-up status by standing up to her full height. Thus, with all children and adolescents, but especially if they are victims of abuse or prone to violent outbursts, a critical dimension of the therapeutic attitude is remembering, at all times, that the therapist and the child are not equal partners engaged in mutual play; they each have their own role in an asymmetric relationship. Commensurate to this position, some fifty years ago, Meltzer (1967) instructively stated that child psychotherapists need firmly to protect their authority, like a director who works out every single detail of the setting while handing the child the task of filling in this framework with his personal inclinations and content.

Once in a while, and, one hopes, at least once in any child's psychotherapy, while scrutinising the ongoing transference–countertransference process, the therapist might have a sudden glimpse of emotional–cognitive insight, a *eureka* moment. In these precious moments, the therapist's mind intuitively correlates several, hitherto separate, observations, feelings, and ideas, which, taken individually, appear quite interesting, but which are suddenly understood as a meaningful whole—a coherent, narrative pattern that combines object-related phantasy, feelings, and defences. This special form of intuitive recognition was described as "selective facts" by Bion (1962b, 1963; Riesenberg-Malcolm, 2001). These moments can become genuine turning points, creating in their immediate wake a benign change in therapy. It is a common clinical experience for us and other therapists that such positive turning points typically occur after a difficult period in the therapy: for example, a crisis in the transference relationship (Carlberg, 2009).

Projective identification and containment

Melanie Klein first introduced the concept of projective identification in 1946, describing this as an especially primitive and extreme form of ego splitting. This splitting is accompanied by phantasies in which the inner world of object relationships is liberated from unbearable parts, generally experienced as bad or "mad" aspects of self. This could, for example, be an envious part of the self that is imagined as being transferred (projected) from the self and into the object, which the child then identifies as envious. However, projective identification might also concern especially precious parts of the self, which the child unconsciously experiences as endangered by other, more destructive, parts of the self. For example, the child might be anxious that his own jealousy and envy, aroused by observing the parents' mutual relationship, risk damaging the good, loved parental couple irreparably. He might also worry that these aggressive feelings risk destroying his own valued creative powers and abilities for love and reparation (see Chapter One on Melanie Klein). In this case, the child might, in a phantasy, project his own good, creative abilities on the parents, who are, thus, idealised and perceived as omnipotent, while the self is accordingly devalued and depleted. The projecting self subjectively holds on to the projected parts, which means that the differentiation between self and object becomes blurred, partly blotted out, for example, by phantasies of controlling the object from within through the projected parts of the self, which are now sheltered inside the object. Klein primarily understood projective identification as a category of radically defensive phantasies, the effect of which might well be a certain relief, as unbearable feelings (e.g., self-loathing) are directed outside the self. As described above, this relief comes at a high cost, as it undermines the self's experience of separateness. Furthermore, projective identification militates against the introjection of the good, nourishing parts of the therapeutic relationship, since the child, in phantasy, comes to identify the therapist with the bad, projected parts of the self (Klein, 1957).

Bion normalised the concept by adding a developmental dimension, positing the mental activity of projective identification as an early, preverbal, interpersonal communication mode, the fundamental paradigm of which is the wordless intersubjective dialogue about emotional states between infant and parents (Bion, 1962a). Projective identification, in Bion's formulation, refers to the emotional, intersubjective connection between the infant's inner, mind–body emotional states and the mother's unconscious world of phantasies about objects. Hence, projective identification could also be thought of as infants' earliest reality-testing activity.

Building on the concept of projective identification, one of Bion's main contributions to modern Kleinian theory formation is the development of the theory of containment. Broadly speaking, this theory on early mental development takes as its starting point the assumption that the infant's first experiential world is comprised by sensory impressions in the raw (denoted β-elements, i.e., beta-elements), pleasurable or disagreeable sensory impressions, which the infant is mentally unable to digest and assign emotional and relational meaning. Hence, the infant's psyche is regularly flooded by undigested sensory impressions, leaving the infant only one way to rid himself of the excess stimulation, which is through sensorimotor phantasy and related actions: for example, by kicking, crying, urinating, spitting, increased muscle tone, and other concrete bodily ways aimed at ridding the psyche of disagreeable sensory impressions and related feelings of falling apart. This sensorimotor communication from the child seeks a recipient and, thus, passes on a commensurate frame of mind to the mother, if she is able to open her mind to the child's primitive communication and, as described above, enter into a receptive, unfocused, dreamlike state. Relative to the relationship between mother and infant, Bion defined reverie as follows: "that state of mind which is open to the reception of any 'objects' from the loved object and is therefore capable of reception of the infant's projective identifications whether they are felt by the infant to be good or bad" (1962b, p. 36).

The container–contained relationship represents an emotional relationship in which a recipient (a parent or a psychotherapist), by means of reverie, makes her mind available as a container for an infant's or (as in child and adolescent psychotherapy) the young client's projective identification of parts of the self that are so unbearable that he cannot mentally process and give meaning to them. In the more mature mind of the parent/therapist, the crude sensory impressions (beta-elements) projected by the child are transformed into reflective and symbolic thoughts, feelings, and phantasies, enabling an intuitive understanding of the child's states and needs. Bion named this ability the alpha-function (α-function). The alpha-function works through largely non-conscious mental processes, in which the parent/therapist uses empathic mirroring and suitable mental and literal care to return to the child the formerly projected, now improved, parts of his inner world in such a way that the new, improved version of the self becomes tolerable (digestible) to the child. The repetition of these benignly virtuous circles constitutes the relationship with the parent/therapist as an inner function—an inner, empathic, and emotionally nourishing parental presence—that contributes to the development of affect regulation, frustration tolerance, empathy, and self-knowledge.

Parental and therapeutic containment will, after all, always be incomplete and sometimes flawed; for example, because of the parent's/therapist's occasional misunderstandings and moments of absence (mental or physical), or because the infant is especially difficult to contain, for instance, because of the weak, indistinct, or disorganised nature of his projective identifications. In other words, dedicated and empathic parents/therapists will also at times fail to meet the child's expectations with an appropriate realisation. Thus, even in the best of mother–infant relationships, at certain moments the child does not introject a relationship with an empathic parental-figure-easing-my-mental-state, but, rather, engages in a relationship with an insensitive parental-figure-worsening-my-distress. Moreover, the child reintrojects his own unbearable feelings into an insufficiently modified, unaltered, aggravated, or fundamentally misunderstood form. In these distressing moments, the child introjects a relationship with a misunderstanding and/or flooding part of the parental object. In early ordinary development, through these processes, the split organisation of object relationships that Klein (1946) named the paranoid–schizoid position becomes constituted in the infant's psyche. (See Figure 1, a graphic representation—inspired by Bion (1962b) and Riesenberg-Malcolm (2001)—of successful *vs.* failed containment.)

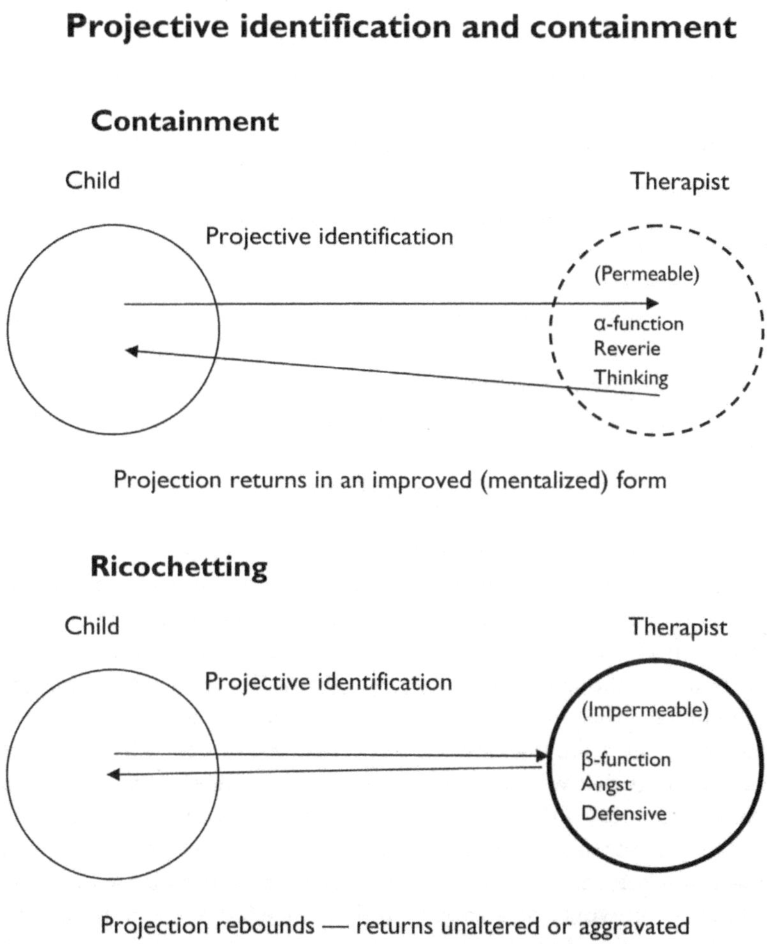

Figure 1. Graphic depicting projective identification and containment: successful *vs.* failed containment.

The container–contained relationship ambiguously refers to both an intrapsychic and an interpersonal phenomenon. As an intrapsychic occurrence, it refers to a subjectively containing, inner structure in the form of an unconscious relationship with an inner object, which enables the person to regulate, represent, and think about, rather than enact, inner states of mind. As an interpersonal occurrence, it refers to a particularly close, non-verbal connection or rapport between two persons, for example, mother and infant or therapist and child. In this relationship, both participants are engaged in, and receptive to, an emotional communication leading up to exploration and mental development. Hence, an interruption of the connection (e.g., a sudden termination of therapy) will be painful to both participants, entailing an experience of loss (Bion, 1962a).

In psychotherapy with children and adolescents, the container–contained relationship can denote the relationship between the therapist's thinking–feeling mind and such parts of the child's inner world that the child is mentally unable to transform into meaningful feelings and thoughts and, therefore, wordlessly communicates to the therapist through actions and attitudes. Yet, container–contained might also refer to the child's introjection and identification with the containing relationship with the therapist; in that case, it refers to an ongoing development constituting, in the child's inner world, an understanding and regulating object, a forthcoming mental structure of self-control and confidence in the mind of the child.

(Clive, excerpt, session 7). He brings his box and asks, "Actually, what are worries anyway?" Before I get around to answering, he finds a little broom and asks, "What do we use this for? Is it meant to clean up everything?" (I remind him that just before, he asked what worries are . . . what are his thoughts about a worry, what is it?) Clive says that a worry is something that gives one a tummy ache, sometimes so much that one has to fart to make it go away again. ("Yes, you're right", I say. "Worries can be things that we think so hard about that we get sad or get all mixed up, and sometimes they can make one's tummy hurt a lot.") "I don't think I have any worries," says Clive, "or, yes, sometimes I still fart a lot, but that's not the reason, I think." He carries on talking about the broom, which he felt would be a good help if one needed to clean up sand from the floor of the playroom.

(Clive, excerpt, session 9). For a while, Clive is very focused on drawing. "This is a fart-shit," he says. He draws a microscopic dot on the paper.

(I suggest that it might be a worry-fart.) Clive confirms and colours a dark green ring around it, making the dot a little bigger. He colours so vigorously that the colour nearly saturates the paper. Then he wants to draw something that makes "the worry-farts a little scary". He colours the border of the dot red ... ("It's just like blood," I say). "Yes," he says, "so it is. This is why, when it comes out it hurts so much if the baby is too big." (I: "Maybe you're wondering if the babies and the worry-farts are coming out of the same place?") "Yes," says Clive, "do they also come out of the bum?" He adds that this drawing is for me, so that I can see what the worry-farts look like. He lifts up the upper paper and sees that the colour went all the way through to the underlying sheet of paper. (I comment, "Yes, those worry-farts take up so much space that even through two sheets of paper, you can still see them.") "Yes, in fact, my worry-farts are only on the bottom paper, where you can barely see them." (I reply that, in fact, there was a much bigger worry-fart on the upper paper, although now it really was not visible any more.) "No," says Clive, "now, it's your worry-fart, just like mummy has a baby brother in her tummy." (I say, "Maybe you're anxious that I won't have enough space here for you?") Clive replies, "Yes, what if you had another baby now, and then you didn't have the time to come here any more—in that case, one would have to give up all sorts of things one used to do."

Symbol formation and relational thinking

A fundamental assumption of psychodynamic theories of early development concerns infants' and toddlers' awareness that, as part of ordinary family life, their parents temporarily leave and return. Thus, on a par with the stable presence of emotionally available parental figures, the young child's recurring experiences of temporary absence are considered an important precondition for healthy emotional and cognitive development. Accordingly, in a context of stable attachment, recurring real-life experiences of a parental figure's physical absence will enhance the child's capacity to contain depressive feelings such as sadness, longing, and mourning, thus helping the child come to terms with developmental dilemmas related to dependence and separateness. On the one hand, it is crucial that the parents provide a containing caring relationship, in which they mirror and respond to their young child's needs, feelings, and intentions in a sufficiently sensitive, congruent, and marked way. On the other hand, the parents' ability and willingness, at regular intervals, to let the child experience limited, not excessively prolonged, absences are equally necessary as an incentive for mental development.

Correspondingly, assumptions of a formative relationship between early anxiety situations, unconscious phantasy, and the ability to explore and seek new learning are already to be found in Klein's early works. In these papers, she explored the connections between the psychogenic inhibition of learning: for example, literacy, and inhibitions related to curiosity concerning gender, sexuality, and reproduction (1921, 1923). Klein argued that curiosity—the urge to explore and get to know—is a central, constitutional drive, calling this "the epistemophilic instinct". She contended that a healthy balance between anxiety and the urge to know is crucial for mental development and the ability of symbol formation, for example, as manifested in dreams and symbolic play. Therefore, a touch of anxiety or concern—provided it is not overwhelming—might encourage the child to seek out other, emotionally more neutral, relationships than the early, sensory-based closeness to the mother. In this way, anxiety and curiosity interact and stimulate the child's search for new knowledge and development (Klein, 1930).

Bion regarded the cognitive capacity as dependent on two main mental developments: a development of thoughts (i.e., ideas, intentions, expectations, reasons, states of mind) and, since these thoughts have to be thought by a thinker, also a development of an apparatus for coping with thoughts (i.e., thinking). He held this development to depend, in part, on the child's introjection of a containing relationship (as described above) and in part on the child's tolerance of frustration, which, in this context, should be understood as the capacity to contain and take ownership of one's own frustrated feelings and behaviour—as opposed to a tendency to evade the experience of frustration (Bion, 1962a,b; Riesenberg-Malcolm, 2001). In essence, how the child copes with frustration stemming from the parent's absence or empathic failure takes up a central position in this model as a precondition for the development of a capacity for thinking (symbolic) thoughts. The implication is that a certain dose of experiential frustration is considered necessary for the development of mental structures (the alpha-apparatus) for transforming primitive emotional experience into wistful recollection and, consequently, into symbolic thinking about relationships. This principle, however, is valid only if these challenges (absence and empathic failure) are not too prolonged or too frequent and if they are, to a certain degree, compensated for by alternative care. Otherwise, there is a considerable risk that absences and empathic failures will lead not to development, but, rather, to early neglect and traumatisation.

As described, when the child is able subjectively to contain and recognise the absence of the good parental object, the child's frustration is transformed to a thought about and a longing for the good, but absent object. By this mental operation, the child takes the first steps towards the development of an inner apparatus with which to think symbolic–relational thoughts. Or, in other words, a cognitive–affective structure capable of recognising emotional experience and adding symbolic meaning in the process. As a result of the child's endurance of the experience of himself as emotionally attached to, and dependent on, a less than perfect object, he gradually becomes able to relinquish infantile omnipotence and omniscience in favour of a self-image as an ordinary human being who is willing and able to seek out and learn from new experiences and knowledge.

Formulations of aims

It is a hallmark of the work with children and adolescents that it takes place amid the flux of an ongoing personality development. As the therapeutic work stirs up the fundamental urge to explore, get to know, and learn through experience, this becomes a central impetus in a process of personal change. With an expression coined by Anna Freud, in psychodynamic literature, this inborn thrust of childhood and adolescence for continuing psychobiological development is often referred to as an "urge to complete development" (A. Freud, 1965, p. 28). This might, for instance, express itself as the child's ardent wish to become as capable as other same-age children in coping with age-adequate anxieties, tasks, and challenges. When such personal (specific) aims of development and learning take shape in the child's mind, they should be noticed, since they provide an essential contribution to the formation of a genuine therapeutic alliance that is acknowledged by the children/adolescents themselves (the challenges of the concept of a therapeutic alliance in relation to children and adolescents are more fully explained and discussed in Chapter Five).

In line with Anna Freud, one could describe the general aims of child and adolescent psychotherapy as restoring the child to the path of normal development (Edgcumbe, 2000; Sandler et al., 1980). In accordance with Klein, the general aims could, instead, be stated as increased synthesis between the contrasting feelings of love and hate followed by a growth in ego integration (Klein, 1950, 1952). As a common denominator, in general, psychodynamic child and adolescent psychotherapy builds on the assumption that every child is to be considered a unique being with his or her own personal developmental path formed on the basis of innate human potentialities and subjective experiences of past and present relationships and life events. The therapist, accordingly, will do his best to establish a viable communication with the child's inner potential for development, addressing the child's unique urge for exploration and development.

In any modality of psychotherapeutic treatment, it is necessary to distinguish between aim and method, that is, between the aimed-for effect and the processes through which the therapist seeks to attain this effect. Although this might seem to be a trivial point, it is a common cause of difficulties, also in explanations of how and why psychodynamic therapy works. This difficulty is related to an inherent paradox in the psychodynamic approach: the demand that the therapist should relinquish her ambitions to cure the child and, instead, adopt a non-directed therapeutic attitude. In psychodynamic child and adolescent psychotherapy, the therapist perceives all verbal and non-verbal manifestations as conscious and unconscious statements that convey information about the child's inner phantasies and object relations, the mood of the child's inner world, and the child's experience of the present relationship with the therapist. Rather than offering teaching and tutelage, the psychodynamic psychotherapist strives to understand the child's life situation and inner world. Thus, in order to understand statements that the child cannot convey verbally but mainly communicates through play and other behaviour, she draws on her own subjective reactions in the therapeutic work.

Consequently, the therapist's state of reverie implies an open, not-knowing state of mind, bracketing information from the parents or the child's file and relating, first and foremost, to the child's communication in the therapeutic here-and-now. Taken literally, since all human perception and understanding take shape and colour from the subjectivity of the inner world, this demand is an existential impossibility.

That is one of the reasons why the ability of therapists to include their own countertransference is an important precondition for any effort to differentiate between the child's and their own perspective. To understand a child's play behaviour in the light of the present transference relationship, the therapist needs to focus on the unknown, as stated by Bion, doing her best to cultivate "a watchful avoidance" of memory and desire (1967, p. 18). For a start, this means that the therapist should meet the child with an open, observing mind, putting aside her preconceived knowledge not only of case history, but also of what took place in the previous session. Second, she must be able to contain her own ambitions, taking care that her own ego does not come to depend on curing the child or guiding her decisions in any particular direction.

Anna Freud explained this attitude of having no specific aim in very straightforward terms:

> Analysts should distinguish between aim and method in psychoanalytic treatment. The analyst's aim is stated in terms of the patient's needs. The analyst's method is not to concentrate on these needs during the course of treatment but rather to direct attention to the analytic process itself. The analyst reaches his aims only if he concentrates on the process. It is very much like driving somewhere. Your aim is to arrive, and if instead of looking at the road, you think how nice it will be when you arrive, you will probably have an accident. Concentrating on the driving process implies steering the car. The aim and the method are different. (cited in Sandler et al., 1980, p. 251)

As seen, this does not mean ignoring the aims of the treatment. As described above, before the start of therapy, it is important to discuss the aims in a dialogue with the parents and, in some form or another, with the child or the adolescent himself. This dialogue about progression and setbacks should continue throughout the course of therapy.

First, however, it is important to remember that the child's or adolescent's own conscious desires for change might differ considerably from the changes envisaged by the people around him. The development of a therapeutic process requires the therapist to make contact with the child's own worries and experiences of himself and his relationships with respect for his uniquely subjective developmental potentials. In practice—as shown in the above vignette about Clive and his therapist—this means initiating the therapy with an enquiring mind in order to get to know the child's own worries and ideas about change. Second, when it comes to children and adolescents in foster care and residential treatment, it will usually be appropriate to involve the foster parents and/or the professional team with the goal of working together to secure the development and general welfare of the referred child by setting appropriate treatment aims and criteria for the desired development (see Chapter Seven on the importance of the parents' commitment).

This leads up to a final paradox: that while the therapist-inside-the-therapy actively excludes any thoughts about the aims of treatment, the therapist-outside-the-therapy needs to be keenly aware of these aims. Hence, it is of paramount importance to the effectiveness of therapy that the agreement about the aimed-for change between the parents, the therapist, and, whenever relevant, the professional team (in the following referred to as the treatment organisation) not only includes the wishes, worries, and anxieties of the parents and other adults, but is also framed by a specific, realistic assessment of the child's or adolescent's resources for development. Further, the treatment organisation also has to consider how the therapy can contribute to remedying or reducing the child's problems or suffering. No less important, at regular intervals the treatment organisation should meet to evaluate the effect of therapy, as this feedback from parents and professional workers who are in daily contact with the child offers a crucial possibility for properly reality-testing the impact of the therapy.

Diverse traditions

It is debatable whether psychodynamic child and adolescent psychotherapy can rightly be described as a uniform therapeutic method, which prescribes certain determinate, predictable principles to demarcate the context, setting, therapeutic philosophy, attitude, and interventions. Accordingly, ever since the first attempts at psychotherapy with children in the early twentieth century, there has been a lively and, at times, heated ongoing debate about principles and methods (A. Freud, 1946, 1966b; Klein, 1927, 1955). Out of these discussions, especially between Anna Freud and Melanie Klein, different traditions and related organisational conflicts emerged. Yet, the debate also gave rise to productive theoretical developments in the form of new concepts that became part of everyday child and adolescent therapeutic practice: for example, object relations, mirroring, splitting, identification with aggressor, projective identification, and containment. Also, despite certain differences, there seem to be obvious affinities between, on the one hand, Klein's and Bion's theories on symbol formation and the development of an apparatus for thinking, and, on the other, the more recent concept of mentalization (Fonagy & Allison, 2012; Fonagy et al., 2002a).

The original discussions peaked in the 1940s with a number of formal meetings at the British Psychoanalytical Society (often referred to as "the controversial discussions") debating various conceptions of fundamental psychoanalytic concepts. The details of these discussions digress too far from the subject matter of this book, but suffice it to say that they included the themes listed below, questions that, to this day and into the future, ought to give child and adolescent psychotherapists food for thought when planning psychotherapy:

- What is the role of symbolic play and phantasy in therapy sessions—and how can the therapist relate to children who neither engage in playing, drawing, nor dreaming?
- In child and adolescent psychotherapy, how might the therapeutic alliance best be conceptualised?
- In child and adolescent psychotherapy, how might the transference relationship and its development best be conceptualised?
- How to find a workable balance between interpretation of positive and negative transference feelings?
- How to find a workable balance between, on the one hand, verbal interpretation of unconscious phantasies and conflicts and, on the other hand, comments related to containment, clarification, and support?
- How to find a workable timing of, on the one hand, interpretation of unconscious phantasies and conflicts and, on the other, interventions aimed at immediate preservation and safeguarding of the setting, in effect, the therapeutic process?
- How best to include and engage the child's parents and the treatment organisation (if any) in a continuous effort of teamwork to support the therapy and promote benign change in the child's everyday relationships outside therapy?

CHAPTER THREE

Referral and assessment

Referral and assessment are important preconditions of any psychotherapy. The feasibility and effect of a given psychotherapy intervention depends on a solid foundation, which means sufficient information about the underlying problems and the involved persons as well as the presence of the necessary conditions for the chosen treatment. If a psychotherapy intervention is initiated on the basis of an insufficient assessment, it will often fail and, perhaps, end prematurely, something that may have negative consequences for the participants. Psychotherapists working with children and adolescents are often exposed to pressures from the persons around the child or adolescent to act fast. It is important to be able to resist this pressure and insist on sufficient time to conduct a proper assessment. A thorough preliminary assessment not only makes the potential subsequent treatment easier, but might, in itself, possess considerable therapeutic qualities. It might be necessary to make an exception and speed up the process, however, if a child is currently subjected to serious maltreatment or abuse; in that case, the safety of the child should be given priority over the assessment and precautions taken in order to prevent continuation of the abuse.

Often, the persons who refer a child or a young person for assessment and possible psychotherapy will expect and, perhaps, wish for the child to receive a psychiatric diagnosis. In such cases, it might be necessary to help them understand what the difference is between making a diagnosis and understanding the problem (or problems). A psychiatric diagnosis is not, as believed by many, the designation of an illness; on the contrary, the *ICD-10* deliberately uses the word "disorder" throughout in order to avoid the many problems inherent in the use of the words "disease" or "illness" (World Health Organization, 1992). The concepts of "illness" and "disease" easily suggest permanence and physiological causes, and it is probably exactly such (mis)conceptions that the authors of the system wanted to prevent. The diagnosis is solely a designation of a certain group of symptoms, a snapshot, so to speak. If the symptoms change or disappear, the diagnosis no longer applies.

As mentioned in Chapter One, the diagnoses are drawn up in such a way that they can be made solely on the basis of observation, without any inferences about inner states within the person. Thus, it is relatively easy to make a diagnosis, but the acquired knowledge is, correspondingly, so limited that it is far from a sufficient foundation of psychodynamic psychotherapy. The implementation of this form of treatment requires a significant amount of additional information. First, it is necessary to understand what the problem or problems are, how extensive they are, and where they are. The symptoms are rarely the problems, but just that, symptoms of something, and it is this "something" that the therapist needs to know more about. Second, it is necessary to get to know the child better, which implies knowing his history, assessing some of his personality functions, and understanding his personality structure. Finally, and no less important, it is necessary to learn about his family, his environment, and his total life conditions. All these aspects will be further developed below.

Characteristics of assessment of children and adolescents

For several reasons, the assessment of children and adolescents is more difficult and complicated than the assessment of adults. Children and adolescents cover an age spectrum from newborn infants to near-adult seventeen-year-olds. Thus, it encompasses children and young persons on widely different stages of development, and, obviously, neither assessment nor treatment can be identical across this age span. In the book, we do not include a description of assessment and treatment of zero-to-three-year-old infants and young children. Usually, they are treated in parent–infant psychotherapy, which, like psychodynamic child psychotherapy, builds on psychodynamic theory, but, of course, uses methods that are adapted to the presence of both infant and parents. In spite of the differences, however, some things are common to all children and adolescents: they are not of age and cannot make decisions for themselves about accepting or refusing treatment, and, consequently, their parents have to be involved in all decisions concerning possible psychotherapy. Besides, children have only a limited capacity to express their problems, feelings, and thoughts in words. Therefore, the clinician needs help in her assessment from the adults who know the child best, primarily his parents, but also, for example, teachers.

The initial contacts

Children and adolescents might seek help for themselves, but, much more often, the grown-ups around them appeal for help because they are worried. That can be the parents, but could also be other persons or agencies, for example, the school or social services. When persons other than the parents refer the child, it is always a good first move to contact the referring agency, which will often have more information than was offered at first, including written records. The referring person or agency might also have expectations about what might emerge from the referral, and it might be wise to discuss these expectations already at this point. Perhaps, there is a wish for individual psychotherapy for the child or other specific treatment modalities. When that is the case, it might be a good idea to clarify to the referring agency that a decision about possible and suitable treatment options cannot be made until the assessment has been completed.

As the next step, the direct assessment of the child and his family may begin. The parents of a child with problems might naturally expect that the assessment primarily concerns the child. However, if the clinician acts on this expectation and initiates the assessment in sessions with the child alone, there is a considerable risk of running into difficulties. Even after several sessions with the child, the clinician will usually be left with an insufficient understanding of the issues. If the parents are subsequently invited to take part in a session, they will often, quite understandably, expect to learn what the problem is and, perhaps, even receive a treatment proposal. As this will not be possible, the parents could end up frustrated, which is, of course, very unfortunate.

The first task actually consists in building a good working alliance with the parents. It is important to help them understand that it is not possible to initiate a treatment right away, solely based on knowledge of the child's symptoms, as this requires more thorough knowledge and understanding and, consequently, a more comprehensive assessment. It is, likewise, important to help them understand the crucial importance they have for their child and that they possess information about the child that the clinician needs to gain insight into. A conjoint family interview is, therefore, often a much better introduction to an assessment and lays a good foundation for understanding the family environment. In addition to learning the basic facts, such as who the family members are, and how the parents and siblings spend their time (work/school, hobbies, etc.), this also lets the therapist gain an impression of the family members and their mutual relations. In such an interview, it is usually also possible to elaborate on the description of the child's problems, how long they have lasted, and—something that is very important to know—how the parents understand them. Do they think that their child suffers from a congenital disease of the brain, that the school treats their child inappropriately, or that they, themselves, might have a part in the child's difficulties? It is, likewise, important to find out what the parents have done to try to remedy the problems, and how these attempts have worked out. It is a good idea to enquire into what kind of help the parents hope to receive. Family interviews might also help to clarify whether it is necessary to involve the school/preschool in the assessment, and, if so, obtain the parents' permission to involve them.

Such an in-depth interview with all members of the family is often a new experience to them and might, in itself, lead to positive processes in the family, as illustrated by the following example:

> A family asked for help for their ten-year-old son, Peter, who had developed encopresis (faecal soiling). Both parents, Peter, and his six-year-old sister participated in the interview. It appeared that, not long ago, the

father had been involved in a serious accident that had left him partly disabled and unable to work. The family members were all eager to explain how well they had coped with this difficult situation, and they were inclined to maintain that it had not had any negative consequences for them as a family. As a result of my persistent questioning, however, little by little, it emerged that Peter very much missed doing sports together with his father and going on bicycle rides with him, something they had both enjoyed. During the interview, it became obvious that Peter tried to protect his father from hearing this; he objected every time I approached the subject. Peter's younger sister also participated actively in the interview, frequently interrupting and, thus, in her own way, showing her resistance to touching the painful topic. Another interview was planned for some time later.

Before the scheduled time for the second interview, however, Peter's mother rang to cancel the appointment. She explained that further sessions were unnecessary, as Peter's encopresis had stopped. They acknowledged that it had been a good experience for them to discuss their situation together and face some facts that they had been inclined to ignore. She also said that, during the interview, they had noticed how much the younger sister dominated her brother, and that they had subsequently made some changes at home, giving Peter more privileges in accordance with his age, with positive consequences.

In a case like this, when a family has been struck by a shared traumatising event, conjoint work with the family is usually the best help to offer, at least in the beginning, even if one of the children might have developed a specific symptom.

If the parents are divorced and find it difficult to co-operate, it might be necessary to talk with them separately. Often, one or both parents will have found new partners, and, in that case, it might be expedient to include the new partner(s) in the interview. It must be decided on a case-by-case basis what is the best approach.

The child's history

Since children, as mentioned, have only a limited capacity to talk about themselves, their background and their development, a thorough history-taking with the parents is a key part of any assessment of a child or adolescent. Ideally, both parents should participate in the interview. However, if this is not possible, the therapist should talk to the parent who has the most contact with the child. The child should not be present at the interview, as this might hamper the disclosure of important information.

It is not our intention to offer a detailed description of how such an interview should be carried out. However, we do want to emphasise the importance of being especially careful in the investigation of the child's first years of life and the enfolding of his relationships inside the family, especially with his parents (and/or other primary attachment figures). It is not rare that a connection is found between the child's current problems and difficulties affecting the child or the family during the child's first years of life, such as maternal depression, marital problems, or other issues that have had long-lasting mental consequences for the child. Such connections are far from always seen or understood by the family members themselves, as the following example demonstrates:

> A nine-year-old boy, Nick, was referred for aggressive and violent behaviour and frequent temper tantrums, particularly in relation to his parents. His developmental history revealed that he had been born with deformities to his feet, and that his parents had been trained to provide the necessary treatment during his infancy. This was difficult, as the treatment was painful for Nick, but it was necessary in order to avoid later disabilities. From Nick's psychological assessment, it appeared that he harboured early-founded distrust and anger towards his parents. In all probability, these feelings were associated with the early painful treatments that, of course, the parents had not been able to explain to him as an infant. Nick was offered long-term individual psychotherapy, and the parents engaged in parallel parent work, with good results.

When the child's history is taken, it is a good idea not only to pay attention to the facts, but also, in particular, to the parents' understanding of them and their attitude to them. The more thorough these first interviews are, the easier it will usually be to agree with the parents about the nature of the problems after the assessment and, in turn, to agree on a treatment proposal.

Assessment of the child

After the interviews with the parents, the child himself must be seen individually by the therapist. If a child or young person is suspected, for example, to have a severe attachment disorder, an autism spectrum disorder, or any other severe developmental disturbances, a full clinical psychological assessment should be recommended. With less extensive disturbances, the child can be assessed by the psychotherapist in preparation for psychotherapy. The parents are asked to prepare their child for a couple or more sessions with the psychotherapist in order for her to get to know him better and understand how he might best be helped with his difficulties. When the child arrives, usually accompanied by one of his parents, the psychotherapist speaks with the child alone. Some children are so anxious at first that they want their parent to accompany them into the room and stay with them there, and it might be necessary to allow this for a little while. The assessment of the child should not begin, however, until the parent has left the room. If the child is quite unable to let go of his parents, this may be an indication that—at this stage—individual psychotherapy with the child is not possible. In that case, it might be necessary to postpone further individual assessment of the child, instead working with the parents' ability to separate from their child. For children older than three to four years of age, this problem indicates a serious attachment disorder, and, hence, a clinical psychological investigation is warranted.

It is a good idea to begin by asking the child what he has been told about the assessment and, if he seems uncertain, to explain the reason to him. An assessment of a child by a child psychotherapist can encompass interviews, and—with young children—a couple or more play observations. If the child undergoes a full psychological assessment, a variety of psychological tests might be included as well. Besides gaining a more thorough understanding of the child's problems, the purpose is to get an impression of key personality functions and the child's personality structure. It is difficult to plan an assessment in detail beforehand.

If psychological testing is necessary, as a rule, it is advisable to begin with one of the more structured tests: for example, a cognitive test such as the WPPSI (Wechsler Preschool and Primary Scales of Intelligence) or the WISC (Wechsler Intelligence Scale for Children), if they have not already been administered. Because these tests are similar to schoolwork, which is familiar ground for the child, they will usually have a calming effect. However, they only provide limited information about the child and usually need to be supplemented with projective tests, such as, for example, drawings, the Rorschach test, the TAT (Thematic Apperception Test), or the Sceno test. Play observation is also an important tool in the assessment of younger children. It would go too far to describe in detail how such an assessment is made; it is a special task that requires training under supervision. Not least, the use of projective tests and play observation requires supervision or experience, because they rest, to a great extent, on the interpretation of symbolic content. With the youngest children, play observation and, for example, the Sceno test are useful instruments for assessing the child's personality structure; for children from the age of six, the Rorschach test is particularly well suited.

It is always necessary to keep an open mind throughout the assessment process; for example, if in the course of the assessment the therapist finds that it is necessary to supplement with neuropsychological tests or other specialised tools, this should be added to the process. On the other hand, an assessment should never be continued longer than necessary; once a sufficient understanding of the child is reached, the assessment should end.

As a guideline in determining which personality functions it is necessary to know, the therapist may rely, for example, on the Profile of Mental Functioning for Children and Adolescents (PDM Task Force, 2006, pp. 181–191). The list is helpful in ensuring that no important functions are missed. It contains the following areas.

1. Capacity for regulation, attention, and learning.
2. Capacity for relationships and intimacy.
3. Quality of internal experience (level of confidence and self-regard).
4. Affective experience, expression, and communication.
5. Defensive patterns and capacities.
6. Capacity to form internal representations.
7. Capacity for differentiation and integration.
8. Self-observing capacity (psychological-mindedness).
9. Capacity to construct or use internal standards and ideals: sense of morality.

In addition to assessing these functions, it is necessary to form an overall picture of the child's personality; this might, for example, be done on the basis of object relation theory and attachment theory. The description of the various functions above might help in this endeavour; for instance, an assessment of the child's capacity for emotional contact, reality testing, and defence structure makes it possible to assess whether the child predominantly functions in the paranoid–schizoid position or if he has continued his development and is (also) able to function in the depressive position.

An assessment of the child's attachment pattern based on CAI (Children's Attachment Interview) requires special training. However, an assessment of the child's capacity for emotional contact, his affect regulation, his ability to form inner representations, and his capacity for imagination (mentalization) will help shed light on the child's attachment pattern.

Planning of intervention

Based on the assessment of the child and the interviews with the parents, it is usually possible both to form an overall impression of the child as a person and to obtain an understanding of the dominating problems, how extensive they are, and where in the child–family system they are located. As mentioned above, the main causes of a child's problems might very well lie outside the child. There are several possibilities, as listed below.

1. The child's symptoms might occur in reaction to an acute problem in his environment: for example, illness in the family, divorce, an accident, or other traumatic experiences.
2. The symptoms might be a reaction to prolonged stress or recurrent trauma inside or outside the family; the child might live in a chronically dysfunctional family, or he might have lived under straining circumstances, for example, in war or as a refugee.
3. The symptoms might originate primarily within the child; for instance, the child might have physical or mental congenital disorders, or a foster child might have severe early attachment problems stemming from the time before he was placed in his current foster family.

Of course, these variants can—and often do—occur in various combinations. From the beginning of life, some infants are easily irritable and difficult to soothe, and a poor temperamental fit between mother and infant might also make the early regulation complicated. Also, if a child grows up in a severely malfunctioning family setting, or under other adverse circumstances, his personality will gradually be influenced and the problems will be internalised in his personality.

The therapist's understanding of the problems can lead to an evaluation of the most appropriate form of treatment. Later in this chapter, we describe when individual psychotherapy to a child or an adolescent is the best, or even the only, possibility, but it should be remembered that this modality is not always the best choice. We have already offered one example, where conjoint family therapy was preferable. When the problem resides mainly in the family unit or in the parents, it is usually a better idea to suggest family therapy or parental guidance. Perhaps the parents find it difficult to show the necessary parental authority and set boundaries for their child, or divorced parents might put each other down when speaking to their child. Such situations can lead to symptoms in the child, which might, however, disappear again if the parents can be engaged in a mutual effort to solve the problems.

If the parents are unable to give their child sufficient emotional and basic care, individual child psychotherapy also is not the right choice—at this point. Psychotherapy can never be a substitute for care. In such cases, a number of steps can be taken to help the parents provide the necessary care for their child. If this is not possible, however, removing the child from the family might be warranted.

Children who have recently lost a parent or other close relative are often referred to individual psychotherapy or, perhaps, to a grief support group. However, this is not always the best solution. Usually, it is best for the child to be helped by the remaining parent. They are both affected by the same loss, and it might strengthen the bond between them to share their feelings about what happened. If the parent feels unable to do it, he or she can be offered support and advice about how to speak with the child about what happened. Joint sessions with the parent and child together are another possibility. If only the child receives help, there is a risk that the parent might feel left out, which could, in turn, increase the risk of division within the family at a vulnerable time.

Response to the family

When the assessment is completed, the therapist is left with a wealth of information about the child, his family, and his overall life situation. The task now is to derive a meaningful pattern from this comprehensive body of knowledge. The information must also be related to the therapist's working theories in order to lay the foundation for a holistic and dynamic understanding of the problems at hand. This is the most demanding stage in any assessment, and it is a task that requires both skill and training. If the therapist is not sufficiently experienced, supervision is crucial. Sometimes, apparently minor details might be very important, such as slight differences in the quality of the emotional contact with the child, while more conspicuous details are not always essential. It is, however, always important to remember that the result must, by necessity, be provisional and of a hypothetical nature. As a rule, the therapist will find that her understanding develops and changes as she works with the child and his family.

When the therapist has, thus, thoroughly considered her findings and determined what she considers the best possible intervention, her conclusion must be communicated to the family, both to the parents and to the child (unless he is too young). It is preferable first to talk with the parents, since they have the authority to decide whether to accept the treatment proposal. It would be unfortunate to speak with the child or the young person first and to hold out a prospect of, for example, psychotherapy that the parents subsequently decline.

The results of the assessment must be communicated in terms that are easy to understand for both parents and child, and psychological and psychodynamic concepts should, as far as possible, be translated into everyday language. If the preliminary interviews with the parents have been thorough, it is often possible to take one's point of departure in incidents and observations originally introduced by the parents while supplementing and expanding on them with observations from the assessment. This links the therapist's understanding with the parents' and, ideally, leaves the parents feeling that they have been understood, and that their understanding has been further expanded and amplified by the clinician. When this link is successfully established, it usually provides a framework for the therapist's treatment proposal. However, it is not always that easy. Sometimes, the clinician's understanding is quite different from the parents', and when that is the case, several interviews might be necessary to reach a mutual understanding. In yet other cases, it proves impossible to reach an agreement.

When the interviews with the parents are finished, the therapist can speak with the child. Sometimes, it is a good idea to see the child with the parents, to let everybody know that everyone is in agreement about the next steps. Usually, what is said to the child or the young client is less comprehensive than what has been said to the parents; however, the same principle applies, of taking one's starting point in, and developing further, what the child or young client has said.

While with grown-up clients, the working alliance is made with the client himself, in child psychotherapy the alliance must mainly be made with the child's parents, and the younger the child, the more this applies. Older children and, especially, adolescents must also, at least to some degree, be motivated for psychotherapy themselves. As described by Carr (2009), the therapeutic alliance is the most important common factor in psychotherapy, and its importance is no less when it is made with the child's parents. Therefore, it is crucial to give the parents thorough feedback, not only about the therapist's understanding of the child's problems, but also about the aims of the psychotherapy and, on a more basic level, what psychotherapy is about. If the parents have had experience with psychotherapy themselves, they might already have some knowledge of the process, but that is rarely the case. Neither is psychotherapy with adults and children completely alike, and most parents will not know the difference. Having a child in psychotherapy often gives rise to a certain degree of anxiety in the parents: they might be worried that the therapist will compete with them about the child, and that, with all her psychological knowledge, she will be a "better" parent than they are. It is, therefore, important to emphasise to the parents that the therapist's task is very different from theirs. It is—as always—their task to give their child emotional and basic care, protection, and guidance. The therapist's job, on the other hand, is to help the child overcome the impediments to his growth and development. The most important goal is not to search for the *reasons* for the child's difficulties, as some parents might fear, but to understand their *meaning*. Parents could also worry that their child will complain about them in therapy; it might be reassuring if the therapist explains that the therapy has only a very limited focus on the child's current daily life. Instead, the therapist might explain to the parents that the treatment revolves around helping the child to play out deep-seated feelings and attitudes in his relationship with the therapist, that the focus is on these fundamental and (usually unconscious) feelings, and that it is possible to help the child by working through these, often quite strong, feelings.

When to use individual child and adolescent psychotherapy

Above, a number of situations are described when individual psychotherapy is not considered suitable, but there are certainly cases when this treatment modality is the optimal, and sometimes it is probably even the only, effective approach. For individual child psychotherapy to be successful, however, a number of conditions must be met. Some of these conditions have to do with the child, others with the parents or other carers, and yet others with the psychotherapist or the organisation offering psychotherapy.

Necessary conditions in the child

In a number of cases, the child will have intrapsychic problems of such a kind or magnitude that an offer of individual treatment is warranted. The results of such psychotherapies are described in numerous case studies, but are now also supported by empirical quantitative research (see Chapter Thirteen). Children with emotional problems, such as anxiety or depression, are good candidates for this kind of treatment, and they often improve relatively easily and quickly. Their treatment does not necessarily have to be long term or intensive; a course of weekly psychotherapy of one to two years' duration will usually be sufficient, sometimes even less, depending on the scope of the child's problems and the co-operation of the persons around the child. Traumatised children, too, stand to benefit from individual psychotherapy (see Chapter Twelve).

In many cases, aggressive children or children with adjustment disorders will also be able to benefit from this kind of treatment, but they often need more prolonged and more frequent psychotherapy, with at least two weekly sessions. As they often think that the problems originate not in themselves, but in the persons around them, they might be inclined to drop out prematurely. A significant effort from parents or other carers is, therefore, often needed to keep them in therapy. If this effort is successful, however, they do stand to benefit from the therapy. Usually, it is easier to keep the child in therapy if, besides his adjustment problems, he also suffers from anxiety and, thus, experiences subjective discomfort.

Children with extensive attachment disturbances—for example, many adopted children or children placed in foster care or residential institutions—were once regarded as being beyond the reach of psychotherapy and were, consequently, often referred to educational or special-needs counselling. The development of psychotherapy theories and methods has, fortunately, made it possible to change this perception. A large number of evidence-based studies now show that these children are better helped through individual psychotherapy than by any other means. This has been described in in-depth case studies (e.g., Cleve, 2004) as well as in quantitative empirical research. These children often need at least twice-weekly treatment of several years' duration, but, in spite of this, the treatment is a low-cost provision compared to the expenses society could incur if they are left untreated. Children with severe disorders, such as psychotic or autistic children, will also, in many cases, be able to benefit greatly from individual psychotherapeutic treatment (see Chapter Eleven).

Necessary conditions in the parents

As mentioned above, it is necessary to be sure that a child who is offered individual psychotherapy receives sufficient care. Having a child in psychotherapy, however, also makes other demands on the parents. They must be concerned about their child and need to understand that the offer of psychotherapy is well founded and necessary. They must understand the necessity of the child's regular attendance without too many breaks and of their own support for the process, also during periods when the child, perhaps, resists attending. Younger children must often be brought in for the sessions by one of their parents, which could be difficult to arrange for a family where both parents are employed in the workplace. This problem can sometimes be solved by an arrangement where the child travels by taxi from his school or preschool. Finally, the parents must commit to participating in parallel parent work, and sometimes in network meetings.

If there is any doubt about the parents' motivation, it is often a good idea to begin work with the parents before the child begins his psychotherapy. If the parent work goes well, the child therapy may be initiated without problems; otherwise, one runs the risk of initiating therapy only to have to discontinue the course after a little while, something that is always unfortunate. In that case, it would be better for the child not to begin therapy in the first place.

Necessary conditions in the treatment organisation

The institution that wants to undertake individual child or adolescent psychotherapy must have at its disposal persons who will commit to a treatment of the planned duration. If short-term therapy is planned, which might often be sufficient and beneficial, that is not usually a problem. If, however, the plan calls for long-term psychotherapy, it could be more difficult to secure the necessary stability. Of course, minor breaks due to, for example, holidays or sick leave are unavoidable in any therapy course, but, if the therapist knows beforehand that she will not be staying with the institution for the duration, she should not embark on a prolonged course of psychotherapy, as a change of therapist is best avoided. In practice, this is not always possible to ensure, but, from the outset, the therapy should be planned to take place without such major disruptions or impediments.

If the therapy takes place in a residential institution or an inpatient ward, the whole staff has to have some knowledge about individual child psychotherapy, so that its members can support the process; for example, by helping the child to attend all the sessions and by being aware of the splitting tendencies that might easily develop between individual staff members and the therapist.

Work with individual child and adolescent psychotherapy may be organised according to different models. In a classical model, two therapists work together, one as a therapist for the child, the other as a therapist for the parents and a co-ordinator for the network. There can be meetings with school, preschool, social services, etc. An advantage of this model is that it lets the child therapist focus on the often quite demanding work with the child without being exposed to the different pressures that the therapist is often subjected to from the persons around the child: for example, by teachers or parents who are impatient with the child's progress. It is an advantage if the two therapists know each other; as a minimum, they must agree on the theoretical framework for the process. It is preferable that they both have personal experience with child psychotherapy and—unless they are very experienced—access to supervision.

In another model, the same therapist works with the child, his parents, and the network. This is often the case, for example, if the therapy takes place in a private practice where the therapist has no colleagues with whom to share her work. In this model, the therapist is protected from the splitting that might otherwise arise between the two therapists. On the other hand, however, she has to endure and contain the often strong opposing countertransference feelings that can easily arise when the same person works with both the child and his parents. Anna Freud (1946) has given a vivid description of this. While working with a difficult and aggressive girl, she wrote that she felt it necessary to side with the child and to make herself the child's ally against her parents. That was the only way she could work *with* the child and not *against* her. She continued,

> The analyst . . . is commissioned and perhaps paid by the parents, and he always gets into an awkward position if he sets himself against his clients, even if it is in their own interest. In fact I never held the necessary consultations with this child's parents without feeling uneasy, and the analysis after some weeks, in spite of the best inherent condition, finally came to grief on account of this unclarified relationship. (p. 8)

By "this unclarified relationship", Anna Freud referred to the potential contrast between siding with the child while, at the same time, providing loyal support for the parents.

When, for example, social services pay for the therapy, and regular meetings with the network are, therefore, required, the total workload might be quite heavy. In that case, it could be difficult for a single therapist to give the parents as much time and support as they need.

Some families pay for their child's psychotherapy themselves, but, in many cases, the service is paid for by the municipality. This is necessary in all the cases when a child has been placed into care, but the municipality can also choose to support the treatment of a child living with his parents. In all cases involving third-party payment, it is the therapist's task, before the beginning of therapy, to provide the entity funding the treatment with a description of the child's problems, clarifying the need for child therapy. Although it might be difficult to give a realistic estimate of the duration of therapy, this should be attempted, and it is important not to underestimate the time required, as that could make it difficult to secure additional funding later. Usually, the referring agency will pay for only a limited period at a time, for example, six months, but it is important to secure reassurance in advance that the funding may be prolonged. It should also be agreed by the participants that a sudden and unscheduled termination should be avoided. It is complicated when other persons or agencies than the therapist and the family together can decide the duration of therapy, and, in such cases, the introductory phase is extremely important. Not all referring agencies know that child psychotherapy necessarily also includes continuous work with the parents and the larger network, and that these activities have to be funded as well. This is usually communicated in writing, but, in addition, it is often helpful to address this issue at a face-to-face meeting. Usually, it is a good idea if regular network meetings can be arranged that also include the referring agencies.

PART II

THERAPEUTIC SETTINGS AND THE THERAPEUTIC RELATIONSHIP

CHAPTER FOUR

Therapeutic settings in child and adolescent psychotherapy

As in other forms of treatment, the setting is an important parameter in child and adolescent psychotherapy. The setting is both a concrete and a mental demarcation of the therapeutic space. The setting protects the psychotherapy and indicates the difference between that and the child's daily life. When psychotherapy goes well, the setting is rarely noticed, and, instead, the attention is directed towards the content of the psychotherapy, what is said and done. The importance of the setting is, therefore, easily underestimated, and it does not always receive sufficient attention. A well-defined and protected setting is an absolutely necessary but, of course, not sufficient precondition for a successful psychotherapy.

The setting may be defined in a narrow as well as a wider sense. In a narrow sense, the setting includes:

1. The therapy room and its furnishings.
2. Play materials.
3. Agreements.
4. Time: that is, frequency and duration.

In a wider sense, the setting includes the institution where the therapy takes place: for example, a residential school, a child psychiatric ward, or a private practice, the larger organisation that these institutions are placed in, for example, a hospital service or a municipal administration, and the broader framework that society provides for psychotherapeutic work.

While the content of a psychotherapy is mainly determined by the child, the arrangement and maintenance of the setting is the therapist's responsibility. That is not always as easy as it might sound, and, from time to time, an otherwise successful psychotherapy process is broken off because of problems related to the setting.

Why is the setting so important? There are several reasons for that.

1. The setting demarcates therapy from other parts of the child's life.
2. The setting is the constant variable in the therapeutic process. When it is constant, the variations of the child's behaviour may be understood as reactions to his inner impulses or to what the therapist says and does. If the setting also varies, for example, with regard to the time and place, it is impossible to know whether these changes are the triggers for the child's behaviour.
3. A stable setting offers security and predictability. It demonstrates to the child that the therapist is trustworthy: for example, that she always arrives on time. It also protects the child from any kind of arbitrariness or boundary violations that might, for example, stem from the therapist's countertransference. The more severely traumatised the child is, the more crucial it is that the setting is safe.
4. A stable setting contributes to the development of structure in the child's thought processes. Many children in therapy have poorly developed ego functions and vague ideas about, for example, time and consistency. During the course of therapy, it is often possible to see how the child gradually begins constructing an understanding of such fundamental qualities.

There is a connection between the outer boundaries of the therapy room and the inner boundaries that the child sets up for himself. The more secure the outer boundaries are, the more the child can allow himself to let go of the control of the boundaries of his inner life.

That said, it must also be emphasised that the ideal of a totally stable setting can never be achieved. There are always holidays, illness, and other causes of breaks in psychotherapy. To deal with these interruptions, the therapist needs to do her best to respect the setting as much as possible, and she needs to notice and respond with empathy to the child's reactions to the breaks. No one can be a perfect therapist, just as no one can be a perfect mother; what the therapist can aim for is to be a "good-enough" therapist.

The therapy room

The therapy room must be adapted to child psychotherapy and should, preferably, be used only for that purpose. As pointed out by Hartnup (1999), the room should communicate both a sense of space and a feeling of containment, providing a setting where children and adolescents can bring up whatever is on their mind, without any objective reason to feel crowded or unsafe. It should provide a space where the child feels seen and accepted as the person he is, and where he can learn to think about what happens between him and the therapist. Preferably, child therapy should take place in a room that does not serve any other functions, such as paper work or sessions with adult clients. Such potentially disturbing elements could cause difficulties in work with oppositional, aggressive children whose inclination for testing boundaries will place considerable demands on the therapist's personal experience and authority. It is, however, not always possible to establish a special room for child therapy, and, in practice, many successful child therapies are carried through under less than ideal conditions. If it is necessary to conduct child therapy in a room with mixed functions, it is important that the furnishing clearly indicates the part of the room that is dedicated to child therapy. It is also important that other children's toy boxes, delicate objects, computers, etc., are placed outside the child's field of vision and reach.

It is unfortunate if the room contains many of the therapist's personal belongings, and it is also not a good idea to put drawings from a child in therapy up on the wall, where other children will see them. Opinions differ as to how neutral the room should be; some therapists prefer bare walls, while others decorate the room with a few neutral pictures.

The room must be located to avoid any disturbance from outside noise. The soundproofing must go both ways, as children in therapy might sometimes scream or otherwise make a great deal of noise. Children might run out of the room during sessions, and it is, therefore, best to use a room that is situated some distance from other offices, so that the child is less likely to disturb others. Windows in the room are, of course, allowed, but it is best if people cannot look in from the outside; also, the windows must be secured to make sure the child is not harmed if he tries to jump out.

The room makes up the physical space of the therapy, which means that therapy should not begin on the way from the waiting room to the therapy room or continue outside the room after the session. It might sometimes be more easily said than done to keep up this boundary, as some children want to begin therapy already on their way to the room.

Children are often keenly aware of changes in the room and comment on them. After a break, they might inspect the room to see if things are the same as they were before the break. The importance of the room for the child is especially obvious if a change of room becomes necessary during psychotherapy.

> Seven-year-old Andrew, who came in for therapy for the first time after a change of room, began to ask me what games we used to play in the old room, as if he wanted to check whether I remembered. He asked questions that he had asked before about what other children I had in therapy, as if to find out whether they, too, had had to change rooms. I began to feel insecure about my abilities as a therapist and whether I was good enough when I could not even safeguard the room.

Play materials

Play psychotherapy is an internationally applied treatment modality for children, and there are, of course, cultural variations as to what is regarded essential equipment in a play therapy room. Usually, considerable importance is attached to the inclusion of water and/or a sandbox (Chang et al., 2005). Therefore, it is necessary that the floor can handle being exposed to both water and sand. The room should have sturdy furniture—also child-sized pieces—and a sofa with a blanket and cushions. There should be easy access to a toilet.

Toys and other materials should be simple and easy to manage. First and foremost, they should be suitable for the symbolic expression of the child's inner world. Hence, unstructured materials, such as sand and water, paper and crayons, plasticine, string, glue, scissors, etc., that may be used to produce a wide variety of things, are useful. Small dolls and animals, both wild and domestic, are suitable for giving shape to the child's phantasies about other persons and himself. The dolls should represent both children and adults in various age groups, so that they can be used to represent families.

In considering the selection of toys, the therapist needs to consider each child's sex, age, cultural background, and subjective life experience. Thus, it facilitates the alliance with the child if the toys include figures and objects that represent both well-known elements from the child's own culture (with regard to, e.g., complexion, hair colour, dress, food, and specific animals) and fantastic and/or foreign elements (e.g., family dolls with a different appearance from the child and fantastic and/or strange figures, perhaps including some resembling monsters). Depending on the child's age, cars, planes, police cars, an ambulance, a fire engine, and a doctor or a nurse might also be suitable. For children who have experienced their own or family members' severe illness, a doctor's bag could be appropriate. A small teddy bear or other soft toy will often be included in the box, especially for work with younger and/or abused children.

Individual toy boxes were originally introduced by Klein (1955), and, in modern play therapy based on object relation theory, it is common for each child to have his own box with materials that the therapist provides for him. In addition, the therapist could include some shared materials, which should be limited to a few things, for example, toy bricks, a doll's house, and a sandbox. It is much better for each child to have his own box with the materials that the therapist has provided for him than for all the children who come to the same room for therapy to share the materials. Otherwise, there will often be too many toys, they will not always be suitable, and they eventually become more or less defective. Many children in psychotherapy are easily over-stimulated and become chaotic, and they are best helped by a limited selection of simple materials.

Precisely the use of personal toy boxes can be considered one of the standardised aspects of psychodynamic play therapy that make it possible to develop evidence-based research into the field. When the child has his own box, the content becomes personal, and the box often functions as an image of the child. The fact that the child is the only one who has access to his box contributes further to demarcate the therapy as a confidential relationship, which is off-limits to others. The box is put away when the child leaves and, thus, kept out of reach of other children.

Many children develop intensely positive and/or negative feelings toward the box and its contents, which are used, for example, for more or less symbolic processing of his varying attitudes to the therapist and the therapy. Self-destructive children often destroy their things and might attack the box, which, consequently, gets to look more like a dustbin than a box of toys. This might be difficult for the therapist to observe and endure, and she might be seized by an urge to repair it and replace the things in the box, but, when this destructive behaviour occurs, the best response is usually to reflect, with the child, on what is happening. The therapist should bear in mind that in the child's imagination, the box itself might stand for his experience of the containment of the psychotherapy, or the lack of containment. It is important to discuss this with the child. It might be necessary to provide him with another (more robust) box if the original box has fallen to pieces. If the box is replaced, it might be a good idea not to remove the scraps of the old box, but to leave them in the new one.

Games are not appropriate materials in object relation-based psychotherapy, as they hinder rather than further the child's phantasies and usually lead to situations where the child becomes caught up in competing with the therapist, which risks seducing the therapist into a dialogue with the child that is more educational than therapeutic.

Agreements

Agreements about therapy concern what is permitted and not permitted for the child as well as the guidelines for confidentiality and the therapist's behaviour in case of any transgressions of the boundaries. The purpose of therapy is to give the child the opportunity to show himself as he is, with both positive and negative feelings and phantasies, but that does not mean that the child is allowed to do anything he wants. Some children are so despairing, furious, and aggressive that it is necessary to limit their activities. Destruction of the room or its contents, attacks on the therapist, or self-harm is not allowed. Sometimes, the therapist might be able to stop a child's (self-)destructive behaviour by offering an interpretation; for example, when the child kicks the wall, and the therapist comments that she is wondering whom the child really wants to kick, and this makes him stop. In other cases, the therapist has to verbally forbid a child to do certain things, for example, opening the window or attacking her. If that is not sufficient, she might have to stop the child physically. Sometimes, the therapist has to remove certain objects, for example, scissors, or impose limits on the amount of water a child is allowed to use. If the child regains greater self-control later, these materials can be reintroduced.

If a child is so out of control that the therapist finds that continuing therapy will do more harm than good, it might be necessary to shorten the session. This is, of course, only possible if somebody is waiting for the child in the waiting room, or if the therapy takes place in an institution where other staff members can be asked to fetch the child. In such a situation, something like the following could be said to the child: "It is too difficult to do psychotherapy today, we'll meet again on . . ." A therapist might worry that a child who generally objects to therapy will take advantage of such an intervention and continually act up so much that therapy will have to be permanently suspended. In our experience, however, the child will actually make an effort to control himself in the future.

It is open to discussion whether it is best to lay down rules for the child's behaviour from the beginning or to introduce them little by little, as it proves necessary. We prefer the latter. For some children, it is never necessary to lay down rules, and, in other cases, an early introduction of restrictions transmits an unfortunate expectation to the child that he is going to transgress. It is better to wait until the situation arises and then set boundaries for the child.

Adolescents, in particular, might be quite preoccupied with doubts about the confidentiality of therapy. If they do not feel they can rely on it, there could be things they will not dare to talk about: for example, criminal offences. Some especially distrustful adolescents might be quite persistent in their enquiry of the therapist, and, in such cases, a thorough description not only of the confidentiality guidelines but also of their limits, might be warranted. If the therapist, for example, learns that someone is harming the adolescent or intends to do so, or if he talks about acts that will have serious negative consequences for him or others, the therapist is obliged to interfere and communicate it to the persons who are responsible for the adolescent. On the other hand, it might be a good idea to remind the child or the young person that the confidentiality only applies to the therapist and not to them; they can share whatever they want from their therapy. This might be especially important to point out to children who have been subjected to sexual abuse, and who might have been coerced into treating the abuse as a shared secret. Precisely because the therapy concerns the child's most private feelings and phantasies, it is important that the therapist remains completely neutral in her behaviour, continually aware of her own countertransference and maintaining a suitable physical distance from the child. That is not always easy, as some severely disturbed children and children who have been sexually abused might communicate their phantasies in the form of sexually challenging behaviour: for example, through more or less undisguised masturbation or by taking off some or all of their clothes. In such cases, it is important to emphasise that therapy is done in a dressed state and, together with the child, to reflect on what he is trying to convey by these actions in lieu of words.

Time

The concept of time concerns both the duration of each session, the frequency of sessions, and the duration of the psychotherapy. The length of the individual sessions is usually forty-five to fifty minutes for children and adolescents. It is important to respect the time for both beginning and ending the sessions as much as possible.

In treatment institutions, children or adolescents are usually offered one weekly session, but this is not always optimal. As demonstrated by research (see Chapter Thirteen), children with more comprehensive problems need both longer and more intensive psychotherapies than children with less severe problems. Fonagy and Target (1996) found that while children with slight disturbances improved through both intensive and non-intensive treatment, the frequency of the treatment was precisely the factor that made a difference for children with more severe disorders. Another study found that children who received insufficient treatment in childhood later demonstrated greater problems than children who had received no treatment at all (Target & Fonagy, 2002). If it is obvious in advance that it will be impossible to offer a sufficiently stable and long-lasting treatment to a severely disturbed child or young person, it might, thus, be better not to initiate psychotherapy at all.

Younger children, too, may benefit from two weekly sessions, as waiting an entire week between sessions might be too long for a young child. Since occasional cancellations are unavoidable in psychotherapy with children and adolescents, the number of sessions could become quite sparse if there is only one weekly session. This will reduce the intensity of the therapy and might cause a delay in the treatment plan. Regardless of frequency, it is important that the time of the sessions stay fixed. It can be helpful for some children if the therapist, for example during the time leading up to a holiday, keeps a calendar where the child can see the number of remaining sessions before the break.

Unless the therapy is short term, where a fixed number of sessions or a certain duration has been arranged beforehand, it is often difficult to predict the duration of the therapy at the outset. It depends on many things: the therapy itself, the support provided to parents or other carers, and what happens in the child's life outside therapy. Many of these variables are outside the therapist's influence. If the child is severely disturbed, however, it is usually realistic to anticipate a duration of several years. That might seem like an unpleasant message to deliver, and the therapist might feel tempted to offer a more optimistic estimation. As described in Chapter Three, however, it is unwise to underestimate the required time, as that might make it difficult to obtain the necessary funds later for continuing the therapy. Further, if it later turns out that the child requires more therapy than initially suggested, this could cause distrust of the therapist's knowledge or skills. Although prolonged therapy is expensive and binding for those involved, it might be worth reminding oneself and others how much greater the cost will be, in both economic and human terms, if a severely disturbed child does not receive help in time.

Boundary transgressions

The therapist establishes the setting, and it is her job to protect it. However, violations of the boundaries occur in any psychotherapy, with both the therapist and the child as transgressors. The therapist will not be able to avoid breaks entirely as a consequence of holidays, illness, training courses, etc. When a break occurs, it is important, as far as possible, to prepare the child for the forthcoming changes and to pay close attention to his reactions to them, including indirect reactions, such as diffuse anger with the therapist or dissatisfaction with coming to therapy.

It is, of course, no less important to be aware of the many transgressions of the boundaries that the children will attempt. Nearly all children will want to test the limits and try to determine how trustworthy the therapist really is. If, for example, part of the room is reserved for office functions and, thus, off limits to the child during therapy, many children will experiment with gradual transgressions of the boundary until the therapist intervenes. At some point or another, many children might also wish to leave before the session ends or, conversely, refuse to leave when the time is up. The therapist's task in these cases is not merely to uphold the limits, but also to attempt to understand and contain the feelings that the child is trying to communicate with his actions and, if possible, to offer an interpretation.

A modest breach of the boundaries can be seen from children who, for instance, want to take a drawing home with them to show or give it to their parents. This might seem innocent, but often these small and insignificant boundary crossings are just the first in a series of steps that continue to grow in number and extent, and a therapist who has allowed an apparently trivial transgression could quickly get into trouble as to where the limit should actually be drawn. Many of the more externalising children are used to having things their way with their parents by continuing to insist, and they might, for long periods, display very challenging behaviour. They seem to see any limitation laid down by an adult as an invitation to try to break it. Therapy under these conditions can be extraordinarily straining, and an inexperienced child therapist who is exposed to such a fight for months will be in sore need of supervision to be able to stick to her conviction that psychotherapy with this child can lead to positive changes. It is important to remember, however, that it is no less straining and painful for the child to feel this inner urge to always be in opposition, and he might feel very relieved if the therapist succeeds in liberating him from this burden.

Although the limits should generally be maintained, situations will invariably arise when the therapist is tempted to break them. Such situations might be due to the therapist's countertransference, as when, for instance, as mentioned above, she feels sorry for a child who has destroyed all his toys and feels like replacing them. In such cases, it is rarely a good idea to act on one's inclinations. However, there are situations when it could lead to a good result to act in another way than usually, as illustrated by the following example:

Eleven-year-old Jack had been in psychotherapy for several years with two weekly sessions. For a long time initially, he had been very aggressive, constantly attacking the setting of his therapy, ordering me around, trying to prevent me from talking to him, and in every way trying to provoke me and have things his way.

Over the past six months, however, a noticeable development had taken place. His behaviour was much less provoking, and—in a no less important development—he had begun to share his thoughts and feelings with me. He now talked about some of the many things at home that worried him. Earlier, he had often been hurt, but I now noted with pleasure that he began talking about the importance of protecting himself. One day, a teacher, N, from the institution where he was a day patient, had his last day of work at the school; shortly before his departure, Jack said to me, "There's one thing that I wish very much, but it can't be done." ("OK, why can't it be done?") "Because the things I make here in therapy have to remain here." ("What would you like to make?") "I would like to write a letter to N. I would like N to come and see me when I stop coming here, at XX." ("You'd like that?") "Mm, I have been thinking about it." ("Have you told N?") "It's difficult to say, but I could write it in a letter, and I don't know if it's possible, but I want to take a chance." ("It sounds like a really good idea. You could write the letter, and then I could think about what we can do with it; you know, it's a good idea to take some time to think matters over when you're in doubt.") "But there's no time for that, for when N leaves today, he won't come back on Monday." He said this with desperation in his voice. At this point, only three minutes remained in the session, and my mind was hard at work trying to find a solution. While I was thinking, Jack continued, "I'm certain that if N can't make it to my final day here, he will have a reason for it . . . not just any reason, but a really good reason." (At this time I said, "Now I am going to make a decision, and this is an absolute exception. I think you should write your letter to N; then I'll make a copy of it that we're going to keep here, and then you can take the letter with you and give it to N.") Jack then wrote his letter, over which he took great pains; he looked up, smiled, and looked at the clock, saying, "We have gone over time." ("Yes, we have, because this is important.") We left the therapy room together and briefed the teacher who was there to fetch Jack about what had happened, so that he would understand that an exception had been made from the usual principles.

As seen from the example, there is rarely time for lengthy considerations about how to act in child psychotherapy; usually, it is necessary to draw a quick conclusion and to consider afterwards whether a suitable choice was made. When that happens, it is important to reflect afterwards—often together with the child—on other possible motives behind the situation that arose; in this case, for example, how insufficiently integrated earlier losses contributed to his current wish.

The wider setting

The wider setting is understood as the organisation in which the therapy takes place, which can involve several very different situations. In the early days of child psychotherapy, most of the work was done in private practices or clinics, whose main purpose was to provide therapy for children and their parents. Not much was known about the importance of the setting then; for instance, Klein had her own three children in therapy, just as Anna Freud, as mentioned earlier, was analysed by her father; however, the therapist was the one who controlled the setting.

Today, psychotherapeutic work takes place in a wide range of settings and in many different organisations, not all of which are equally well suited for child psychotherapy. The enormous work pressure and narrow time constraints in many institutions and organisations prevent long-term therapeutic work and only allow for short-term psychotherapy. Sufficient time, however, is not the only necessary precondition for the implementation of individual psychotherapy; an institution that wants to offer psychotherapy must possess what might be called a therapeutic culture: that is, knowledge of the necessary conditions in the overall institution to be able to serve as a setting for psychotherapy. It is especially important that the leadership has sufficient awareness of what it takes.

In such an organisation, the many elements at play in the child's treatment must be taken into consideration with due regard for all the different staff members working with him. The staff should be introduced to all the implications for the institution of having a child in individual psychotherapy. They should, for instance, know about the importance of the setting, including the child's regular attendance, and about the therapist's duty of confidentiality. They should understand that the child decides what he wants to bring up in therapy, and that the therapist cannot bring up subjects that have been suggested by other staff members. They should be familiar with concepts such as splitting and projective identification, so that they will be able to understand the child's possible attempts to play the therapist and other staff members off against each other. This will usually require continuous supervision for the staff in order to protect the therapeutic work.

However, even in institutions with a good understanding and protection of individual therapeutic work, it might be difficult for the therapist to maintain her own inner boundaries. If she also has other functions in the institution and, for example, participates in regular treatment conferences, the knowledge she acquires about the children she has in therapy might influence her work with them.

An example of this is Donald, who lived in an institution and spent much of his time in an inner phantasy world. At a treatment conference, it was decided to try to limit his escape into this inner world. In her supervision, the child therapist discovered that she had been influenced by this decision in her own work with Donald and had begun to set similar limitations for him.

Adopted children and foster children often have significant mental problems and require long and intensive psychotherapy. A local or national health service will often offer to pay for this psychotherapy; in most cases, this is an economically sound decision, as these children, if left untreated, might, in the long run, be very costly for society. Ultimately, it is always the referring agency (municipal services or the parents) that decides for how long and to what extent it is going to fund the child's or young person's therapy. In the above-mentioned cases, however, careful preparations in planning the therapy have played a crucial role. First, it is important to ensure that the child and the people around him are thoroughly assessed before any therapy is initiated (see Chapter Three). Second, an understanding must be established that therapy with a child must also include work with his parents, whether birth parents or foster or adoptive parents. If two therapists work together, the funding has to cover the time they need for co-ordination and co-operation and for participating in regular network meetings with the referring agency, parents, school, and other institutions. Finally, the referring agency needs to understand that it is a long-term therapy that, once it is begun, should not be broken off suddenly or prematurely, as that could leave the child worse off than if he had not begun in therapy in the first place. It is important to have reached a sufficient mutual understanding of the problem with the referring agency before the start of therapy that the funding can be trusted to continue for a sufficient period and will not be discontinued without due warning.

CHAPTER FIVE

The therapeutic relationship

The therapeutic relationship can be understood from three perspectives: as a transference relationship, a current, real-life object relationship, and a therapeutic alliance. In the therapeutic process, these aspects are interdependent, continually interacting and, thus, in no way clearly distinguishable from one another. The psychodynamic approach implies that, in order to understand the child's unfurling relational experience, feelings, phantasies, and mental states, from the very beginning, the therapist devotes her full attention to the therapeutic relationship. In time, this will bring out as salient the transference aspects of the relationship, as the child, for instance, develops highly subjective ways of relating to the therapist, the therapy, and the clinic. There is, however, great variability in how fast, how comprehensively, and around which central relational themes this gathering of transference-related aspects of the relationship happens. This topic is in dire need of open-minded qualitative research; however, our experience as therapists and supervisors points to the complex interaction of a number of causative factors, including the therapist's approach, skills, and personality, the quality of the child's or young person's early attachments, current care relationships, and ability to mentalise, and, last, but not necessarily least, the context, frequency, and duration of the therapy.

The transference relationship: a subjective, two-way relationship

As outlined above, the psychodynamic child and adolescent psychotherapist's continuous attention on her interaction with the child facilitates the development of a transference relationship, that is, the particularly intense, phantasy-linked, emotional aspects of the relationship. This concept encompasses, from the one perspective, the child's transference to the therapist of subjective feelings, thoughts, and phantasies and, from the other perspective, the therapist's countertransference to the child of her similarly subjective, personal reactions to the child's transference. Hence, the transference relationship can be understood as a subjective two-way communication, which in the therapeutic process creates, maintains, and contains the mental interconnections between the child's and the therapist's unconscious, inner worlds. In the course of the therapy, this subjective communication process leads both participants to introject and internalise the other as a contribution to their pre-existing inner worlds of unconscious object relationships. Hence, the transference relationship forms a continuous undercurrent in the therapeutic process, which—in more or less powerful ways—at certain times takes centre stage in the process.

In the transference, children and adolescents (and adults) in unconscious phantasy assign certain complementary roles to their therapists and themselves. Through play, verbal dialogue, actions, and their general attitude, children actualise these subjective roles (complete with feelings, phantasies, and defensive patterns derived from the inner world). Hence, they relate to their therapist not only as a real-life, external figure but, in unconscious phantasy, add certain feelings, phantasies, and defences deriving from their own inner world. The therapeutic relationship consequently becomes suffused by the child's subjective experiences and memory traces from earlier and current relational experiences. Thus, at any given moment of a therapy session, a child's attitude, verbalisations, play, and actions will contain certain aspects derived from his subjective phantasies, fusing subjective, relational experience dating from earliest infancy to present-day relationships (in and outside the therapeutic space).

The therapists' countertransference has been conceptualised in two ways: (a) as the therapist's unresolved personal issues interfering with her work, and (b) as the therapist's emotional reaction to the client's unconscious projective identifications, which, through introjective identification, gives rise to corresponding feelings and phantasies in the mind of the therapist.

The therapist's unresolved personal issues interfering with her work

All therapists have unresolved personal issues, which act as blind spots in their field of vision and interfere with their therapeutic stance and understanding by causing, for instance, over-involvement, confusion, antagonism, or indifference and neglect. Even so, however, therapists are bound to have personal emotional reactions to their clients, who at times in the therapeutic process are very likely to project parts of themselves into the therapist (projective identification). Hence, countertransference is unavoidable, and, although it is set in motion by the client, it is caused by the therapist's state of mind rather than by the client's mind. Accordingly, a continuous task for psychodynamic child and adolescent psychotherapists is to discover what is going on in their own minds. To the best of their abilities, they have to differentiate between their own and the child's contributions by studying their own mistakes and becoming wiser as to what personal difficulties are at stake. This was Sigmund Freud's and, according to Spillius, also Melanie Klein's view of countertransference (Freud, 1910d; Spillius, 2007).

The client's unconscious projective identifications give rise to corresponding feelings and phantasies in the mind of the therapist

This additional meaning was introduced by Paula Heimann (1950), who stressed countertransference as a useful therapeutic tool. It anticipated Bion's development of projective identification from a pure phantasy phenomenon into a relational model, a primitive form of communication actualising the child's unconscious phantasies through evocative acts towards the therapist (Bion, 1962b, 1970, see Chapter Two). This meaning implies that any of the therapist's impressions, as experienced in a psychotherapeutic process (i.e., thoughts, feelings, perceptions, sensations, and other mental and psychosomatic reactions), may be considered potentially important as sources of information about the client's states of mind. In this broader meaning, the therapist's countertransference can be considered an essential tool for her ability to mentalize what is taking place in her interactions with the child. Thus, at all times, the therapist needs to be (privately) attentive to her own feelings and phantasies, applying them as a means of enriching her empathic understanding of the child. This broader understanding of countertransference has become widely accepted in contemporary psychoanalytic and psychodynamic work with children and adolescents (Lanyado & Horne, 1999; Pick, 1985; Sandler & Sandler, 1998; Spillius et al., 2011).

In the reality of the therapeutic space, it is hardly ever possible to clearly differentiate between the two forms, which, rather, seem to coexist in some sort of mutual equilibrium. Thus, good therapy is a two-way, bi-personal communicative process with the power to change both parties. Children, adolescents, and even adults in psychotherapy often show a strong tendency to actualise precisely the kind of feelings that their therapist seems responsive to. Even experienced psychodynamic therapists might, at times, find it hard to differentiate between the two forms of countertransference, especially in child and adolescent psychotherapy, where events sometimes not only move pretty fast but might also seem to follow their own logic. It is important to understand just how complicated is the formation of the countertransference states of the therapist, created by the interplay between the child's projective identifications, the therapist's introjective identifications, the therapist's interventions as derived thereof, and the subjectivity of both participants as derived from their personalities and life stories.

In this process, the child's transference and the therapist's countertransference are continuously present as emotional undercurrents that colour the child's communication at all times, regardless of what manifest theme is being presented. Consequently, whatever the child brings into the therapeutic relationship, this may be—and, most often, should be—understood from several perspectives, including the here-and-now state of the transference relationship. It is crucial for child and adolescent psychotherapists to be just as attentive to the emotional statements implied by children's way of relating and acting as they are to the thematic, narrative content of play and verbalisations. A superficial, one-dimensional perception of the goings-on—for instance, in an exclusive focus on manifest themes of play and verbalisation—will lead to the loss of important information about which inner object-related scenario the child is externalising in that moment, including which transference roles are being actualised. Content and relationship form a whole, and the therapist's awareness of these factors is, therefore, a key precondition for capturing the present moment's total information about just how the child relates to, wishes to relate to, or fears to be related to by, his therapist. This conception of the transference relationship (i.e., both transference and counter-transference) presumes a process taking place in any present moment of the session. While its form and emotionality draw on the individual's subjective containment and mentalization of the experiences of past relationships, the transference is created and lived in the therapeutic relationship of the here-and-now (Spillius, 1994).

The child's transference as phantasies relating to the therapist

In the course of therapy, the therapist, in the phantasy of the child, might come to represent a variety of aspects from the child's inner world of object relations. At a more or less symbolic level, children in therapy tend subjectively to insert their therapist into pre-existing emotions and phantasies about the self *vis-à-vis* inner figures: for instance, paternal, maternal, and sibling figures, etc. These inner scenarios can speak to the therapist through the children's play and drawings.

> In session after session, five-year-old Nabil, a child of severely traumatised refugee parents, created a flooded world, in which his dolls persistently drowned or disappeared in ceaseless streams of poison rain, meanwhile creating chaos in the playroom by flooding his toy box, the sandbox, the paint, the basin, and the floor with water. In the first session after a break in therapy, I noticed that, half hidden in a corner of the usual chaos, Nabil acted with a more concentrated focus, narrating in a doll's play the privations and sufferings of an infant doll that was left to perish from thirst, hunger, and loneliness in the sandbox desert. In addition, the infant doll's survival was threatened by poison rain from the sky and scary pursuers occupying all safe places, grabbing all available edible nourishment and life-saving, protective relationships.

It is important to remember that the child's transference most often has complex origins, spanning both past and present. Thus, Nabil's play in the sandbox no doubt was set in motion by the therapy break, stirring up pent-up longing for affectionate care paired with sibling jealousy; however, his play also contained elements that probably represented introjective identification with the sufferings experienced by a parental figure, who had experienced real-life atrocities of genocide and war.

Sometimes, rather than the manifest themes of play and verbal dialogue, the child's attitudes and actions imply that the child, in phantasy, transfers object or partial object relationships to the therapist. At some point, the child might, in phantasy, equate the therapist with projected parts of his own self: for instance, a harsh superego, consequently casting the therapist in the role of a punishing and forbidding parental figure rigidly upholding law and order, or, conversely, the child might relate to the therapist as if he himself were a strict, omnipotent parental figure, harshly calling a naughty child-therapist to order.

Especially at session beginnings and endings, some children tend to initiate plays or actions that appear vividly illustrative of traumatic loss: for instance, repeatedly losing and recovering a specific object that has become immensely important to the child, maybe a specific parental or sibling doll, a cuddly toy animal, or even a hard, lifeless thing such as a specific car or the shovel for the sandbox. The loss, or aspects of the loss, can be repeated in disconnected fragments of actions or play, as, for instance, a ten-year-old girl who, after breaks, regularly arrived in a confused state of mind, unable to recognise the therapist or remember her name. Memories of traumatic breakdowns could be represented as ceaseless flooding of the playroom, as, for instance, in the example above. Aggressive fortification of the self might be represented by a child appearing deaf to the therapist's comments, while being endlessly preoccupied with preparing buildings with solid walls, no way in or out, and unbeatable machines without a human driver, crunching everybody and everything to pieces on their way.

The possibilities of transference are, in principle, legion. Therapists need both empathic intuition and sensitivity to transference and countertransference processes to understand the full emotional and relational meaning of play themes and repetitions. A fundamental task of therapists, therefore, is to engage in reflective thinking to elucidate what kind of inner scenario preoccupies the child at a given moment, and what role the therapist is assigned in the play activity. In other words, therapists need to continuously ponder their own role *vis-à-vis* the child, questioning what part of the child's self is in what kind of relationship with what parts of the objects, and how these roles are distributed between therapist and child (Klein, 1929; Sandler, 1976).

The emotional atmosphere of the therapeutic process fluctuates constantly, generally between positive and negative transference, according to what parts of the child's inner world were kindled in the here-and-now relationship. At one moment, the child might transfer loving, longing, soft, sad (depressive) object relationships; in the next moment, the atmosphere might shift towards anxious, empty, indifferent, stubborn, rejecting, or openly aggressive (paranoid–schizoid) states of mind. These shifts in emotional atmosphere are related to the role of the therapist in the child's phantasy, as it is actualised in the present moment.

The child's initial attitude

Over time, the transference relationship undergoes certain changes. The therapist's divided attention—partly on the child's activities and states of mind, partly on her own inner emotional and reflective process, and partly on the interaction between the child and herself in the present moment—plays an important role in transforming the relationship into a transference relationship. Thus, the therapist's management of countertransference contributes to the development of the child's transference and *vice versa* in a spiral movement that acts as a dynamic impetus for change.

The child's initial transference attitude is often profoundly instructive. In a one-to-one situation with an adult stranger who is supposed to be helpful, most children's and adolescents' initial (conscious and unconscious) inclination is to display fundamental relational expectations. This tendency is already conspicuous in the first encounters with a psychodynamic therapist, both because of her attentive and containing attitude and non-judgemental willingness to wait and see what is on the child's mind and because of the implicit invitation and relatively loose structure of the setting. Thus, practically all children and adolescents, when they first enter the therapy room, unconsciously begin to project their inner world, and, through their attitude and actions, they subject their therapist to a certain interpersonal pressure, thus unconsciously trying to actualise certain complementary roles. Children's initial attitude to the therapist might demonstrate abiding, ossified contact patterns that they present to everyone, or, at least, everyone who in their mind belongs to a certain category (e.g., all grown-ups, authority figures, women, foreigners, dark-haired persons, doctors, do-gooders, etc.). This is not yet a personal transference relationship based on a specific relationship with the therapist, but, rather, a case of character transference (Reed, 1990; Sandler et al., 1980).

In addition, the initial transference attitude often reflects factors related to the background context of the therapy, for example, the child's perception of the parents' attitude to the therapy, what spare time activities he had to sacrifice in favour of therapy, and, especially, the risks that the therapy implies for the child's perceived sense of personal safety. For instance, children with earlier experience of care arrangements might believe the therapist to be in control of such decisions:

> Four-year-old Joseph spent his first year of life in almost total isolation with his severely mentally ill mother and was then removed from the home and placed in a residential institution. From that point on, he never saw his birth mother again, and, at two years of age, he was placed with his birth father and his new wife, who had visited the institution during his stay there. In this new family, he was the only child. He was referred for psychotherapy partly for severe separation anxiety, which prevented him from attending nursery school, partly because of a tendency towards intentional, sadistic abuse of animals and younger children, and partly because his general development seemed delayed, even if he did not generally appear developmentally challenged. This is an excerpt of his therapist's notes from the first session:
>
> Joseph is brought into therapy by both parents; he hides behind them, unable to let go. (I suggest that they join him in the playroom.) In the playroom, he catches sight of a police car, lets go of dad and then proceeds to ignore both parents. He does not react when the parents say goodbye after a while and leave the playroom, at my suggestion. Joseph examines several cars carefully, finds defects in them all and asks a lot of questions without waiting for me to answer. He has not yet looked me in the eye and mostly keeps his back turned towards me. (I answered his initial questions, but as I become aware that the answers are of no consequence, I say, "What a lot of questions you are asking—

maybe you don't know why you're here to play with me?") To my surprise, Joseph answers in a pseudo-adult, mocking tone of voice, "No, but I should like to know." He finds a doctor figure, knocks it against the driver's cab of a tractor and says without pausing to breathe: "Who is that? Why him . . . it . . . not going in there, who is in charge of this"? (I: "You would like to know who decided that you're going to play with me?") "Yes." He continues his search and this goes on for some time. Then Joseph finds a lorry with a tiny hole in the body. His movements become frantic; suddenly, he appears terribly anxious: "What is this, why is this hole there, I don't want it." ("You don't like the hole?") "The sand runs all the way through." ("You think that you yourself might go through this hole and get lost?") For the first time, Joseph now looks directly at me: "Yes, how do you know?" He takes another lorry and an excavator to the sandbox, digging with the excavator, feeling with his fingers at the big teeth of its shovel: "Are they sharp? The man says, don't come too close. Are they big and dangerous when the man drives it? He's in there, isn't he?" ("You think my excavator may get mad, biting you to pieces. You think that I have dangerous things in here.") He drives the excavator so fiercely that the caterpillar tracks come off. He is struggling to put them back on and does not ask for my help. Then he points to the caterpillar tracks: "Don't like these, get all crushed if the man is driving." He buries the excavator and the caterpillar tracks in the sandbox, taking care to cover it all up and noting with a contented smile, "Now, he can't." (I move closer but realise that Joseph appears alarmed if I get too close.) He reacts by turning his back to me, keeping his distance.

Later in the session, Joseph unearths the excavator and plays with it, digging up sand, which he dumps at the border of the sandbox. The sand trickles on to the floor through a tiny chink between the box and the border. Joseph anxiously eyes the sand dripping on to the floor. He points to the chink: "What is this there, why does it have to be there?" He discovers a wet lump of sand in a corner and asks in a pseudo-adult, indignant voice, "Who done this?" He fetches a dustcart lorry: "Don't like this either, one bin's trash into, me too will be binned, says dad." ("You think dad may throw you away like trash if I make you do something wrong?") "Yeah, in fact, but now I'm cooking, plenty good food." He pours sand in a saucepan, finds a lump of plasticine in the sand: "Watch it, green potato, not good, hey, fell on the floor." A little later, "Look out, very hot, don't get too close, you'll get burned, this is boiling water I make." At the end of session, he goes to the doll's house and looks through the doors into the house: "Can't come in."

First, Joseph appeared scared and sceptical, full of negative expectations and phantasies. He did not dare to let go of his parents, but, never the less, he barely noticed it when they left the playroom. He began the session by walking around, exploring the playroom, keenly alert to even minor defects, visibly anxious if the therapist came too close. This fearful, primarily visual exploration can be understood as reminiscent of very early survival-related vigilance, perhaps born in the interaction with a severely mentally ill mother (Grünbaum & Gammeltoft, 1993).

Joseph's initial transference attitude is suggestive of a suspicion that the therapist and her playthings were too damaged and brittle to contain him and his aggressive feelings but also dangerous and unpredictable, waiting to bite him to pieces with sharp teeth, bulldoze right through him, or maybe enticing him to do vile, sadistic things that would cause his dad to reject him. From this perspective, it was no wonder that he needed to keep some distance from the therapist. Thus, Joseph had little faith in the capacity of a containing space to regulate his anxiety and aggression. On the other hand, he was also looking for an understanding relationship, eager to talk about his anxiety and paranoid–schizoid phantasies of rejection and destruction of the self by damaged and dangerously aggressive objects. This receptive, object-seeking part of Joseph showed clearly, for example, the few times that the therapist was able to grasp the meaning and formulate her intervention in ways that Joseph was able to recognise. Even so, a split second later, he was flooded by anxious suspicion that nothing good would result from "coming into" a doctor person's awareness.

Joseph seemed profoundly confused about the difference between himself and his objects, and, in parallel, the therapist found it difficult to determine whether the doctor figure and the tractor, respectively, represented the self and/or the objects. However, it seemed very clear to her that Joseph conceived of the relationship between a helping doctor figure and the tractor as impenetrable, blocked to the reception of projective identification, without an inner space for the self to nest (literally and mentally). This was evidenced, for example, by his comments about the impossibility of getting into the tractor and, at the end of the session, the doll's house, as well as his resistance to going to nursery school.

None the less, from the first moment, Joseph initiated a communicative process, projecting both the suspicious self that lacked good, available objects and the explorative, help-seeking self into the therapeutic relationship and setting. At the end of the session, he even showed a glimpse of hope that maybe, after all, this new, strange relationship might prove helpful. Thus, he embarked on preparing food, in phantasy swapping the roles so that he himself became a good, caring mummy-therapist, simultaneously shedding the identity of an unwanted, naughty child and passing that role on to the therapist.

A personal transference relationship

From the outset, one of the therapist's central tasks is to intervene in such a manner that, in time, the diffuse, object-related endeavours of the child become focused on the therapist and transformed into a personal transference relationship, in which the child and the therapist are constituted in each other's minds as subjective personal objects. Stated somewhat differently, over time, an intensive relationship forms between them, in which the unconscious of both participants is engaged, and in which transference and countertransference form recurrent patterns, unique to precisely this child–therapist pair. In this process, positive and negative transference feelings are intensified, coloured by the subjective traces of former relational experiences and related unconscious phantasies. At times, this might cause the child's actions towards the therapist to become quite unrealistic, tenuously related to the therapist's actual behaviour and personal characteristics. Yet, it is important to recognise that, from the first meeting, most children and adolescents have a keen, perhaps preconscious, sense of their therapist's countertransference states. Therapists, therefore, need to recognise the complexity inherent in the transference relationship, which also implies that even the most distorted transference phantasies could contain a kernel of realistic perception.

As described, the child's transference comprises an unconscious repetition of emotionally coloured, subjective inner traces of both earlier and current relational experience and phantasy. The transference is not a literal repetition of these relationships or of the infantile self's emotional states, wishes, disillusionments, conflicts, etc. Rather, we might think of transference as total inner scenarios, in which subjectively processed, condensed memory traces combine and condense the emotional experience of earlier and current interactions, transferring these experiences as a whole together with the emotional atmosphere and context of these past and present relationships. The transference includes the child's unconscious communication to the therapist of condensed memories of past relationships as well as his subjective (more or less unconscious) communication to the therapist of the way in which these memories are fused with his experience of the relationship with the therapist in the present moment. Hence, within the therapeutic space, the child's mental processing of past and present relationships outside the therapy will be coloured by the emotional experience in relationship to the therapist in the present moment (Joseph, 1985; Klein, 1952).

It goes without saying that we do not witness the infantile attachments *per se* in the playroom, only the subjectively processed traces and representations. The appearance of these traces is created in the present moment, their vitality and form coloured by the child's here-and-now experience of his relationship with the therapist. The infantile object relations can, thus, be understood as an inner template that somehow shapes the current spontaneous responses to impressions. The methodological implication of this is that therapists need to focus their interventions on what takes place here-and-now in the therapeutic relationship—especially the transference relationship—rather than on past events and relationships (see also Chapters Eleven and Twelve).

In the above example, four-year-old Joseph's fear that the therapist might bite, crush, and dump him like trash should not be understood as Joseph's displacement on to the therapist of an originally experienced dread of his psychotic birth mother. Far from it—in fact, in the present moment, he is scared to death that the therapist might actually attack him in these ways. Thus, if the therapist were to interpret Joseph's anxiety as derived from past relationships outside the playroom, this will neither ease Joseph's anxiety nor help him achieve better self-knowledge. More likely, Joseph's acute persecutory anxiety presumably points backwards in time, to characteristic phantasies experienced in his early care relationships. In other words, his present-day, acute, persecutory phantasies presumably have parallels with the inner, object-relational template created by the one-year-old Joseph's subjective processing of his interactions with a severely psychotic mother.

Specific crises in the transference relationship

If the therapist follows the guidelines defined above, most children will gradually gather and focus their transference feelings and phantasies on a uniquely subjective, painful core of object relations and defensive phantasies, conflicts, and enactments bound up with these (see Chapter Ten). In the course of this development, one or more particularly critical periods of dissonance in the relationship might arise and potentially endanger the therapeutic alliance, not only with the child, but sometimes also with the parents. This development is caused by the child's increasing anxiety and desperation as he compulsively picks at this deep-rooted complex of painful object-related phantasies and related defences. As a contributing factor, for a time the child typically perceives these problems as being caused by the therapist. This belief probably stems from the experience of increased dependence on the therapist in combination with the therapist's persistent insistence that the feelings engendered in and by the therapeutic relationship are important and should be verbalised. The emotional atmosphere of these fundamental, unconscious themes and conflicts vary and might, for instance, be predominantly loving, hateful, paralysed, or pervaded by emptiness, or they might oscillate between such states of mind. The emotional intensity of these experiences could frighten not only the child, but also the therapist. In these difficult transitions, both the child and the therapist might come to harbour wishful phantasies about ending the therapy. Unfortunately, this phantasy complex can, if it is not contained by the therapist, affect both the parents and any professionals involved in the care for the child.

There is a certain parallel between this phenomenon and Freud's original notion of an intensive transference crisis, the relationship gradually intensifying until it reaches a peak where the client, with a new desperate intensity, repeats rather than remembers his subjective infantile sufferings and conflicts, for a time experiencing these as originating in his relationship with the therapist (Freud, 1916–1917). Since the beginning of child psychotherapy in the early nineteenth century, questions of whether and how this working theory might be applicable to psychoanalytic child and adolescent psychotherapy have given rise to animated discussions. Klein, on the basis of clinical experience, held that the concept of a transference crisis was relevant also in psychotherapy with young children, describing the phenomenon in clear and instructive detail:

> When analysing children I observe that their symptoms change, are accentuated or lessened in accordance with the analytic situation. I observe in them the abreaction of affects in close connection with the progress of the work and in relation to myself. I observe that anxiety arises and that the children's reactions work themselves out on this analytic ground. Parents who watch their children carefully have often told me that they have been surprised to see habits, etc., which had long disappeared come back again. I have not found that children work off their reactions when they are at home as well as when with me: for the most part they are reserved for abreaction in the analytic hour. (1927, p. 152)

Today, there seems to be an agreement that specific, intensive crises in the transference relationship are not unusual in child and adolescent psychotherapy. It can, for instance, be mentioned that Sandler and colleagues (1980), from an ego-psychological perspective, defined a specific transference crisis like this:

> . . . a very special intensification of the transference involving an externalization of a major pathogenic internal conflict onto the therapist, so that the conflict is felt by the patient to be between himself and the therapist. His interest, attention, concern, and symptoms related to the conflict diminish in intensity or may even disappear" (p. 92).

Readers interested in the historical discussions between Anna Freud (1946, 1966a), and Melanie Klein (1927, 1955) are referred to King and Steiner (1991).

Specific transference crises in child and adolescent psychotherapy will naturally reflect the intensity and predominant emotional atmosphere of core themes in early relational experience. Thus, for some children, this development might concern an intensification of predominantly affectionate, positive feelings, possibly followed by a flourishing of infantile psychosexual phantasies (Grünbaum, 1989). For other children, phantasies might develop of being the therapist's only, special, favourite baby, entitled to perfect care, understanding, or other forms of attention, out of range of a therapeutic relationship. For children whose early relationships have been emotionally ambivalent, unstable, and/or traumatising, this development can lead predominantly to an intensification of unbearably painful, persecutory feelings. Such a child might, for instance, feel ignored, controlled, suppressed, and deeply cheated by the therapist, convinced that other children are getting all the goods. Painfully unsettling feelings such as these might be accompanied by confused and frightening phantasies, in which aggressive and sexualised themes become mixed up. At certain critical moments in these therapies, the therapist might get the impression that the child has completely surrendered to a subjective reality of depriving and scary figures from the traumatising past. In these moments, the therapist might come to feel that the child quite literally, but unconsciously, is re-enacting before her eyes a personal version of old relationships, conflicts, and states of mind (Grünbaum, 2014).

When such new or re-edited versions—rooted in the child's personal history of inner core themes and related phantasies—come alive and repeat themselves in the transference relationship, the therapist has to take upon herself the differing roles subjectively experienced by the child in family life. This was probably what Freud essentially meant by the term "working-through" (1914g). Thus, the therapist's ability to contain and (at least partially) understand the child's emotional experience plays a crucial role. The repetitions of these intense transference manifestations offer therapists a golden opportunity for working through and influencing the child's present self-image, relational assumptions, and ways of relating. Recurrently working through core object relationship issues has a parallel in normal early development, as the infant and his parents return to the same issues over and over, repeatedly working through them, at times despairing, for example, at the thought that maybe this particular child will never be able to sleep through the night.

As described above, children's early curiosity—the urge to observe, explore, and get to know especially their parental and sibling figures and their mutual relationships—is the basis of all subsequent learning and especially important for the development of the ability to think and mentalize (see Chapter Two). However, children with problems often find it much easier to explore these feelings in relation to the therapy and the therapist than outside the therapy in the relationships of everyday real life. Through the transference relationship, the therapist is offered a role as stand-in for the primary relations. The therapist takes on these roles, reflecting upon their impact and meaning and inviting the child to explore relational phantasies and conflicts mentally with her as a stand-in. Hence, as the relational problems come to cluster around the therapist, this provides relief to the child's real-life relationships and offers the child a second chance of working through intense feelings that were perceived as far too risky to explore with the parents or other primary carers. As eloquently framed by Winnicott, the special feature of play and its roles and relationships is its localisation in the potential space of the transference, created by, and in, the intersubjectivity of transference–countertransference, rather than created unilaterally in the mind of the child or the therapist (Winnicott, 1971a).

An actual, real-life relationship between two persons

From the vantage point of the transference, the psychotherapeutic relationship is entirely different from any other relationship experienced by the child in his everyday life. However, from sociological and sensory-based perspectives, the therapeutic relationship may be compared to the child's relationship with any other adult. It is, for instance, delimited in part by an external, sociological reality compounded by differences of gender, generation, and appointed roles, and in part by a sensory-based reality, compounded by perception and observation, which, likewise, demarcates the separateness and dissimilarity of the therapist and the child. Furthermore, universal social psychological group dynamics linked to other given characteristics and roles, for example, related to social class, ethnic, or cultural group, can also influence the relationship.

Yet, the therapeutic relationship creates something more: an actual two-person relationship that develops between child and therapist during therapy. Thus, even if the child and the psychotherapist are assigned different tasks and roles, both are in a position to observe the other. Because they meet regularly to address emotionally important issues, a mutual, interpersonal process develops alongside the therapeutic process. Through introjection, both participants take in observations of the other, and through containment they are able to make these introjects part of their inner world of object relations. From this perspective, in the two-person relationship, it is not only the therapist who observes the child; the child also observes the therapist, and, through recurrent, social and sensory-based observation, the child forms more or less acute impressions of the therapist as a person.

The therapist's actual demeanour and genuine personal characteristics, therefore, also influence the therapeutic process. As pointed out by others before us, in the process of a psychodynamic interpretation of children's statements, play, and reactions in the therapy room, it is not sufficient to strive to understand their underlying transference phantasies about the therapist. Rather, to the best of her ability, the therapist also needs to identify how the child's realistic, preconscious, sensory-based observations of his therapist contribute to the formation of these phantasies (Ferro, 1999; Searles, 1975). Children (and adults) in psychotherapy are not only looking for the therapist's understanding; in this new situation, they also try—in every way they can—to figure out what kind of person the therapist is, and what it might take to make her react in certain ways. Thus, children and adolescents, more or less deliberately, constantly observe their therapist, who cannot (and should not) avoid showing her personal individuality as a human being—for instance, through facial expressions, phrasing and tone of voice, clothes, bearing, etc. As children watch and listen to their therapist, not only do they take notice of the meaning of her words and how they are said; they also take notice of how the therapist feels: for example, whether she feels comfortable or out of sorts. Children and adolescents do not primarily pay attention to the therapist's good intentions in intervening but have a keen eye for contradictions, unspoken implications, and the general emotional context out of which the intervention was born.

In the early stages of therapy, most children and adolescents more or less consciously look for hints from the therapist about how to solve this as-yet unknown task of "going to psychotherapy". Moreover, they compare the therapist with other grown-ups in their personal life and, as mentioned, notice her looks, clothes, voice, moods, and when and how she intervenes. In other words, most children relate to their therapist as both a transference figure and an actual person in their present reality. This seems especially to be the case for children who have experienced unstable, depriving, abusive, or inverse care relationships early in life: for instance, on a background of unpredictable parental mood swings and loss of self-control, drug or alcohol issues, a personality disorder, or mental illness.

In principle, the child's perception of the personal characteristics of the therapist belongs in the borderland between interpersonal and intrapsychic domains and has accordingly, aptly, been called "the perceptual edge of the transference" (Smith, 1990, p. 219). As with transference, the child's sensory-based introjections of the therapist's actual appearance, manner, and behaviour act as a continual undercurrent in the psychotherapeutic process, which is always present as a potential dynamic force, whether or not the therapist and the child are aware of it. The child and the therapist's mutual exploration of the child's observations of the clinic, the therapy, and the therapist is, therefore, an important therapeutic means of facilitating the child's reality testing, paving the way for a development of a stable ability to differentiate between the inner world of phantasies and the outer reality of other people.

As mentioned, an important part of therapists' work concerns their willingness in the therapeutic space to act as stand-ins for primary figures in the personal life of the child, allowing and encouraging the curious exploration of their personal appearance and manner. This area is often the cause of certain countertransference-related confusion and difficulties, however, especially so for therapists in training. It is important to note that the therapist's encouragement of the child's exploration of her personal appearance should not be mistaken for a willingness to share information about her personal life, whether it is about the therapist's family or her private reflections on her own state of mind (including countertransference feelings). Children, and even some adolescents, tend openly to voice quite hard-nosed and sometimes very apt observations of their therapist, and they are far more likely than most adults to spontaneously share their observations about the therapist's looks, eccentricities, and mood. This is a delicate and important balancing act, since the therapist should avoid transgressing the boundaries of her own privacy while, at the same, permitting the child, in phantasy, to invade her personal and narcissistic space with comments that she and the child together will consider and discuss seriously. Thus, a competent psychodynamic child and adolescent psychotherapist possesses a certain resilience and keeps an open mind, remaining curious and willing to learn new knowledge about herself from the child. A therapist who is able to make room for these unpredictable aspects of child and adolescent psychotherapy will be personally enriched by each therapeutic process.

Therapeutic alliance: possibility or necessity?

Last, to some extent, the therapeutic relationship between child and therapist may also be described as a therapeutic alliance. Alliance is, however, a difficult concept to define in a clear and meaningful way, particularly in relation to child and adolescent psychotherapy. In this book, the therapeutic alliance in child and adolescent psychotherapy is conceptualised as an aspect of the total therapeutic relationship. From this, it follows that it must be understood as a continuous, relational phenomenon, waxing and waning throughout therapy, dependent on the contributions of both therapist and child.

As described by Kjærgaard and Westergaard (2015), a conceptual review of definitions of the therapeutic alliance in child and adolescent psychotherapy shows that many definitions do not differentiate clearly between process and outcome; for instance, they define the alliance in terms that might just as well be an outcome of therapy (e.g., the child's ability to co-operate with the therapist). Definitions could, for example, also be ambiguous in explicating with whom the therapist has reached an alliance, the child or the parents. (See Chapter Seven on the role of parents in child and adolescent psychotherapy.)

The significance of the therapeutic alliance for the effect of psychotherapy with adults has been shown empirically in a great number of quantitative studies. In these studies, the alliance is typically described as the task-orientated, purposeful dimensions of the co-operation between client and therapist, although some definitions also include their emotional or personal relationship (Elvins & Green, 2008). Accordingly, the alliance is generally supposed to be located in the reality-orientated part of the client's personality, the part of the mind that is able, during periods of intensive positive or negative transference, to differentiate between the transference relationship and the real-life relationship, the purpose of which is the client's psychotherapy.

More often than not, children and young people with psychological difficulties and/or mental disorders are not referred for psychotherapy because they themselves feel a need to change, but instead because the adults around them are worried about their development, mood, and behaviour. As an exception to this rule, some children are motivated by subjectively painful symptoms (e.g., anxiety, compulsion, emptiness, and traumatic re-experiencing). Even so, in psychotherapy, children and adolescents are typically less stable than adults in their motivation, which often comes and goes. Thus, their ego-functions (especially frustration tolerance and their capacity for long-term planning) might still be too immaturely developed to maintain a consistent level of motivation and preserve the alliance through periods of working through painful feelings.

How to facilitate a therapeutic alliance with children and adolescents?

Questions about how best to create and maintain a therapeutic alliance with children have been widely discussed over time, and, as mentioned, even today the issue cannot be said to have reached an unambiguously valid resolution.

As an example of a definition that focuses solely on the child's contribution to the alliance, Sandler and colleagues (1980), in *The Technique of Child Psychoanalysis. Discussions with Anna Freud*, defined the alliance as a product of "the child's conscious or unconscious wish to cooperate and his readiness to accept the therapist's aid in overcoming internal difficulties and resistances" (p. 45).

Klein focused explicitly on the therapist's technical contribution to the alliance. She felt that what mattered most was the therapist's ability to link as fast as possible to the child's unconscious world of phantasies through interpretation, easing his anxiety, shame, and guilt (Klein, 1927, 1955; Segal, 1957, 1977). In this formulation, the alliance is primarily created and maintained through the therapist's ability to understand the symbols of play as meaningful statements concerning the emotional condition of the self and its inner objects. In so far as the child is able to make sense of the therapist's interpretations, these will create a deep—not necessarily conscious—experience of relief, and, according to Klein, this is presumably what primarily binds children to their therapy by increasing their unconscious wish to bring more and more aspects of their inner world into the relationship.

In line with Winnicott's (1971a) understanding of the ability to play as a precondition for the child's mental development, the development of an alliance can also be linked to the therapist's support of the child's genuine enjoyment of play. According to this point of view, the therapist's ability, as a real person, to lend the child active aid in play might be crucial for the development of an alliance. Thus, as exemplified by the work with children whose ability to learn was impaired,

Cohen and Solnit (1993) held that a therapeutic alliance is primarily fostered by the child's internalisation of the therapist's aid in play, as this identification enhances the child's motivation and ability to develop through playing.

By the same token, but taking into account the child's cognitive–emotional capacity for developing and entering into a therapeutic alliance, the American tradition of ego- and self-psychology typically emphasises as crucial the development of sufficient inner frustration tolerance and mental structure as factors that enable the child to recognise ownership of his own emotional states and feelings (Furman, 1992). This point of view has recently experienced a renaissance through the theory of mentalization, in which the therapeutic alliance in child and adolescent psychotherapy is often conceptualised in terms of the therapist's ability to offer the child empathic support by recognising and containing the child's feelings (Fonagy et al., 2002a; Slijper, 2008).

Alvarez (2010) has suggested a flexible integration of these differing points of view, pointing out that children's abilities to enter into a therapeutic alliance vary with the personality of the child, especially with differing levels of pathology and capacities for contact and mentalization. Accordingly, she proposed that, in relation to the single, unique child, therapists need to reflect in detail to determine on which mental level a binding therapeutic relationship can be established. In line with this, Kjærgaard and Westergaard (2015) concluded the therapeutic alliance to be a complex phenomenon to which the therapist, the child, and the parents each render their—mutually reinforcing—contribution.

Observations inside the consulting room

In summary, irrespective of the therapist's preferred definition, the above suggestions include processes that are not fully conscious to the child. Thus, across traditions, it seems safe to conclude that an implicit agreement has developed that a therapeutic alliance with a child cannot be based primarily on the child's conscious motivation for treatment.

To a practising child and adolescent psychotherapist, the most important concern might be to reach an operational working definition of the therapeutic alliance based on observable characteristics or dynamics that appear in the therapeutic process that enable the therapist to assess whether the child is working on his own development in a spirit of enquiry. In our experience, the concerns and reactions described below, as observed in the therapy room, could indicate that a therapeutic alliance is in the making rather than on the decline. We must, however, admit that the perspective outlined in the proposal does make it difficult to differentiate between the manifestations of, on the one hand, a therapeutic alliance and, on the other, the development of a specific transference relationship and a motivation for working through inside this relationship. Perhaps, though, that concern should not be viewed as a liability, but, rather, as one of the crucial constituting features distinguishing psychodynamic psychotherapy from other forms of psychotherapy. Whether such reactions are construed as alliance or working through in the transference, a critical condition for this motivation to emerge is probably that the child was able to recognise himself and his intentions, feelings, and phantasies in most of the therapists' previous interventions.

Thus, at times, when the features mentioned below are observed in the therapeutic relationship, a therapeutic alliance might be in the making.

1. The child becomes preoccupied with other children, wishing to become like them. Some children seem motivated by (not necessarily conscious) wishes to be like other same-age children, including developing the same skills and being able to deal with the same challenges. Despite objections, they might long for an ordinary family where adults take responsibility and make decisions for the children. Thus, even very disturbed or defiant children who, in their manifest behaviour, seem to eschew reality testing, might secretly hold subjective wishes of development and skills on a par with their birth-age peers. This could, for instance, concern self-regulation, making friends, school or sports achievements, and longing for dependent relationships with caring, regulating parental figures. In some—often tragically disillusioned—children, the motivation for personal growth and development might seem quite absent or very, very difficult to sustain, emerging only in brief glimpses. This could be because the impetus for development remained immaturely fixed in

infantile, disturbed relationships. Alternatively, it might be caused by disintegration in the wake of recurrent trauma and neglect, in which case any change might be feared as a change for the worse, and wishes for development have consequently been "locked away" in a brick-solid defence of detachment and denial of any dependence (Henry, 1974). Such children might, for long stretches, demonstratively display an aggressively or indifferently dismissive attitude to the therapist and the therapy, but, even so, in tiny glimpses they might show a dependent longing, which, if given proper attention from the therapist, might develop into a therapeutic alliance. It should be noted that, in our experience, neither a therapeutic alliance nor a positive treatment outcome presupposes positive transference feelings—or *vice versa*. This paradox might be specific to child psychotherapy, but, if a sustainable alliance with the parents of the child has been built, in spite of manifest and loudly declared antipathy, the child might show a degree of active participation that can be understood as nothing but a tacit alliance. Such a child might, for instance, regularly show up smiling, eagerly running into the therapy room, but, once inside, he immediately switches off the motivation, reverting to aggressive, devaluating behaviour. Another child might almost never miss a session, despite loudly voiced protests and ample opportunities for missing public transport to therapy.

2. The child begins to relate to the therapist and/or the therapy in a highly personal way. At some point, perhaps surprisingly early in therapy, some children begin to relate to the therapist and the therapy in new ways. The shift might appear in different modes of expression, not necessarily unambiguously positive, but distinctive and easily recognisable, since the children begin to talk and/or act in new, highly personal ways. Even young children can, after a few weeks or months, from one session to the next simply begin to pick up the same play scenario, as if there had been no break in between the sessions. At home, some children reportedly refer to the therapist when trying to elicit special favours from their parents. The parents might report that the child carefully watches appointment times and reacts to cancellations by acting out or verbal objections. Some children, in or outside therapy, might reportedly refer to their therapists as "my

therapist" or mention her full name in a special tone; they might compare what they hear about other children's therapies with their own experiences in therapy; they might vehemently question the therapist about her private family relationships or other child patients. For some children, it becomes crucially important that certain play set-ups that are too big or fragile to go into their play box are not dismantled, but are cared for by the therapist between sessions. Some children unconsciously appropriate aspects of their therapists, for instance, copying certain mannerisms, verbal modes of expression, or items of clothing. Sometimes, this becomes noticeable as the child begins to use particular turns of phrase that are pregnant with subjective meaning: for example, assigning to the therapist specific personal qualities, for instance, calling her caring, neglectful, consistent, deplorable, admirable, etc.

3. The child takes the lead, adding essential personal experiences to the therapist's interventions. As described in Chapter Two, psychodynamic child and adolescent psychotherapy works in and through an onward progressing, spiralling process of cognition. In this process, the therapist reality-tests her intuitive conjectures of the child's inner world by offering verbal suggestions (interpretations) and then waiting to see what happens next, observing whether and how the child relates to the intervention. In this way, over time, she will get to know the child's life experience. Sometimes, such a more or less verbal interchange is suddenly enriched by an unexpectedly precise answer from the child, who, as in the example below, spontaneously adds new, deeply genuine, personal knowledge (Grünbaum, 2014).

Five-year-old Samantha was referred to psychotherapy by a community childcare worker. When she was eighteen months old, she was removed from her home and placed in a residential institution, and, at the age of forty-two months, she was placed in permanent foster care. She was referred because her development had come to a standstill; she had reportedly stopped playing, and her language was deteriorating into meaningless parroting and copying of the defiant behaviours of her five-year-older foster brother. She was seen for psychotherapy twice weekly. The examples appearing below took place in the tenth and eleventh sessions. (See Chapter Ten for more detailed information on Samantha.)

(Session ten, first session of the week.) At the beginning of the session, Samantha eagerly hurries in, starts painting, paints herself as a big, happily smiling figure but, shortly after, covers the figure's mouth with black paint. (I suggest this to be confusing, the Samantha in the painting is smiling, but at the same time, her mouth is black.) Samantha points to the painting, "Something bad went into her mouth." (I suggest that this bad black might be as if something bad from me got inside Samantha, maybe because it has been five days since the last session.) Samantha confirms, "Yes, she gets fire." She then looks at the furniture in the doll's house, which had been moved around since the previous session, asking, "Was someone in here?", immediately moving away from me to build ambitiously high brick towers, which crash to the floor.

(Session eleven, two days later, second session of the week.) Hurrying into the playroom, Samantha paints a yellow female figure, says that this is her, looks at me, then changes her mind; now this is not herself, but me. She says, "Look what happens to you," and pours black paint all over the female figure, until it is no longer visible. She makes more paintings of me, attacking them in similar ways, in a flat voice threatening to soil and stab me. (I suggest that since the last session, I turned into something bad inside Samantha.) Gradually, the smearing gives way to an intense activity, as she scoops all the paint up into a single container. (I suggest that Samantha wants to use up all the paint to prevent other children from getting any.) Samantha gazes intently into my eyes, asking whether she is the first child to come, because if she is, I am not stupid, but if she is not, she will cut my throat. She mimics drawing a knife across her own throat.

Therapeutic alliance: a conclusion

The therapeutic alliance evidently plays quite an ambiguous role in child and adolescent psychotherapy. Among other uncertainties described, children—and even some adolescents—are not necessarily conscious either of a need for personal change or of a need to co-operate with the therapist. All in all, the conclusion seems to be that with children, conscious, task-orientated co-operation plays a less pivotal and much more equivocal role.

However, to perform any form of psychotherapy, the therapist obviously needs to enter into an alliance with someone. This is also the case in child and adolescent psychotherapy, where the alliance probably originates in the complexity created by several forces, among them the attitude of the parents, the organisational and economic context of the psychotherapy, the therapist's willingness and ability to communicate at a level that matches the child's age, the child's own concerns and capacity for mentalization, and, of course, to some degree, the child's own, more or less conscious, experience of suffering. Concerning the age of the child, with few exceptions, a good rule of thumb seems to be that the younger the child, the more important is a firm and durable alliance with the parents. On the other hand, the older the child, the more important it is to engage the child in an alliance.

CHAPTER SIX

Understanding drawings and symbolic play

In this chapter, we describe how the spontaneous symbolic works of children and adolescents—drawings, play, and other creative products—can be understood as communication about their inner world, which is activated in and by the therapeutic process. First, various characteristics of pictorial production are reviewed, second, symbolic play is described, and, finally, a model is suggested in which these forms of production are understood as intentional linguistic expressions.

Drawings in child and adolescent psychotherapy

From the beginnings of child analysis, drawing has been an essential element in both assessment and psychotherapy with children and adolescents. In Klein's (1961) description of her analysis of ten-year-old Richard, which was carried out during the first years of the Second World War (but not published until later), many of his drawings were reproduced. Richard's works were paper-and-pencil drawings, but that is not always the child's chosen medium. Children can produce pictures done in crayons or wet paint, and sometimes they make objects out of clay or plasticine. Therefore, the concept of pictorial representation is often to be preferred to the narrower concept of drawing.

Drawing can be a valuable part of the assessment of a child or young person and offers important information. Usually, children are familiar with drawing, which means that the task is not frightening to them. Young children, in particular, often enjoy drawing. Space does not allow a thorough treatment of this subject, but see, for example, Brafman (2012) and Jolley (2010).

It is important to remember that drawings made during an assessment or in a psychotherapy session are never casual but are—often unconsciously—addressed to the person the child is with, and, as such, they are part of a transference relationship. The child or young person might often convey things in his drawing that he would not be able to express in words.

Some children and adolescents never draw, some do occasionally, and, for some, drawings are their main channel of communication. Sometimes, the message of a child's or young person's drawings is surprisingly straightforward. For example, a ten-year-old girl, whose main problem was that she could not sleep without wetting her bed, drew a ship with water gushing out from a row of portholes (see Figure 2). A lonely boy of the same age drew a small, isolated house in an empty, snow-covered field.

It should be noted that the use of drawings in psychotherapy is not the same as art therapy. The art therapist is not a psychotherapist, but has special training in art therapy, which places significant emphasis on artistic expression and the process of picture production. As described by Kramer (1971), one of the pioneers of art therapy, pictorial representation is the key element in art therapy; this stands in contrast to psychotherapy, where creative expressions are a tool. Art therapists usually rely less on interpretation than psychotherapists do, and although they might respond to unconscious as well as conscious elements in a child's behaviour, their work is usually more about providing support than about uncovering unconscious phantasies. According to Kramer, by itself, art therapy is usually not enough to solve more deep-seated emotional problems. The challenges of the creative process and the occupation with colour and form that speaks more directly to senses and feelings than words do might, however, be a very valuable supplement for many children.

Figure 2. Drawing by a ten-year-old girl who was a bedwetter.

Children's drawings develop with age, and, naturally, it is important for a psychotherapist to know what can be expected of children at different ages. Children with mental problems often have a delayed drawing development compared to other children.

To produce any kind of pictorial product, its creator must possess an impulse, an inner drive to express himself. That alone is not enough, however; for the picture to have any form and structure, there must also be a controlling or structuring force to modify the raw impulse. There has to be a suitable balance between these two forces. If the impulse is too strong, compared with the controlling force, the product will be formless and chaotic; if the opposite is the case, the result will be rigid and lifeless.

Kramer (1971) distinguished between (1) predominantly formless and chaotic works, (2) conventional and stereotyped works, and (3) what she named "formed expression", that is, complex, aesthetically successful works that are genuine expressions of the child's emotions and have a suitable balance between impulse and defence.

The following example concerns a child who had difficulty controlling his impulses.

Eleven-year-old George used wet paint to make a picture that he explained represented an oasis in a desert. It showed a very simple house, consisting only of a square, a palm tree, and an elephant with a raised trunk. The second picture featured a similar motif in an even simpler execution. In the third picture, he painted a big blue square, representing a lake, surrounded by a thin green stripe and with a small white duck in the middle. In the fourth picture, he abandoned symbolic content entirely, filling the paper with rows of closely spaced circles. In the fifth picture, he eschewed structure, daubing the paper with a thick layer of paint. In the sixth picture, he stopped using the brushes for painting and, instead, immersed them in the paint until the paint flowed from them, then rolled the brushes between his hands, causing part of the paint to drip on to the paper and part of it to splatter around. Finally, in the seventh and last picture, he gave up the use of tools completely, putting his fingers into the paint and smearing it all over the paper, with great pleasure.

This is a clear example of regression, where the symbolic representation is abandoned in favour of a pattern, and, next, even this basic structure is abandoned. The impulse to represent something disappears in the course of the process and is substituted by a pleasure in feeling the paint on his hands and smearing it—a form of exploration of the material that one would expect from a much younger child. Children with such extensive control problems often need limitations on their activities, for example, by not having access to wet paint.

Conversely, an over-controlled child might shrink from using paint in the first place in favour of a (faint) pencil, use a ruler to draw, or draw stereotyped comic strip characters. Some children become expert at drawing certain cartoon figures and, thus, completely avoid showing more personal traits. It might tax the therapist's patience to wait for a very inhibited and perhaps obsessive child to allow himself to reveal more of his phantasies and personal life, but he needs space and time to do so. It is important to keep in mind, however, that the child should not open up with the purpose of pleasing the therapist, so she has to be very careful not to encourage him directly.

Pictures are more closely connected to the body and emotions than our spoken words. As illustrated by the following examples, sometimes, unconscious material might make itself known in pictures before the drawer is conscious about what it is he is expressing.

Eleven-year-old Joanna was adopted from a distant country. She was anxious and inhibited and rarely demonstrated any anger. She had significant generalised learning problems. During the psychological assessment, among other things, she drew a furious face, which, however, was captioned "To sweetie" (Figure 3).

Sally, a severely neglected child, who had been placed into a foster family at the age of three, was defiant and aggressive but never showed any signs of sadness, not even when there were obvious reasons for it. For many years, however, she drew a large number of pictures of weeping girls.

Sometimes, such pictures help the child to recognise the emotional content, but that is far from always the case. Therefore, it could be perceived as invasive if the therapist is too quick or too direct in interpreting the content of a picture.

Below, we provide an example of the inclusion of drawings in the dialogue between a child (here a teenager) and the therapist.

Figure 3. Joanna's "To sweetie" drawing.

> Sixteen-year-old Tom had a very difficult childhood, including the loss of both his birth parents and his foster parents. He often made drawings during his therapy sessions. Once, he made a big black blot on the paper, using a crayon that he pushed hard into the paper. I commented as to whether this might be how he felt inside. He answered, "Can you tell from my drawings what's the matter with me?" ("What do you think is the matter with you?") "They [the teachers in the residential unit where he lived] say that I'm paranoid." ("I think you feel persecuted by all the misfortune and all the losses that you have suffered.") In response, he painted a beautiful rainbow with light, delicate colours.

The above vignette can illustrate several points. My first comment was too direct and sparked a paranoid response in Tom. It would have been a good idea if I had commented on the anxiety my remark aroused. However, we had a long-lasting collaboration behind us, and, perhaps for that reason, Tom seemed to forgive me and accepted the subject I suggested. In his last drawing, he very delicately showed me that he had felt understood.

Therapists who are not used to working with pictures often ask what to do with the drawings. The question is not easily answered. As may be seen from the above example, it is necessary to be very careful when interpreting a drawing. It can be frightening to realise that others discern meanings in one's work that one might not have been aware of; something that the child might both desire and fear. On the other hand, the drawings also should not be neglected, as if they were of no interest. The therapist should feel free to enquire about details that are not immediately understandable. Often, it is a good idea to ask the child to comment on his picture or to mention the feelings that the picture triggers in her.

Playing and symbolic representation

The freedom of spontaneous play facilitates the externalisation of the child's unspoken or unconscious concerns and relationships with objects, enabling him to communicate his innermost feelings, thoughts, and unconscious phantasies through symbolic representation. Like drawings, symbolic play contains highly subjective communication and, thus, contributes uniquely valuable psychodynamic insights into the child's inner world. Whether part of a psychological investigation, an assessment for child psychotherapy, or a therapeutic process, psychodynamic observation of the child at play enables an essential understanding of his inner world that cannot be obtained in any other way. Space does not allow us to elaborate on the many aspects of psychodynamic play observation, but see, for instance, Björn and colleagues (2011) and Schaefer and colleagues (2010).

The playing child unconsciously creates a mental bridge that connects the gap between the social relationships of his ordinary, external world and his inner world of object relationships and related phantasies. Through non-directed pretend play, he communicates, explores, and works through feelings and phantasies related to his everyday experience of either ordinary happenings or troublesome events and experiences that are so fragmented or traumatic that he cannot speak about them in words. In this way, play not only gives the child singular opportunities for practising numerous perceptual, motor, and cognitive skills; in developmentally important ways, it also helps him reality-test feelings and phantasies, thus furthering his ability to learn from experience. Hence, as pointed out by several authors, the ability to mentalize through symbolic play presupposes a healthy early personality development (Caper, 1996; Fonagy et al., 2002a; Winnicott, 1968).

Accordingly, a precondition for successful child psychotherapy is the therapist's understanding that the child's spontaneous language of feelings, phantasies, and object relationships is action-orientated rather than verbal. Hence, an important difference between psychotherapy with children and, on the other hand, adolescents and adults is that while the natural medium of communication with adolescents and adults is verbal associations and narrations, this is only partly true for children. In general, children only have a limited capacity for verbalising their feelings, phantasies, and experiences directly, but they can fluently communicate these in representative play, in a process that is only partly governed by conscious intents and, instead, draws mainly upon unconscious creative and symbolic sources.

In other words, play is a quintessential medium of both the psychotherapeutic process and the verbal exchange between the child and the therapist. As a curiosity, it might be mentioned that, in the early days of child analysis, this status was not assigned to play, and the child's partiality to playing might even be considered an obstacle;

for instance, in 1913, Ferenczi allegedly terminated the treatment of a child because he constantly interrupted the therapist's business by indulging in play (Bernstein & Sax, 1978). Fortunately, as is well known, the work of Melanie Klein and Anna Freud changed this perception, and today the important functions of play in both child development and child psychotherapy are generally acknowledged.

As mentioned above, before puberty, for most children in psychotherapy, it is not natural to reflect on their subjective experiences, feelings, and phantasies in words alone. However, they are able—at least to a certain degree—to communicate through play, representing relationships and actions by toy figures and, thus, symbolically revealing feelings, subjective phantasies, and relationships that they need the therapist's help to sort out. Hence, inside the transference relationship, disturbances in the process of play, whether manic enactments, inhibitions, repetitions, or actual blockages, are not considered accidental events but are, instead, understood as events stemming from the child's unconscious phantasies about object relationships, including phantasies related to therapy and the therapist (Klein, 1929). This places the child psychotherapist in a unique position to gain insight into the child's inner world, enabling an indirect but emotionally meaningful dialogue with the child about pent-up or unconscious feelings and object experiences.

Thus, when we provide a box of toys to a child who is in psychodynamic psychotherapy, the intention is not to provide him with the means to amuse himself while he converses with the therapist. On the contrary, the intention is to provide the child with a medium that allows him to engage in detailed, personal dialogue with his therapist about emotional intentions, ideas, and phantasies. Toys and creative materials such as plasticine, felt-tip pens, and crayons should, thus, be understood as additional means of expression—offering a larger, more flexible vocabulary—that enables an emotionally committed, reflective dialogue, even with young children.

It is, for instance, hard to imagine any child entering the therapy room saying, "I feel so tense today, you have to help me find out why . . ." Instead, any child at any age is much more likely to kick off the session with an angry accusation: "Who messed up my box, where is my little green car?" while desperately searching for the car, which, in fact, sits right under his nose.

The child's use of the materials in his box needs space and time to unfold in a way consistent with his inner process. In psychodynamic psychotherapy, the therapist's task is neither to push the play in any specific directions nor to play with the child like a peer. That does not mean, however, that the therapist should not assist the playing child, for instance, by taking on specific roles, as assigned by the child. None the less, the therapist should never forget her primary task, and, while she engages in play, she needs to keep up an inner, reflective process about why the child allocated this role to her. At all times, the therapist needs to remember that her main task is to facilitate the child's communication of his inner world. Through her attitude, interventions, and interpretations, she therefore aims to further the child's communication and help him work through his feelings, such as anxiety, grief, anger, and confusion, as related to subjective relational experiences and phantasies.

Immaturity and disturbed thinking

While the manifest narrations and themes of a specific play activity yield important information about the child's inner world, it is equally important for the therapist to consider the underlying aspects of how the child applies and relates to the toys. These more formal aspects of the child's activity have an important story to tell about what cannot be symbolised in plays or drawings, that is, a story of disturbances or inhibitions in the development of symbol formation and relational thinking (mentalizing).

As early as 1957, Segal described a specific, pathological form of thinking, which she called symbolic equation. It describes a relationship between symbol and symbolised, in which the symbol is handled as if it were the original object. This lack of differentiation between object and symbol can be understood as the consequence of a defensive fusion between self and object, brought about by excessive splitting and projective identification (Segal, 1957). There is a certain parallel to this in normal development, since, in early childhood, the child is not yet able to represent mental states independently of physical reality and might confuse inner thoughts and phantasies with what exists in the outer world, and *vice versa*. Hence, the young child's ability to differentiate between, on the one hand, his own feelings, ideas, and phantasies, and, on the other hand, the external reality of other human beings, their feelings, and intentions is blurred and unstable. This mode of thinking has been named psychic equivalence mode by Fonagy and his colleagues (Fonagy & Allison, 2012).

For some children, the immature mode of thinking lingers way beyond its normal stage of development. This could be due to an intellectual disability; however, it might also be that, in the mental aftermath of severe, early traumatisation, collapses occur in the child's ability to differentiate between the symbol (e.g., the pretend character of a toy) and the symbolised (the original real-life object).

> At the age of one and a half years, Christian had suffered severe accidental scalding with extensive damage, leaving him immobilised and in pain for several months in a specialised hospital ward, partially separated from his parents. At the age of five years, he was referred for clinical psychological examination and possibly psychodynamic child psychotherapy for severe separation anxiety and delayed cognitive development, especially of language, and, consequently, also for observation of possible general intellectual disability. After nine months of twice-weekly psychotherapy, Christian had developed significantly in cognitive, social, and emotional terms. However, he was still not stable in his mode of functioning. At this point, it became clear, both to me and to his teachers, that his immature levels of functioning were no longer a fairly persistent phenomenon but, instead, emerged as sudden, delimitated relapses:
>
> During a stressful moment of the psychotherapy, Christian absent-mindedly tries to eat a tiny, red plastic apple on a toy tree. Once the apple is in his mouth, he discovers the mistake, spits it out into his hand, staring at it in amazement, saying: "Yuk, just thought it was a real apple." (Details of this case study were published in Grünbaum, 1989.)

In the case of more profound disturbances of reality-testing and thinking, the child might use toys in odd, distinctive ways, disregarding their immanent aims and functions in favour of private, not easily understandable, meanings. He might, for instance, over-construe a non-essential aspect as a central characteristic of the object: for example, the colour, texture, name, sound, form, or other superficial attributes. Such dreamlike, condensed, or expanded uses of specific toys or words point towards underlying, dissociated pockets of disturbed, private thinking about object relationships. It is, therefore, crucial for the therapist to pay close attention to possible eccentric uses of toys, not with the aim of intervention and correction, but because they contain crucial information of the child's way of thinking and, thus, offer important opportunities for insight. Such thought disturbances appear in many degrees and forms, and, during the course of a session, the child's cognitive level of functioning might fluctuate from ordinary mentalization to severe disturbance.

For example, children pained by repeated loss, early neglect, or unstable early attachments might often comprehend a reel of string or adhesive tape as not only a practical aid for tying or taping objects together, but might often subjectively include the additional emotional meaning of linking subject and object together. Hence, during the last sessions before a break, it is common for a child in a mode of symbolic equivalence to be obsessively preoccupied with taping or tying things together: for instance, applying pieces of paper to drawings and furniture or tying their drawings to the toy box, to the therapist's chair, to the couch, to the doorknob, etc., perhaps even, in the heat of the moment, having a go at tying up the therapist.

If the child is severely disturbed or confused, the painful yearning for caring and understanding parental objects—and, in the transference, an available therapist—might take on much more opaque, condensed paranoid modes of expression.

Eight-year-old Paul was referred to psychotherapy with three weekly sessions because of fierce conflicts with his adoptive mother, his resistance to bathing and to tidying his many collections, and a tendency towards idiosyncratic behaviour, which had escalated during the preceding six months. During this period, he had also developed paranoid ideas about possibly being poisoned or choked by his food. He did well at school, but remained aloof from peers and often felt that the others were teasing or bullying him. During his first year of life, Paul had lived in isolation with his psychotic birth mother, who, at the time of referral, had been chronically hospitalised due to severe mental illness. Until recently, Paul had regularly visited his maternal grandparents, and, during these visits, he had probably sometimes met with his birth mother.

In therapy, Paul rarely played and often preferred to talk. While playing, he allocated private and highly idiosyncratic meanings to some of the things in his box. This tendency was evident from the very first therapy session.

Paul is sitting in a chair, crossing his legs like an adult, earnestly talking about his problems. He says that at night he cannot go to sleep, because when he lies in his bed, the furniture and things in his room change and turn against him, which is really frightening. Sometimes at night, he is convinced that evil people outside his house are looking at him; in fact, the whole world is looking at him. Also, he cannot stop quarrelling with his mother. While he is talking, Paul begins to examine the contents of his toy box, sorting the animals by species. At a certain point, he hides a monkey behind a ball of string, placing a giraffe directly in front of the string. He points to the monkey and says, "This one was all alone. Something was missing. And it's afraid to be eaten by this one [the giraffe]."

In the next session, Paul sets up the same scenario; the monkey is still afraid of being eaten by the giraffe and hides behind the ball of string, which Paul now refers to as "food". Over the following months, he consistently refers to this ball of string as "food", which to him seems analogous to good feelings of connectedness with an understanding other. During the same period, the bad feelings go into a pencil sharpener, which he calls the "sharpened stick of a bad, dangerous commander-voice-king".

As the first Christmas break draws near, Paul talks about his thoughts, describing them in fairly concrete terms, as physical entities passing back and forth between himself and me. He tells me, "The good thing about coming here and talking about bad thoughts is that then one doesn't have them any more; as if they left one and went inside someone else, who now has them . . . making more space inside for good thoughts. But then, when one comes back on Monday, one thinks that maybe the bad thoughts will have won, making you all different . . ."

In the last session before this break, Paul appears very withdrawn. (I suggest that he feels so alone because of the forthcoming break.) He is silent, but after a while, he says, "If anything, it's like you disappear and never existed. One gnaws into you, and then you're gone, but this is not like images, more like commander-voice thoughts, and then one cannot see you when one is at home . . . but, like, sometimes, then this bad thought appears that when I come here, you'll be gone, and there's going to be a new one, and every time I come to see you, there will be a new one, and a new one, it's not you at all . . . or maybe it is you, really, but suddenly it's not you any more, but you changed into someone else, even if you look like yourself."

Some children animate inanimate objects but shrink away from dolls and animals. This might have a defensive function linked to an aggressive, inner organisation of object relationships. In an excessive paranoid–schizoid mode, these children apparently feel safer in relation to things-as-human-beings than human-beings-as-human-beings, probably partly because this makes it easier for them to convince themselves that these dehumanised objects are unable to feel pain, even from the most gruesome, sadistic attacks, and, hence, they are not likely to retaliate (Rosenfeld, 1971). Parenthetically, the same sort of defensive dehumanising is often encountered in connection with atrocities committed during civil war and ethnic or religious cleansing.

Carlo, who was nine years old at the time of referral, spent the first two years of his life at an orphanage and was then returned to his birth father and stepmother. In the therapy room, he was very hard on the toys, and during the first few months he transformed his box and its content to a chaotic mess of damaged objects. Even the box, which was made of sturdy cardboard, was about to fall apart, because it had been pierced by scissors and pens. After a good six months of twice-weekly therapy, this sequence took place.

Carlo begins the session by finding and carelessly brushing aside an adult, female doll, then takes the washing machine from the doll's house, shaking it while he sings, "And then we butcher the washing machine, oh, my lovely washing machine." He grabs the vacuum cleaner from the doll's house, pulling at the hose, as he sings, "And now, we drag out its long, long neck, so it says ouch, ouch." He opens the doll's house toilet, placing a potted plant in the toilet bowl, while he sings, "And this one here, the cry baby, she goes down to the shit." (I say, "Above all, you wish to get completely rid of her, flushing her down the toilet.") Carlo: "Yes, but only her. And you can't flush her all out, she's too big to pass through." ("But you like the thought of doing it.") "Oh, yes, a little. My, I'm so hungry."

The plant in the toilet bowl was a comprehensible symbolic reference to his little sister, of whom he was terribly jealous, but, at the same time, it is probably also a reference to the therapist and other children who come in for therapy, towards whom he had felt quite hostile for some time.

Not all uses of play and toys are rooted in the child's creative resources and, accordingly, applied as means of genuine mental work in the therapeutic process. Some children play only sporadically, in short, disconnected, or enigmatic sequences, or not at all. They might use the toys for other ends, including the desperate destruction and devaluation of a therapist whom they perceive as useless. Or maybe for taking cover, hiding their aggressive, vulnerable, or empty self in endless, stereotyped play and drawings, while, at the same time, rejecting genuine contact with the therapist: for example, turning their back to her or sneeringly thumbing their nose at her attempts at establishing a dialogue about what is going on.

The therapist's task is to do her best to understand the nature and functions of the child's play during the sessions in relation to his emotionality, self-knowledge, and perceptions of the therapeutic relationship. The play of some children generally communicates rich narratives of inner meaning and intentions. Conversely, other children's play mostly conveys a sense of as-if-play to the therapist, perhaps in the form of a completely shallow negation of a painful inner scenario of, for instance, loss or loneliness, a scenario that the child seeks desperately to blot out and annihilate. The play of some children at times seems to impart no meaning at all, such as drawing abstract lines, endlessly counting marbles, or shifting sand from one jar to another.

There are many different forms of as-if-play. However, even the most concrete, unrelated repetitions usually contain possible, if tiny, starting points for establishing a meaningful relationship based on some level of object-related, pre-symbolic communication. To get into this form of relational development, the therapist needs to maintain an open mind, ready for reverie, the reception of projective identifications, and containment (see Chapter Five).

The language of pictures and symbolic play

Both pictorial production and symbolic play may be regarded as a language, but it is a different kind of language than spoken and written words. A suitable distinction is Watzlawick and colleagues' (1967) differentiation between digital and analogic communication.

In digital communication, arbitrary signs are used as symbols, and they are handled according to a logical syntax that does not presuppose any similarity between the symbol and the symbolised. This is characteristic of ordinary spoken and written language.

In analogic communication, on the other hand, there is a certain similarity between the sign and what it signifies. An analogic language will be more or less generally and immediately understandable, according to the degree of similarity between the sign and the object it represents.

Analogic language is regarded as rooted in a far earlier stage of development than digital language. Digital language is particularly well suited for the exchange of information about objects. However, when it comes to relationships, it is often necessary to use analogic communication. As expressed by Watzlawick and colleagues (1967), "Whenever relationship is the central issue of communication, we find that digital language is almost meaningless" (p. 63).

Digital language has the advantage of being precise and logical. It has so far found its most extensive use in the digital media (the similarity in naming being no coincidence). Conversely, analogic languages have nothing that compares to the logical syntax of digital languages. They have no way of expressing such important relationships as conditions (if . . . then), choices (either . . . or), or, perhaps most important of all, negations. Neither do they have any capacity for indicating time; for example, to distinguish between past, present, and future.

Another, related way of characterising the different forms of language is Freud's (1900a) distinction between primary and secondary process. In describing the laws governing dreams (which are predominantly pictorial), he used the primary process. The unconscious functions mainly at a primary process level. Conscious language and thinking, however, usually follow the so-called secondary processes, which designate a logical and ordered way of thinking, which appears in its purest form in mathematics, logic, and scientific thinking. It is further characteristic of secondary processes that the emotions have a relatively stable connection to their objects. In primary processes, emotions have a more unstable connection with their objects and may be displaced to other objects. Here, for example, we find the phenomenon of *pars pro toto,* that is, that part of an object may represent the whole object. Also, condensation can occur, where different objects with shared characteristics fuse into one. Closely connected to this is the phenomenon that two things that have a strong similarity to each other, or which have something in common, can be regarded as identical. Ambivalence and splitting are also characteristic of primary processes. The same is true of the primary process that was described above for analogic language, where there is no possibility of information about time or negation.

The concepts of primary process and analogic language are useful in connection with the understanding of pictures and play as symbolic production in psychodynamic child and adolescent psychotherapy. For example, they make it clear that it is impossible to know where these products belong in time and place. A scary monster that appears in play or in a drawing could, thus, be a representation of someone or something the child has encountered before; it might be an expression of the child's perception of himself or the therapist in the here and now, or it might be a representation of something he is afraid of encountering in the future. It is, likewise, impossible to know if it refers to the inner or the outer world, inside or outside the therapy room, in the home, or in other places. It is impossible to know if the child is producing something he fears or, conversely, something with which he wants to identify. Often, the most likely situation is that the representation contains several of these possibilities, since, as mentioned above, splitting and ambivalence are characteristic of analogic communication. A drawing or a play sequence could be understood as a statement, but it could also constitute a suggestion or a question.

Verbal interpretation

In relation to the question about verbal interpretation of pictures and play sequences, it might be helpful to introduce some of the considerations that Watzlawick and colleages (1967) had regarding the translation from analogic to digital language. They wrote that since analogic material lacks many of the elements of digital language, these elements must be supplied by the translator. Since analogic material is ambiguous, as described above, however, this process of translation implies a risk of arriving at interpretations that are too clear-cut or simply erroneous. There is also a risk that the therapist chooses possibilities that fit her own understanding, without sufficient regard for what the child has actually said or communicated in pictures or play.

The transference relationship is, thus, as described in Chapter Five, the pivotal point for the therapist's ability to formulate and reality-test hypotheses. Especially at the beginning, her verbal interventions are, therefore, primarily focused on the aspects of play sequences or pictures that might symbolically represent the child's current phantasies about, and experiences of, his relationship with the therapist. Three important conditions are required for the child to accept interpretations of symbolic production and use them to drive his development.

1. The therapist has to be in contact with the live emotions of the present moment, her own as well as the child's.
2. What is said has to be sufficiently specific, that is, based on the therapist's actual observations of the child's play or pictures and of the interaction between the child and herself.
3. The therapist has to understand that verbal interpretations are not isolated interventions, but constitute a continuous open dialogue, which develops over time, where the child is allowed the opportunity to correct or fill in the details of the interpretation.

CHAPTER SEVEN

Work with parents

From the early days of child psychotherapy, few descriptions exist of the therapist's work with the child's parents. Of course, there were sessions with the parents before the beginning of therapy and ongoing contact with them during the course of therapy, but systematic work with the parents is not described. One reason for this might be that the children in therapy were often the children of friends and colleagues, who already knew what psychotherapy was about. It is also conceivable that it might have been difficult for a therapist to work with parents who were friends or acquaintances.

In the early days of psychoanalysis, the knowledge we now have about the child–parent interactions had not yet been developed; this is evident, for example, in Freud's case studies, where much of the focus was on the child's own contribution to the development of his neurosis, while obviously problematic behaviour from the parents, such as long absences, was not attributed any importance.

In 1989, the American child psychotherapist, Morton Chethik, wrote that work with the parents had received relatively little attention although "it is obvious that no child in treatment can prosper without the sanction of the parents, and it is the parental support of the treatment that *allows* the child to use the therapy experience"

(p. 217). He added that this part of the work had often been completely neglected or left to staff members with limited knowledge of psychotherapy.

Baldwin (2014) also maintains that although the therapist's relationship with the child's parents is one of the most important facets of child psychotherapy, it is also one of the least emphasised aspects in empirical and theoretical literature as well as in psychotherapy training programmes. She refers to some comprehensive reviews of the history of psychoanalytic parent work that highlight the relative lack of focus on parents in the literature on child psychotherapy, suggesting that a combination of factors have contributed to minimising parent work in clinical theory development (Horne, 2000; Novick & Novick, 2005; Siskind, 1997).

As mentioned above, one factor was that the intrapsychic nature of early psychoanalytic theory did not emphasise the influence of parents (or the external world at large) on the child's psyche. Another reason was that early child analysts tended to model their theories after the adult models of psychoanalysis, leaving little room for the exploration of parent roles and family dynamics (Novick & Novick, 2005). This led to a historical tendency within psychoanalytic training programmes to minimise parent work. Minimising parent work in theory and training is followed by a lack of focus in seminars, articles, and supervision. Without a framework within which to conceptualise the role of parents in a child's life and in child psychotherapy, as suggested by Baldwin (2014), powerful countertransferences can emerge, such as rescue fantasies on the part of the therapist or a desire to be a "better parent" than the real parents.

Today, our knowledge about children's development and the importance of the parents is radically increased. The literature on work with parents has grown considerably (e.g., Novick & Novick, 2005; Siskind, 1997; Tsiantis et al., 2000) and research into child psychotherapy has demonstrated the importance of involving the parents in the treatment (see Chapter Thirteen). A natural consequence of this development should be the inclusion of work with parents as a necessary part of all child psychotherapy. As demonstrated in Chapter Three, in some cases it is even possible and appropriate to work with the parents alone, without including the child.

However, there have also been movements in other directions. Earlier, it was common practice in child and adolescent psychiatric wards and in child guidance clinics for a psychologist or child psychiatrist to undertake psychotherapy with the child while a social worker worked with the parents. The social workers in question had training and experience in this particular work, which was usually effective. As stated by Horne (2000), however, changes in social work in the 1980s gave rise, on the one hand, to an emphasis on cognitive behavioural therapies and, on the other, to a preoccupation with child protection work of a more managerial, co-ordinating nature, to the detriment of the capacity to undertake psychodynamic parent work. She further writes that cuts in local budgets led to serious difficulties in multi-professional staffing in many child and family mental health settings. Moreover, the current diagnostic systems, with their emphasis on symptoms-based diagnoses and corresponding neglect of family and environmental factors, even with children and adolescents, have also contributed to a state where work with parents is assigned a low priority.

The complexity of work with parents

In traditional child guidance work, the mother usually had regular sessions with a staff member other than the child's therapist, while the father only occasionally participated. As fathers are now generally much more involved in the daily life of their children, this picture has, fortunately, changed, and now, as a rule, both parents participate in the sessions if they live together. When the parents are divorced, however, it is necessary in every single case to consider how the work with the parents is best organised. In some cases, it will be inappropriate or even impossible to see both parents together, as the result might be open conflict or attempts to hide the difficulties each of them has with the child, for fear of appearing as an incompetent parent. When divorced parents have joint custody, both of them must be involved in all decisions about the child, and it might be necessary to have sessions with each of them, although not necessarily to the same extent. On the whole, it is important to be well informed about current laws and rules regarding custody and to make sure not to breach the rules of confidentiality in working with divorced parents.

If the parents have found new partners, it is often a good idea to include them in the sessions, too, as they are of great importance to the children. It is, for example, often necessary to clarify to which degree they are allowed to be involved in the children's life and participate in their upbringing. This is something that the biological parent has the authority to decide, but that is not always clear to everybody, and it could be very useful to discuss it.

When foster children are in therapy, their foster parents will often already be receiving supervision. In the fortunate case that their supervisor is familiar with child psychotherapy, it will often be uncomplicated to continue this supervision and supplement it with a few meetings involving the child therapist. If, however, the foster parents' supervisor is not aware of the possible complications that child psychotherapy could cause, the child therapist, besides her work with the child, should also meet with the foster parents and their supervisor. That is usually a better approach than to introduce yet another person in the work.

If the child lives in an institution, it is important, as described in Chapter Four, that the staff at the institution knows something about how best to co-operate with the child psychotherapist, and, *vice versa*, that the therapist knows something about what goes on at the institution and how to co-operate with the staff. In many cases, the workplace will be providing ongoing supervision for the staff, where child therapy can be discussed, and often it will also be useful to have regular meetings with either the parents' or the child's therapist.

Some general comments

Altman and colleagues (2002) describe the complexity of the parent's role as "variously partner to the therapy, adversary to the therapy, part of the system, sources of guidance as well as resistance for the therapist to respond to, a patient of the therapist, and the employer of the therapist" (p. 287).

Although all parents are different, as is the nature of their children's problems, it is common for most parents who have a child in therapy to feel guilt and shame for failing to prevent their child from developing problems. In the course of events, they will often have been met with direct and indirect criticism, and they could worry that this might happen again.

Shame is more primitive, more pathological, less conscious, and more isolating than guilt. Shame induces feelings of worthlessness, powerlessness, exposure, and inferiority. On an interpersonal level, shame is associated with distancing behaviours such as withdrawal and avoidance, attack or externalised anger, and tendencies to be secretive in an attempt to avoid exposure. Because it is so painful, shame is mostly concealed and is, therefore, difficult for others to notice. A common defence against shame is rage, which can be externalised and transformed into blame directed at others. When parents use externalisation as a way of dealing with shame, the target is often the therapist. Both aggression and passivity could be indicative of defensive reactions to underlying shame.

Guilt is generally considered to be less debilitating than shame. It is often more conscious and might motivate the parent to behaviours such as making changes, apologising, or confessing, as well as to self-reflection. Although guilt is painful, in parents it might also be an empirical predictor of more adaptive parenting.

Shame and guilt usually occur together and might not be easily separable. Baldwin (2014) suggests that it might be more accurate to say that every individual is prone to shame or guilt in varying degrees. It should be assumed that feelings of shame, guilt, and isolation are almost always present in parents of troubled children. Therapists should, therefore, become adept at recognising and addressing guilt and shame with parents from the early stages of the parent–therapist relationship.

Guilt and shame are important sources of rupture in the parent–therapist relationship. Baldwin defines a rupture as "a deterioration in the quality of the relationship between patient and therapist; and an interpersonal marker" (2014, p. 6). Child therapists will inevitably encounter ruptures in their therapeutic relationships with parents of the children they see, and there is evidence that these ruptures are often overlooked or inadequately addressed. One way to manage such ruptures is for the therapist to predict parental ambivalence and desires to drop out early and to encourage parents to talk about (rather than act on) these feelings when they come up.

There are at least two major types of communication that might indicate the occurrence of a rupture. In withdrawal ruptures, the parent might withdraw or disengage his or her emotions or self. An example might be when parents pull back by dodging the scheduling of a meeting, by being hard to reach, or by avoiding the therapist. In confrontation ruptures, the patient directly expresses dissatisfaction in some way. Parents might, for example, express that they are dissatisfied with a perceived lack of progress or suggest that therapy might be exacerbating the child's symptoms.

For some parents, this process of relational destruction and repair in itself promotes growth and positive outcomes. At the very least, attention to ruptures enables the therapeutic work to continue and helps prevent early termination. At best, it could add depth to the child's psychotherapy and the parents' understanding of the child.

Work with parents of children in individual psychotherapy is not easy to characterise briefly. It is necessary always to keep in mind that the parents seek help because they are worried about their child, but that they did *not* ask for help with their personal problems and would probably not have come in if not for their child's problems. Therefore, the parents should not be offered psychotherapy, although their involvement in the child's therapy does hold therapeutic qualities for themselves. Neither should they be offered counselling or psychoeducation, although some information may be provided, for instance, about general characteristics in children's development.

Rustin (2009a) emphasises some important points related to the work with parents, including how the adult way of thinking sometimes breaks down, causing the parents to be overwhelmed by infantile feelings and, thus, losing their ability to be responsible parents. An example could be a mother who has herself been neglected as a child, and who is seized by jealousy and rage when her own child expresses his natural and legitimate need for care. To recognise this and to realise what provokes it might be an important aspect of the parental work.

Rustin also emphasises the importance of being aware of two kinds of parental behaviour, both of which are necessary: the receptive, nurturing, and relationally orientated mode *vs.* the limit-setting mode, where greater emphasis is placed on the environment and the child's curiosity, ambitions, and potential achievements. She calls these respective behaviours the maternal and paternal attitudes, and it is probably true that the caring mode will often be most noticeable in mothers, while the more demanding mode is more commonly expressed by fathers. However, it is important to remember that both modes are found in both mothers and fathers, and that it is beneficial if the division between the modes is not too sharp. Single parents, for example, need to be able to function in both modes. Some parents, however, find it difficult to strike a good balance between the two modes and could either provide too little care or be reluctant to make age-adequate demands. It might be helpful to draw the parents' attention to this double parental task and to support the implementation of it.

Two different models

Several authors distinguish between different forms of work with parents. The following briefly discusses two models, one by Chethik (1989) and one by Rustin (2000).

Chethik's model

Chethik operates with the following four forms of work with parents:

1. Parent guidance.
2. Transference parenting.
3. Treatment of the parent–child relationship.
4. Treatment of the child via the mother.

The fourth form will not be described here, as the chapter deals with work with parents in parallel with child therapy. The first three forms can be seen as stages of increasingly in-depth forms of work with the parents.

Chethik describes that most work with parents begins as parent guidance, a form that is mainly concerned with conscious thoughts and feelings. He describes this form of parental work as "a continuum from simple information or education through advice, permission, and clarification, depending on what is necessary" (p. 219). He suggests the following outline of the domains that belong to the various forms of work with the parents.

1. Parent guidance.
   A. Issues that affect the emotional balance in the family, including:

- working with general difficulties in either parent's life that affect his or her ability to parent;
- working on differences between the parents regarding how they relate to their children and consider proper parenting;
- working with stresses that emerge in parents caused by the fact that their child is in treatment; for example, a sense of failure, suspicion, or jealousy of the child's attachment to the therapist, etc.

B. Issues that primarily concern the child, including:

- information from the parents about the current reality of child and family events;
- imparting to the parents a *general* understanding of child development and the internal affective life of the child;
- imparting to the parents a *specific* understanding of their child's symptoms or behaviour changes that emerge (the purpose is to help parents cope with the behaviours or symptoms or with the changes emerging within the treatment);
- clarification with parents of their problematic interactions with the child (the purpose is to alter parental handling by highlighting specific interactions, advising changes, and providing explanations for the changes) (p. 220).

2. Transference parenting.

   In a number of cases, however, the parents cannot make use of the above-mentioned parent guidance. That is, for example, the case with parents who, as a consequence of acute stress or personal problems, need more support than parent guidance can offer. It might, for instance, be a question of acute problems in the family related to bereavement, illness, divorce, or problems at work. The therapist then has to function as a caring parent for the parents, intending, through understanding and emotional support, to enable the parents to take better care of their children. In such cases, it is necessary, first and foremost, to listen to the parents' own difficulties and temporarily focus less on the children's problems. Parents who did not receive sufficient affectionate care as children might find it difficult to show empathy to their own children. They will not feel helped by an explanation of what is missing, but probably experience this approach as a form of criticism. Instead, the therapist needs to meet the parents with empathy, thus helping them to feel what empathy is about. Through this process, they might gradually be able to show corresponding feelings for their own children.

3. Treatment of the parent–child relation.
   Chethik (1989) described many cases of unconscious conflicts and/or unconscious relationships between children and parents, noting that, in these cases, the guidance described above is not sufficient. He cited Ackerman, who, as early as 1958, described the need for "a hierarchy of levels of contact, categories of psychotherapeutic process differentiated in accordance with the depth of influence to be exerted on the personality of the parents" (p. 73). Chethik likened treatment of the parent–child relation to a process of limited insight therapy, through which the parents can gain insight into the unconscious meaning they ascribe to their child. Like Horne (2000), he emphasised that this form of parental work was widespread in the 1950s and early 1960s, but that later changes moved the work with parents more in the direction of reality-orientated treatments.

Rustin's model

Rustin (2000) describes the following four categories of work with parents:

1. Work, the prime aim of which is to gain the support of parents to protect and sustain the child's therapy.
2. Support for the parents in their parental functioning; that is, work with parents who need help to understand and make sense of their child's behaviour and relationships and/or parents who struggle to cope with difficult life circumstances.
3. Aiming at changes in family functioning. This might include marital therapy, individual work with a focus on the intra-family relationships, or family therapy.
4. Individual psychotherapy for one or both parents.

The two models are similar in the sense that they both operate with a number of stages, from a relatively conscious level towards increasingly deep and unconscious levels. The last of the four categories mentioned by Rustin, individual therapy for one or both parents, is, however, not unproblematic in child psychotherapy if—as in the model—it constitutes the only support available to the parents. Rustin describes that in such cases, one of the disadvantages is that too little attention might be paid to the damaging projective processes currently going on in the family. In her experience, referring the parent to psychotherapy sometimes creates a painful split between the priority placed on the infantile needs of the (adult) patient and the protection required for vulnerable children and young people. This is true especially if the parents' therapy takes place in a different context than the child's therapy. In general, therefore, it might be better if parents who need psychotherapy can wait until their child has finished his.

In the models, there are several references to the aims in work with parents. In the following, we will go into more detail about some of these aims and exemplify how they translate into practice.

Aims for the work with parents

The overall objective of the work with parents is to safeguard the child's therapy process and the setting around it, but, in addition, a number of intermediate aims may be described.

Mutual exchange of information

Parents continuously need to be informed by their therapist about the development of their child's therapy. That does not mean, however, that the therapist may breach the confidentiality of the therapy, only that she briefs the parents about the progress in general terms. She may also discuss some of the basic conflicts and themes that the child struggles with. This aspect of the work is not always easy. Some parents want more insight into details of the child's therapy than it is helpful for the child to disclose, and, in general, it might be difficult to describe what is going on in a child therapy in terms that are easy for the parents to understand. The more the parents have been prepared for this beforehand, the easier it will be for everybody.

It is, however, not only the parents who need contact with the therapist; the child therapist also needs contact with the parents. First, she needs to know what is going on in the child's life outside therapy, something that few children spontaneously talk about, but which naturally influences them. Second, the therapist needs to know how the child is developing, both at home and in school/preschool settings, including after-school programmes. This cannot always be deduced from the child's behaviour in therapy. Often, the child's problems will be intensified in the transference to the therapist while he improves in his daily life. Such a development outside the therapeutic space cannot be uncovered solely through the contact with the child in therapy, and, naturally, the same applies if the child is actually growing worse, which is, of course, also a possibility. The child might also develop an idyllic and fairly conflict-free relationship with the therapist while his everyday problems either remain unchanged or deteriorate. It will, of course, be essential for the therapist to know about this, if it occurs, in order to regulate her work with the child. Hence, it is crucial that the persons who are together with the child on a daily basis contribute to the assessment of his development. If two therapists work separately with the child and the parents, they need to co-operate closely to ensure that important information is passed on between them in a timely fashion.

Improved understanding of the child

Under this heading, we include both information to the parents about the child's general development and efforts to promote a sensitive understanding of the child. When it comes to knowledge about children's general development, direct information is sometimes relevant. Parents might, for example, need to know what can be expected from children of certain ages, such as when they can stay at home alone or be trusted with various responsibilities. There could be a need to discuss child sexuality, the existence of which some parents might be inclined to deny. It might also be relevant to tell parents that it is common and natural for children to be jealous of their siblings, a fact that some parents find difficult to see or accept.

Parents need to discuss the problems they have with their child at home. In other contexts, such as school/preschool and after-school programmes, they might have received counselling and, perhaps, direct advice about how to handle these problems. They might, naturally, also expect instructive advice from the therapist and, in some cases, even put pressure on her to provide it. It is, however, important to help parents understand that the therapist's methods would not necessarily work for them, since they are different persons. The best way to help parents in such situations is usually to join them in considering how their child's reactions can be understood, and what it is that provokes them. With this support from the therapist, the parents will often be able to find alternatives to the ineffective responses they have relied on so far. When parents receive help to work out better solutions, this strengthens and affirms their parental confidence, while passively receiving advice might be experienced as humiliating and erode their belief in themselves as good parents while underlining the perception of the therapist as a "superior" parent.

A discussion of the reasons behind, for example, a child's school phobia might lead to a beginning understanding by the parents that their child stays at home from school because of concern for one of them. This understanding might lead to new ways for them to relate to the child. Other parents might need to learn to understand that their child uses his tantrums to have things his way, and that the tantrums are, thus, not caused by anxiety. A child might show symptoms when a conflict between the parents is approaching, or feelings of guilt towards the child might make it difficult for a parent to set relevant limits to his behaviour. Discussions of such situations can often make up a considerable part of the work.

It might be useful to teach the parents to anticipate and prevent difficulties. When, for example, a child has separation issues, the parents can learn to anticipate situations that involve a separation and prepare the child for it. They can help the child work out what he and they can do in order to prevent the separation from developing into a problem.

Parents also need help to understand and accept the changes taking place in their child during treatment. This might sound like a paradox—presumably, change is what they were hoping for in the first place—but it is not always that simple. As often as not, the child's problems are bound up with corresponding problems for one or both parents, and when the child lets go of his symptoms, the parents could feel these issues more clearly in themselves. For example, many parents of children with separation anxiety suffer from a similar anxiety themselves and as the child grows more independent they feel their own fear of separation more clearly. Another example might be a child who has been overly inhibited and who receives help through therapy to connect more with his own feelings, including anger, which he then begins to demonstrate more openly in the family. If the parents are inhibited and anxious themselves, they might be alarmed by the changes in their child and worry that the therapy is going to change him in ways they find unacceptable. In such cases, it is important to help the parents understand what is happening and, if possible, to help them to connect more with their own feelings. To the extent that it is possible, it is also helpful to prepare the parents for what to expect before these changes occur.

When a child improves in therapy, this puts pressure for change on the family, in various ways, because the disturbed child often is a container for displaced problems from other family members. Thus, at this point, new problems often become manifest, such as marital conflicts or symptoms displayed by another child. It has already been mentioned that a child can function as a kind of "lightning conductor" in the family and, thus, demonstrate symptoms if the parents show signs of an emerging conflict. If the child no longer fulfils this function, the parental conflicts might become more evident.

It is also not unusual in families that one child is idealised, while another is seen as the "problem child". If the latter improves as the result of a successful therapy process, the parents might begin to find fault with the idealised child, either because he actually changes, or because the parents now see him in a different light.

Support for the parents

This aim was discussed under item 2, "Transference parenting".

Helping the parents change

One of the aims mentioned by Chethik (1989) is the work with differences between the parents regarding their relationship to the child and their view of child-rearing in general. The starting point for both parents, as parents, is their own early childhood experiences and their relationship with their parents. These early experiences naturally differ, and, thus, negotiations between the parents are usually required to find a common parenting approach. If their early experiences are very different, it might be difficult to reach a mutual understanding. Also, parents are not always aware of the need to negotiate. If, for example, one parent tends to be too lenient, this might push the other parent to be the one who always exercises control. At worst, these mutual differences could lead to a polarisation of the parents' respective attitudes, followed by conflicts. Such matters are very well suited for the work with parents.

Sometimes, a child might become the recipient of unconscious projections from the parents. A child might, for example, come to represent a former member of the family of one of the parents, often a sister or brother, who might have been especially admired or who aroused special anger or envy. In the subjective phantasy of the parent, this representation could overshadow the real child, who cannot be seen as he actually is.

An example of such an unconscious projection was found in a mother who fought a seemingly hopeless fight with her rebellious daughter. The work with the mother gradually revealed that she secretly admired her daughter for her rebellious attitude. As a child, the mother wanted to protest openly against her own mother, but she had never dared to do so. As this connection became clearer to her, she was better able to relate to her daughter.

Methods

Along the way, different methods in work with parents have been mentioned, among them some that are rarely used. It might be useful, however, to round off with some additional remarks about the methodology of work with parents

It is important to remember that the work with the parents must take its starting point in the parents' own difficulties with, and worries about, their child. In that respect, the work is basically similar to what happens in psychotherapy. It does not rest on information from the child therapist or on whatever questions the therapist working with the parents might think of asking. If, in the preparations to the work, it has been clearly communicated to the parents that the therapy will focus primarily on the meaning of the child's symptoms and behaviour, it has, one hopes, also been possible to convey to them that their information about what happens in the daily life of their child is important material to bring to their sessions.

As mentioned, work with parents is not psychotherapy with parents. One crucial difference is the rare use of interpretations of transference and countertransference in the work. This, of course, does not mean that the therapist is unaware of transferences and countertransferences, but they are usually not explicitly verbalised in the work. In addition, however, a broad spectrum of methods is applied, ranging from education through a number of supportive methods to methods that offer the parents insight into unconscious parts of themselves. It is common practice to alternate between different levels and methods in the individual case. The quality of the rapport between the therapist and the parents and the parents' capacity for mentalization also play key roles in determining the choice of methods.

As already said, advice is best avoided. An area where advice is appropriate, however, is regarding the choice of treatment. This is the therapist's area of expertise, thanks to her training, and, therefore, direct and well-founded advice is relevant both when she suggests a treatment based on the initial assessment and if she finds that later changes to the treatment plan are indicated.

Rustin (2009a) highlights certain core elements that are central to all work with parents. The first element is the establishment of a secure and stable setting that allows space and time to discuss difficult subjects in private. The work should, therefore, preferably take place at the therapist's office, not in the parents' home, and it should be predictable with regard to duration and frequency. The other element mentioned by Rustin is the joint creation of a language that is suited for talking about emotions and other psychological states, subjects that many parents are not accustomed to discussing. A third element is the appreciation of differentiation—between parents and children and between adult and infantile aspects of the adults themselves. As the fourth element, she mentions a sufficiently complex understanding of emotions and relationships. Last, but not least, all forms of behaviour must be seen as meaningful. This also holds good for cases where we have not (yet) succeeded in understanding the meaning.

Co-operation with other institutions

If schools/preschools and after-school programmes are involved in a partnership with the family and the treatment team, it might be necessary to arrange regular network meetings with them, in which the parents also participate. There is a built-in asymmetry in these partnerships, as the therapist needs open communication from the teachers while, for the reasons of confidentiality, she cannot offer the same kind of openness. This is not always an easy balance to keep. It can be a relief for the child therapist if the parents' therapist participates in these meetings, as she does not run the same risk of violating the confidence of the child. However, the other members of the network are not always content with that but want to hear directly from the therapist how the therapy is progressing.

Quite often, the therapy will be paid for by a public agency, in which case its representatives should also be part of the ongoing teamwork. The referring agency typically not only needs oral reports, but often requires written progress reports and written statements about the need for any further sessions. It can be a difficult balance between, on the one hand, describing the child's progress and, on the other hand, convincing the referring agency of the child's continued need for psychotherapy. This is not least the case for children with serious attachment problems, who need several years of psychotherapy, and where the initial progress is small, until the child develops a trusting relationship with his therapist. The therapist has to be careful not to exaggerate the description of the child's progress in the beginning, as this makes it difficult later to convince the authorities of the need to continue the work. It is a good idea, if possible, to provide a relatively realistic estimate of the duration of the therapy during the initial contact with the referring agency.

It is often difficult to decide when a child is ready to end his therapy. This decision requires co-operation between the therapist and the persons around the child in his daily life. One important criterion, of course, is that the child's symptoms have disappeared, but that in itself is rarely sufficient. Often, structural changes in the child's personality are also necessary, and this could take longer to accomplish. It is important to ensure that everyone who has been involved in the teamwork is engaged in the discussion about when the child is ready to conclude his therapy process.

In spite of the therapist's best efforts to ensure continuity, it is not always possible to avoid the premature termination of therapy. Parents can have many good reasons to want to be relieved of the inevitable practical and financial burden of having a child in psychotherapy. In a study on premature termination in child therapy, Kazdin and colleagues (2006) also found that early ruptures in the relationship between the parents and the therapist that went unidentified by the therapist were one of the factors contributing to premature drop-outs. Therapy with children who are fostered or placed in residential institutions is usually paid for by the community, and, in these cases too, premature termination can occur. If the caseworker changes jobs, someone who had a good understanding of the necessity of psychotherapy might be replaced by someone who has a different view of the matter; the municipality might change its policies regarding referrals; a foster placement might break down, and the child might move too far away to be able to attend therapy. In all such cases, the best thing to do is to try to secure a brief termination period with the child to at least allow time to talk with him about his feelings about the ending and to say good-bye to him (see Chapter Nine).

CHAPTER EIGHT

Psychotherapy with adolescents

Adolescents aged about thirteen to eighteen differ in some respects from pre-pubescent children. These differences also result in variations between the two groups with regard to content and methods in psychotherapy.

For girls, physical puberty generally begins around the age of ten and a half and reaches its climax around the age of twelve, while boys, on average, enter puberty about two years later. Today, puberty occurs a couple of years earlier than it did a few generations ago. There are considerable variations, however; for example, the onset of menstruation can vary between ten and a half and fifteen years of age and might even occur earlier or later than that (see, e.g., Berk, 2009; Bjorklund & Blasi, 2012). Besides actual sexual maturation in puberty, many other important physical changes take place during adolescence, including increase in height, changes in build, change of voice, etc. We will not go into details about these changes but might refer, for instance, to the above-mentioned publications for a more thorough description.

The onset of puberty is determined by biological processes and could, as described, vary considerably among individuals. Consequently, there is no clear-cut boundary between childhood and adolescence at the onset of puberty. The end of adolescence, on the other hand, is clear-cut and determined by legal and formal criteria when the young person comes of age and enters adulthood. This transition has significant psychological meaning, a point we shall return to later. This, of course, does not mean that the young adult is also psychologically mature in every respect. The British psychoanalyst Moses Laufer, who was the director of the Brent Adolescent Centre/ Centre for Research into Adolescent Breakdown, considered adolescence to last from the onset of puberty until about twenty-one years of age. Not until then, in his estimate, have predictable mechanisms for handling anxiety been developed (Laufer, 1997).

Psychotherapy with adolescents has received less attention than the treatment of children, despite the fact that adolescents probably make up the age group that is most difficult to treat with psychotherapy. The parents do not have the same power to make decisions for them as they have for younger children, which means that the adolescents themselves must be motivated for psychotherapy. Conversely, adolescents do not yet have the self-awareness and maturity that adults have, and, hence, do not always have sufficient understanding of their problems to realise their need for psychotherapy. Last, but not least, they are at an age that is characterised by both physical and psychological separation from adults and growing independence; hence, the very process of attachment, which is such a central part of the therapeutic relationship, stands in contrast to the natural age-relevant inclination towards separation and might be felt as a threat to the adolescents.

Key developmental tasks during adolescence

Adolescents face a number of key tasks to be mastered:

1. Both physically and psychologically, they need to adapt to their changing body, appearance, and stronger sexuality.
2. They must change from dependence on their parents to independence. This applies in a physical sense, for example, by taking personal responsibility for their own needs and by preparing to move away from home. It also applies in a psychological sense, as their primary attachment has to shift from their parents to their peers.

3. Although today, many adolescents still go to school even after coming of age, they must at least begin to think about their future and what they want to do for a living. They need to prepare for the change from being a schoolchild to becoming a student or an employee and attaining a certain professional identity.

Under positive circumstances, children undergo a rapid development during childhood as they acquire a wide range of physical and mental skills in motor, cognitive, emotional, and social domains. All these preconditions are important for being able to meet the challenges of puberty on a firm footing. For the adolescents who have not had the good fortune of obtaining these skills to a necessary degree, puberty presents a greater challenge than for others.

Laufer (1997) drew attention to the fact that the developmental challenges of adolescence imply a greater risk of breakdown of the process of development than those that occur during childhood. He described that even though healthy adolescents might feel guilty or ashamed of some of their thoughts and feelings, and although they might feel a sense of emptiness and anxiety in the process of becoming less dependent on their parents, there will be sufficient inner self-love carried on from childhood to enable them to look forward to the future. Adolescents who "break down", on the other hand, might feel unable to maintain their self-respect and never feel free of thoughts and feelings of being abnormal. Their sexually mature body becomes one of the main sources of their feelings of abnormality, madness, or worthlessness. Laufer, thus, used the term "adolescent breakdown" to refer to a developmental breakdown that causes the adolescents to reject their sexual bodies. The consequences of this breakdown will vary enormously—from withdrawal and isolation to the wish not to go on living, the belief that destroying one's physical body will be the answer to the problems, or the move to break with the world and the consequent psychotic organisation. It is, therefore, not strange that a number of psychological disturbances appear now that are not nearly as frequent in childhood: for instance, schizophrenia and other psychoses, eating disorders and other self-destructive activities, abuse, violence, severe depression, and suicide attempts.

As Horne (2006) points out, the task of taking ownership of one's body and sexuality poses a special challenge for adolescents who have experienced early trauma. Such adolescents' defences are often preverbal, pre-representational, and centred on the body self. This results in a risk of different forms of acting out: for example, self-destruction and self-harm or violence and aggression towards others.

However, adolescence also offers a possibility of "a second chance" to master and integrate conflicted aspects of earlier development, provided that the present environment offers sufficient support and possibilities for development (Tonnesmann, 1980). It could, however, place great demands on the environment to strike the right balance between tolerance and demands. If the right balance is not found, the young person's development might come to a standstill, or his difficulties might even increase in adulthood.

The first phase of adolescence is particularly characterised by protests and separation, while the second phase, from about sixteen onwards, revolves around building and consolidating a new identity.

Psychological consequences of physical development

The greater drive pressure and the feeling of not having the same mastery of one's body as during childhood can, as mentioned above, be unsettling, and, for some youngsters, it might lead to the concern that they are "going mad". This is, naturally, particularly so for adolescents raised in families where mental disorder has actually been present. However, the feeling that the sexual development and growing strength is an inexorable and unstoppable process might be so frightening to some adolescents that they end up perceiving their own bodies as an enemy threatening to overwhelm them.

Many adolescents are dissatisfied with their body and alarmed about the changes they experience, and they might worry about whether they are "normal", and whether they will be able to function adequately sexually. The young person's most important, more or less consciously formulated, question is, "Am I normal?" (Wrangsjö & Salomonsson, 2007). The interpretation of all new changes of the body, visible as well as invisible, is framed by this fundamental question.

Both sexes have a fear of not being "good enough", not being able to function sexually, or not being accepted by the people around them. In boys, the anxiety often represents as a fear of being homosexual, while girls try to maintain a difficult balance between, on the one hand, being seen as prudish and unsexed and, on the other hand, being regarded as "cheap", based on the nature and number of their sexual relations.

Wrangsjö and Salomonsson (2007) find that girls often have a more difficult puberty than boys. Throughout childhood, the physical skills have not differed much between the sexes, but girls now see boys overtake them in regard to, for example, physical strength. At the same time, the physical changes in the girls, such as the development of breasts and broader hips, are conspicuous to others and often commented on. Some girls perceive these changes as shameful or embarrassing. The girls also see themselves moving away from the predominant ideal of having a very slender body. A study (Levine & Smolak, 2002) found that almost every second teenage girl is dissatisfied with her appearance and tries to change it, for example, by dieting. This dissatisfaction with their bodies emerges between twelve and fifteen years of age but does not necessarily change later. Girls with an early development often feel greater dissatisfaction than those who develop later.

In a recent study of Danish high school students, Ottosen and colleagues (2014) concluded that the level of psychological dissatisfaction is high, and higher among girls than among boys. Boys are more likely than girls to demonstrate their dissatisfaction through aggressive acts or self-destructive lifestyles, while girls tend to turn the problems inward. Girls report a lower degree of satisfaction with life, and they feel more insecure and stressed than boys. They often experience loneliness, stress, guilt, and demands of perfectionism, frequently supported by the social media.

For adolescents with disabilities, puberty is often particularly difficult, as they are already compelled to answer the question of their normality in the negative. In a different way than before, they now become aware of, and mourn the fact, that they are different from others (Lagerheim, 1988). It is, for example, not rare to see adolescents who, throughout their childhood, have handled their diabetes well now begin to deny it and fail to take their medication or in other ways take the necessary precautions.

Not only sexuality but also anger might be difficult to handle for adolescents. It might be violently expressed, both physically and mentally, directed at themselves as well as others. Because of their increased physical strength, it is particularly important for them to get to know and recognise their feelings, learning how justified anger can be handled in an acceptable way.

As a consequence of the many physical and psychological changes that occur during and after puberty and as a result of their changed position in and outside the family, adolescents are compelled to construct a new image of themselves. During this work, they might fluctuate between overestimation of themselves, often of a clearly defensive character, and feelings of worthlessness and incompetence.

Separation from the parents

The change from dependence on the parents to independence is a complicated process that also implies loss and mourning. Adolescents not only have to separate from the real, living parents but also need to readjust their inner constructs of the parental figures, which might be more or less idealised or devalued and more or less realistic. The strong feelings and attachments that the child has felt towards his parents must be attenuated in order to make room for new attachments. This process can leave the young person with a feeling of emptiness that can sometimes be described as "object hunger" and a need for new emotional investments, which might initially be fleeting and somewhat random (Sandell, 1997).

Separation is easiest for adolescents who have been securely attached to their parents and who have had the opportunity during childhood to develop the physical and mental skills that they need in adolescence and adulthood. Adolescents who either have not become sufficiently independent during childhood, or who have been neglected, are facing a much more difficult task.

Separation from the parents can assume many different forms. Some adolescents loosen their tie to their parents, but simultaneously attach to, and even idealise, other adults who do not differ much from their parents: for example, a teacher. Other adolescents seek out adults with qualities and attitudes that are in contrast to those of their parents and, perhaps, to the general norms of society. If this kind of protest is taken too far, the young person runs the risk of self-destructive behaviour, such as abuse, criminality, or other kinds of antisocial behaviour. Still other adolescents do not separate from their parents but continue their close dependence on them. This can, again, take on different forms. Some turn their positive feelings into negative feelings and overwhelm their parents with protest and anger, while others maintain an excessively uncritical relationship with both or one of their parents; a typical example might be the daughter who shares all her thoughts and feelings with her mother and also functions as her confidante. Such a lack of separation could be just as harmful as overly fierce protests. There are many variations of separation and lack of separation, and the therapist has to sort out the constructive and destructive elements of the process on a case-by-case basis.

Usually, adolescents partly form their ideas and wishes for the future through identification with their parents. This could create difficulties for adolescents whose parents, for example, suffer from chronic physical or mental illness, have been abusers, or have a criminal record. These adolescents must inevitably question whether they have inherited these negative characteristics from their parents, and whether they are going to be like them. It might be difficult for them to see or believe that other possibilities exist for them, and they might even feel guilty if they do better than their parents. The therapist needs to have an eye for such ideas in her adolescent clients.

As mentioned earlier, the change from dependence on the parents to independence also has consequences for adolescents' attitude to psychotherapy. The establishment of a close attachment with another adult person in the shape of a therapist in some ways conflicts with adolescents' movement away from the close dependence on their nearest parental figures. Adolescents might perceive this development as threatening and regressive and, therefore, resist it. Sometimes, it might be easier for adolescents to join a therapy group, where they can feel supported by peers, than to work one-on-one with a psychotherapist.

About referrals

While children are almost always referred by the adults around them and do not personally take the initiative to enter into psychotherapy, some adolescents actively want, and apply for, help. This occurs especially if the opportunity for psychotherapy is easily available, for example, at their place of education. Still, most adolescents are referred by the adults around them. In these cases, as described in Chapter Three, it is important first to investigate what the referring person wants. The adults around the young person might have many different motives for encouraging him to enter psychotherapy. They might view him as troubled, anxious, depressed, or self-destructive. If that is the case, it will usually also be possible to establish a good working alliance with the young person himself. However, the adults might also initiate the referral process because they feel that they do not have sufficient control of, or contact with, him. This can apply both to parents and, for example, to teachers in a residential institution. In these cases, the young person might be far from feeling in need of help. If it is not possible to motivate ham and establish an alliance with him, it is hardly possible to initiate psychotherapy. Consultation with the parents or supervision of the teachers and other close adults is usually a better idea, helping them to obtain better control of, or contact with, him or to realise that this does not appear to be a realistic aim.

It is, likewise, important to investigate what the adults have discussed with the young person, what prospects have been held out, and, not least, what he wants help with. In some cases, the adults have only asked the young person whether he would like to see a psychotherapist, but have offered no explanation as to the purpose or what psychotherapy is all about. The young person might be curious to find out what it will be like and accepts, thinking that the therapist can do something to offer immediate relief. When, instead, he is met by a question about what he wants help for, he is surprised and has nothing to say. It is important to prepare the young person, clarifying his difficulties as they are viewed by the adults around him and making him aware that there are steps that he can take to feel better or improve his situation.

General characteristics of psychotherapy with adolescents

The life tasks of adolescence also influence psychotherapy with adolescents. The first point that we mentioned was the adaptation to the changing body and developing sexuality. Already, during pre-puberty, sexual content often emerges in therapy, as symbolic or direct pictures, as referrals to sexual organs, or as questions about sexual topics. Adolescents can also speak about boys or girls they are attracted to and to whom they want to draw the therapist's attention. Sometimes, the allusions to sexuality are more obscure, but it is important to be aware of them and show that these issues, too, are welcomed in the conversation. This is usually also what the young person wants, although he might be too shy to bring up the subject explicitly.

The relationship with the parents is an important subject for most adolescents. They often express contempt or devaluing attitudes towards the parents, but this is often a defence against their own continued attachment to them. The therapist might have to strike a delicate balance between listening empathically to the young person's complaints about his parents while, at the same time, avoiding the countertransference risk pointed out by Wrangsjö and Salomonsson (2007) of seeing the adolescent as a victim. If that happens, the therapist could fail to see the adolescent's own manipulative, or even sadistic, traits. It might be helpful to reflect, with the young person, on what he could do differently and what he cannot change. It is necessary to be cautious about accepting everything he says about his parents at face value. Also, although adolescents often ask for the therapist's opinion about what they tell her, she should be careful not to voice her own opinion too quickly. Sometimes, however, it is crucial to express one's opinion. This holds good, for example, if the young person says that he has been subjected to physical or sexual abuse or other totally unacceptable conditions. When the therapist has ascertained that these events actually took place, and if the person is unsure as to whether these acts are acceptable, which might well be the case, she must wholeheartedly declare that such actions cannot be tolerated. In these cases, the adolescent might need the therapist's capacity for reality testing to be able to trust his own judgement.

Adolescents often feel split between the desire to grow up and the wish to hold on to the privileges of childhood: for example, to escape responsibilities that feel overwhelming. As much as they might look forward to coming of age and, thus, escaping the adults' control, they might also doubt their own ability to administer the new-found freedom. This applies particularly to adolescents who have had a difficult childhood: for instance, growing up in residential homes. In most cases, they were not offered the possibility of gradually adapting to the conditions of adult life that most parents will help their children attain while they are still living at home. As a rule, they will not be followed by their teachers in the same way as other young persons can be followed and helped by their parents, also after coming of age.

Therefore, they might be justifiably worried about how they are going to manage all the responsibilities of everyday life. For the therapist, it is important to be aware of the ambivalence about coming of age and to engage with the young person in a process of exploring and coming to terms with expectations and fears in a life situation with limited support. The following example might serve as an illustration.

> Seventeen-year-old Robert lived at a residential school, which he had to leave when he turned eighteen. His mother suffered from severe chronic psychosis, and he had never known his father. As an infant, he had been placed in a foster family, but while he was still a child, he lost his foster parents. He was first placed in a children's home and from there he moved to the residential school where he was living now. He received weekly psychotherapy. As the date for the move came closer, he began to talk about how much he was looking forward to leaving the school. At the same time, he expressed growing anger towards the staff, to whom earlier he had been attached. Among other things, he accused them of stealing his and his friends' pocket money. It was not difficult to understand his feeling of being robbed and persecuted by the teachers, who, in his experience, deprived him of the possibility of attachment and security that was all he had.

Adolescents who have been forced to assume adult responsibility for their parents too early because of their parents' mental or somatic illness or substance abuse can often delude both themselves and the authorities into believing that they are more mature than they actually are. This might cause them to be treated as adults and given greater responsibility than they are, in fact, able to cope with, for example, by having to live alone and manage their own economy and other obligations. In such cases, it is an important task for the therapist to gently draw the adolescent's attention to his vulnerability and also to try to make sure that the authorities take sufficient responsibility.

Many adolescents have difficulty enduring inner emotional tension and try to transform it into action. They are, therefore, inclined to act fast and impulsively and do not always have time to think about the consequences of their actions, which can sometimes be of a destructive or self-destructive character. The losses and conflicts that are part of development might be painful, and adolescents commonly defend themselves with a manic defence, often expressed as a need for vigorous action.

If it proves impossible to help the young person to endure his feelings better and begin to reflect on them, psychotherapy could turn out to be impossible. As Wrangsjö and Salomonsson (2007) write, the question of whether adolescents should be offered psychotherapy or not is not mainly a question of formal criteria or indications, but, rather, of the chances of a process to develop between the young person and the therapist. The therapist's flexibility, creativity, and experience are crucial. It might be necessary to step outside the usual setting of psychotherapy, but that will require the therapist to pay special attention to the deviations she makes, and why she makes them.

Methodological distinctions

In child psychotherapy it is possible, if necessary, to plan for a long-term intervention from the beginning. However, such a time perspective might seem unsettling for an adolescent. Here, too, it could be necessary to show flexibility: for example, initially discussing after each session whether the adolescent is interested in coming back for another session, and, if so, when. Another possibility is to agree on short-time therapy to assist with some of the most readily accessible problems, while the more comprehensive issues are left until the adolescent has, ideally, come to trust the therapist more and dares to commit himself for the long term. It might also be necessary to shorten the sessions with some adolescents, who may find that forty-five or fifty minutes is more than they can handle.

As described by Wrangsjö and Salomonsson (2007), therapy with adolescents often centres on the subject showing up or not showing up for sessions. Staying away is common, with or without prior cancellation, more so than with children or adults. Horne (2006) describes adolescents as "escapologists", perhaps particularly in relation to experts. To seek distance from adults is part of normal adolescence, but closeness feels particularly threatening to adolescents who have grown up with severe relationship issues. She writes that it is difficult to create a space for thinking when the urge is towards action and non-thinking. She recommends trying to awaken the adolescents' curiosity about themselves and points out how curious and exploratory neutral comments about acts for which they would expect condemnation can often awaken the adolescents' interest.

She offers an example where the therapist uses gentle feedback with an adolescent who is trying to trigger conflicts with the people around him and eventually succeeds in getting him to accept the conflict as his own. A young man was always fifteen minutes late for his therapy. After pointing out and acknowledging how important it was for him to control the situation, she also pointed out how annoying it was for him that this robbed him of a substantial part of his time. In conclusion, she outlined to him that he was facing an interesting dilemma. In this way, she handed the conflict back to him but without reproof or criticism, which might have resulted in an interpersonal conflict (Horne, 2006, pp. 153–154).

It is often harder for adolescents than for adults to keep a dialogue going, but, on the other hand, they cannot, like children, express themselves through play. Moreover, it is difficult for them to tolerate long pauses. It is the therapist's responsibility to limit the duration of the pauses. Consequently, the dialogues often require the therapist to be somewhat more active than in psychotherapy with adults. The adolescent's lack of words can sometimes "infect" the therapist who, consequently, also finds it difficult to think clearly, let alone to articulate her thoughts clearly in words. Meeks and Bernet (2001) point out how important it is for the therapist to strike a suitable balance between talking and being obliging while, at the same time, avoiding being intrusive or controlling the direction of the conversation. Being more active might entail a risk of getting into the role of an investigator, which could further strengthen the young person's reticence and result in the therapist directing the content of the sessions, neither of which is desirable. It is, however, important to be aware of how the young person experiences the pauses and to take an interest in what goes on in him during the moments of silence. Instead of asking, the therapist could, for example, make suggestions about what she imagines the young person is thinking or feeling. He then has the opportunity of correcting her, if she is wrong. It is often important to be flexible and inventive when working with young persons. Dramatic and humorous remarks can sometimes promote a better climate. As the capacity for self-observation is not yet as developed as it is in adults, adolescents do not easily tolerate interpretations of unconscious material. That might make them suspicious and worried that the therapist might "see through" them.

Adolescents have usually outgrown the use of toys in psychotherapy, and toys should not be offered; on the other hand, they are rarely as verbally articulate as adults, and it is, therefore, difficult for them if the psychotherapy is exclusively based on conversation. For some adolescents, drawing might offer a helpful middle ground between symbolic play and spoken dialogue, and it might also be a help by offering them a break from having eye contact with the therapist, which some adolescents could experience as being too intense. Some adolescents base much of the therapy on drawings, while others only use them sporadically; it is, however, always a good idea to have drawing materials available. It is not unusual, either, for an adolescent to bring in poems he has written.

Adolescents can be dramatic in their presentation and like to provoke, sometimes also by their appearance, as when a glaring new hair colour or a drastically different hairstyle can take the therapist by surprise at the beginning of a session. Adolescents also often like to bring different objects in to therapy, including, of course, the ubiquitous smartphone or other kinds of electronic devices, but also things such as skateboards or other types of sports equipment. The therapist needs to be tolerant of such things.

Adolescents often express themselves in a lively body language where they can demonstrate both aversion and defiance: for example, through their seating position or the way they throw themselves into the chair, and they might display marked motor restlessness and have difficulties sitting still. Conversely, it is also not unusual for the young person to settle into the chair and go to sleep. This might, of course, be understood as a defence against contact with the therapist, but, in many cases, it feels more like an expression of trust. It could be a sign that the adolescent dares to trust the therapist by so completely letting his guard down.

In psychotherapy with adolescents, one must be prepared at times to become more personal than one would in psychotherapy with adults, expressing one's views on right and wrong. However, since it is important to distinguish clearly between a moralising attitude and a realistic emphasis on the risks implied by certain behaviour, this always requires careful consideration. If, for example, a young person has unprotected sex, the therapist should warn against it, not for moral reasons, but because it might have serious negative consequences for the person himself. The same holds true for criminality, abuse, etc., and it is important to explain the difference between these attitudes, something that the adolescent is often not aware of.

Characteristic countertransference feelings

The countertransference feelings that arise in therapists who work with adolescents are often intense; therapists can, for instance, and sometimes with good reason, feel helpless and afraid of what the young person might do to himself or others, including attempting suicide, committing crime, or engaging in acts of violence. Often, the therapist will wait in vain for an adolescent to show up, which can give rise to annoyance or anger as well as concern.

As described by Wrangsjö and Salomonsson (2007), there are some typical risks for those who work with adolescents, whether they are psychotherapists, teachers, or other professionals. One risk is to underestimate signs of self-destructive impulses, eating disorders, or compulsive behaviour and regard such features as part of normal adolescent behaviour. Also, adolescents who appear reserved and shy can cover up severe psychopathology, such as strong anxiety or paranoia.

As a psychotherapist for an adolescent, it is easy to end up in certain characteristic positions generated by countertransference feelings. One of these positions is to become overly familiar with the adolescent and, for example, use a language that belongs to the adolescent's age group rather than to the therapist's. This can, of course, especially be a risk for a therapist who is young or not much older than the adolescent. As adolescents often talk about older persons with contempt, the therapist might wish to distance herself from her role of a (dull) grown-up and responsible person and try to show her understanding of the adolescent's worldview by expressing herself in a way that does not differ much from his.

Another risk is to adopt the position of the good parent. While adolescents are often critical towards their own parents, they can, as mentioned earlier, idealise other adults, including the therapist—at least for a while. The therapist could, to some degree, be seduced into this idealised parental role and, for instance, take on a consultant role. She might also accept the young person's descriptions of his parents at face value, having, and maybe even expressing, negative perceptions of them. No matter how inappropriately the parents might act, and no matter how much they might fail their child, he has no other parents, and it would be very unfortunate if the therapist supported a dissociation that is already considerable. Conversely, as mentioned, the therapist should not approve of behaviour that is obviously inappropriate and perhaps even harmful to the young person; sometimes, it is necessary to confirm that what the parents said or did is in no way acceptable. It can be a difficult balance, and it might be necessary to think twice before expressing one's opinion about what is going on. It is often difficult because the young person will insist on knowing the therapist's stand and whether she is taking his or his parents' side in a conflict.

As Meeks and Bernet (2001) point out, the therapist's (and other professionals') own unresolved puberty conflicts can complicate their work with adolescents: for example, a therapist might unconsciously identify with an adolescent's rebellious urges if she has an unresolved need to protest. This implies a risk of overlooking the young person's own contributions to conflicts. Some therapists might not find it appealing always to be on the side of sensibility, but that side is no less important than the protest. It is important to be aware of this risk, not least because persons with unresolved puberty conflicts could be especially inclined to choose to work with troublesome adolescents.

Just as the therapist might be seduced by the adolescent's rebellion, she can also be seduced by the adolescent's vitality and energy. These qualities are usually regarded as positive, and it is, therefore, possible to miss the element of manic flight into action which they sometimes represent.

Working with parents and other adults close to the adolescent

When preparing for therapy with an adolescent, it is just as important to consider the relationship with the family as it is in therapy with a child. Carlberg (1999) claims that our knowledge of work with parents in relation to child psychotherapy is less developed than our knowledge about what happens in child therapy *per se*, and Wrangsjö and Salomonsson (2007) add that our knowledge of the parallel work with parents is even less explored in relation to individual psychotherapy with adolescents. We completely agree with these observations.

Some parents, both birth parents and foster parents, are good-enough carers for their children but might find it difficult to cope with their task when the children reach puberty. They might become insecure of their role in relation to their older children and run the risk of either withdrawing too much or rigidly sticking to trivial rules, which could result in unnecessary and exhausting conflicts. Some adolescents try to look and behave more like adults than they can actually live up to. This might lead both parents and other adults to hand them too much responsibility. In other cases, parents might oppose the young person's relevant attempts at separation far too much. Bailey (2006) maintains that some parents underestimate their children's continued need for them during their teenage years, while other parents find it hard to dare to let their children go. The parents' own adolescence will inevitably come into play, consciously or unconsciously, and influence the way in which they treat their children.

Some parents misunderstand the young person's withdrawal and protest and see it as an indication that their children no longer love them, and that they are now superfluous as parents. It is important to help such parents understand how important they still are for their children, and how crucial it is that they do not resign their role as parents. The British psychotherapist Charlotte Jarvis (2005) mentions that many studies have shown the need for parents to maintain or develop their authority. It is an important task for the therapist to help parents understand what is behind the young person's behaviour and to distinguish between relevant care and protection and a lack of respect for their child's boundaries.

The general principles described above for working with parents also apply for working with adolescents. The work might, however, at times take on a more acute, almost dramatic character, partly due to the adolescent tendency towards (sometimes hazardous) action and partly due to conflicts between the parents, which might always have existed, regarding the upbringing of their child, but which were less conspicuous during childhood.

If the problems primarily concern difficulties with the young person's separation from his parents, and with co-operation within the family, the best approach will often be simultaneous work with the whole family in the form of so-called conjoint family therapy, that is, therapy sessions involving all the members of the family (see, e.g., Micucci, 2009; Sachs, 2013). If, however, it is decided to offer individual psychotherapy to the young person, it is still important to be sufficiently aware of the family and to assess what the family needs. Continuous contact with the place where the adolescent lives, whether it is at home or in an institution, is necessary in any case, not only for the sake of the adults around the adolescent, but also for the therapist.

Work with the family of the young person may span from a limited effort to thorough family work. Precisely because separation from the parents is such a key task during adolescence, and because this process is painful for everybody concerned, even for the most well functioning family, the relationship with the parents will necessarily take up considerable space in the work with the young person. In many cases, work with the parents will be a prerequisite for successful psychotherapy with adolescents. When less extensive contact with the parents is needed, the simplest solution might be for the same therapist to be in contact with both the young person and his parents. Whether that is the right solution depends, among other things, on the contact between the young person and his parents.

Regardless of which model is used, it is, however, often helpful to arrange joint sessions from time to time that involve the young person, his parents, and one or two therapists. This might, for example, be advisable if each of the parties wants the therapist's direct help to resolve conflicts. A joint session could offer a good possibility for working with the family's general co-operation in conflict resolution, where the therapist or therapists may act as role models. Such joint sessions always require good preparatory work to ensure that all the participants agree about what will be discussed, and what not.

No matter which format is applied for the work with the parents, the preparations require at least as much care as work with the parents of a younger child. The parents need to understand the background and purpose of the therapy and agree with it, and the limits of shared knowledge and confidentiality must be clear to both parties. Not least in cases of adolescents where intense and acute problems might arise, the parents might feel a need to be able, with short notice, to get in contact with the therapist by telephone or email, and it is usually a good idea to offer them this opportunity. In return, this requires an agreement that the young person is always informed if the parents contact the therapist. Such a possibility of contact is often used, but, in our experience, very rarely abused.

Adolescents with externalising symptoms could be particularly inclined quickly to break off contact with their therapist, unless it is possible to convince them that they also have intrapsychic problems. Jarvis (2005) describes how parents often hold on to their own treatment, even after their children have ended theirs, and that it is possible to support them even if the young person terminates his treatment. It is also our experience that work with parents of adolescents who do not themselves want psychotherapy can be very useful. As Bailey (2006) describes, however, such work is not easy. The therapist is often confronted with overwhelming anxiety, hate, hopelessness, and insistent demands for advice and help to find quick solutions for the problems.

Sometimes, however, there is no family to work with. Sometimes, the young person does not live with his parents and has not done so for many years, and sometimes the parents are not willing or able to participate in more extensive collaboration. In some cases, perhaps as a consequence of mental illness or abuse, parents are unable to enter into a continuous collaboration with the therapist. In our experience, however, even a brief contact at the beginning of the therapy with the young person, where the parents are involved in the decision and informed about the background and aim of the therapy, is usually a very positive experience for parents who might often have felt sidelined in relation to their child. Their support for the therapy can be more important for the young person's willingness to embrace it than is widely imagined. Conversely, some adolescents initially reject having their parents involved in the treatment or being informed about their request for help. This is usually untenable in the long run, unless they have a very peripheral relation to them, but, for a period, it might be a necessary condition of the adolescent's willingness to show up for sessions.

PART III

THE EXPERIENCE OF TIME IN THE PERSPECTIVE OF OBJECT RELATIONSHIPS

CHAPTER NINE

Beginnings and endings of child and adolescent psychotherapy

This chapter concerns the characteristic themes of beginnings and endings in child and adolescent psychotherapy. These themes are related to the establishment, early in therapy, of space and time as shared relational concepts framing the work with the child and his parents. The chapter discusses guidelines for preparing both the child and the parents at the beginning and ending of psychotherapy. At the beginning, certain anxieties related to the unknown need to be contained, and, even with careful preparations, there will often be practical issues that require further clarification. Correspondingly, ending therapy and parent work is a process of mourning that needs sufficient time to be worked through, both between the child and the therapist and between the parents and their therapist.

Beginnings

From a psychodynamic perspective, the child's early experience of space and time, and, in due course, his consequent development of corresponding emotional–cognitive concepts, are closely interwoven with the emotional quality of his early object relations.

The earliest experiences of time presumably are rhythmic and somato-psychic in nature, structured by sensory experiences, needs, and rhythms, such as sleeping/awake, light/dark, together/alone (presence/absence of human contact perceived through the eyes, ears, skin, mouth, kinaesthetic sense), full/hungry, soaked through/clean and dry, warm/cold, and, perhaps at a slightly more integrated level, containment/fragmentation. The later introjection and recognition of time as a linear phenomenon—as measured by a watch—seems to be a developmental achievement closely connected to the existential human task of reconciling oneself to the limitations and possibilities offered by external and internal realities. In the course of their development, most children come to recognise that their own feelings, thoughts, and fantasies are subjective experiences with continuity over time, localised in their own, inner space—the psyche—and separate from other people's inner world. If this early development was disturbed, however, the relationships between the self and its objects can become tenuously rooted in time and space. For example, the objects might be felt to be fleeting, elusive, volatile, unpredictable, falling apart, flat, rigid, impenetrable, or otherwise lacking sufficient permanence, solidity, flexibility, accessibility, and openness for the self to relate to them in trustful confidence.

The child's way of relating to the geographical and temporal boundaries of the therapy, accordingly, reflects the qualities and state of his inner objects, that is, his subjective experience of their movements in time and space in relation to himself, each other, and, in the transference relationship, to the therapist (Rey, 1986; Rose, 1997). The establishment of a fixed time frame and geographical space for the psychotherapy sessions is important because it marks that there is a certain, delimited time and space for the phantasies and relationships of the inner world, and other times for carrying on one's everyday life, with its tasks and relationships.

Especially at the beginning of the therapy, time and space attain a pronounced relational importance, and the therapist's management of these aspects of the setting is important (see Chapter Four). Thus, at the beginning of the therapy process, time and space frequently occasion certain discussions and can give rise to a variety of issues: for instance, involving many different attempts at testing the solidity of the therapist and the therapy process. The time structure especially can give rise to objections and questions, for instance, in regard to the duration and frequency of sessions and breaks. Hence, it is important that the parents have been sufficiently prepared for the possibility of such protests, and that they fully understand why they have to stick to the scheduled appointments. Most children abandon these attempts to test the reliability of the time structure relatively early. Others, however, especially children and adolescents with a volatile inner structure and fragile or vaguely outlined object relationships, continue to attach more importance to the clinic, the therapy room, and the time structure than to the therapist as a person, investing their feelings in the more tangible aspects of the therapy process. Similarly, children and adolescents with rigidly controlling inner objects can react as if the time structure were a cruel prison, and therapy process itself a period of forced labour they cannot possibly survive.

Preparing parents and child before the beginning

As part of the assessment, the parents have, one hopes, been told what to expect from their child's psychotherapy, and what demands this will make on their resources and co-operation. The therapist working with the parents cannot, however, be sure that this was taken care of. Even with proper preparation, most parents need guidance on how to prepare the child for his first session with the child psychotherapist. For the same reason, the first session with the parents should take place before the child begins in psychotherapy. In addition, the parents could have met the child psychotherapist and been introduced to the therapy room during the initial assessment; if this is not the case, however, it needs to be arranged in connection with one of the first meetings between the parents and their therapist.

During the first parent sessions, an agreement concerning the aims and scope of their work must be negotiated and reinforced. The work of the parent therapist, thus, is primarily about forging and maintaining an alliance with the parents aimed at supporting their own development as parents. Thus, during the first session, the therapist will encourage the parents to talk about their hopes for change in their relationship with the child. An alliance with the parents that places this topic at the centre of the work is a necessary foundation, which the ensuing parent work will endeavour to expand on and discuss in greater detail (see Chapter Seven).

Even if the parents were carefully informed about the implications of child psychotherapy during the assessment, the first weeks and months of the child's therapy will bring new doubts and questions about what exactly it is the child psychotherapist is doing with the child. It is crucial that the parents' therapist facilitates a genuinely open dialogue about the parents' reservations and questions, creating a space where they can be freely discussed and addressed. This discussion, including possible interpretations of subjective thoughts and feelings, should be carried out with due consideration for the parents' comprehensible concern as to whether bringing the child in for treatment with a child psychotherapist is the right decision. The parents need a chance to discuss with their therapist what to say to their child, for instance when he asks, after the first meeting with his therapist, why he has to go to therapy or if he complains about what she does. Usually, the best way to support the parents is to help them think about how best to tell the child directly—in a concrete and digestible way—of their real concerns for his wellbeing and development: for example, that he appears sad, miserable, and passive, shuts himself off from peers and family, is afraid to go to sleep and sleep in his own bed, has difficulties concentrating, is always nervous and objects to any change in daily routines, is liable to get very upset and scream the house down, or is constantly argumentative, getting into fights with peers and teachers at school, etc.

From the outset, the parents should be told about the teamwork between the parent psychotherapist and the child psychotherapist, since they need to be sure that they will be informed if anything happens in the child psychotherapy that they should know about. However, the parents must also be told that the child psychotherapy aims to develop a close emotional relationship between child and psychotherapist, where the child works with infantile phantasies and notions. Child psychotherapy is, therefore, not primarily concerned with the child's everyday life outside therapy, but, rather, with his private, inner world. For this reason, it is important that the parents respect psychotherapy as the child's private space, just as the parent sessions are the private space of the parents. Thus, in general, the therapists do not share specific information from therapy about the child with the parents or, *vice versa*, about the parents with the child.

For the same reason, it is usually helpful to agree with the parents, from the outset of therapy, that the child's progression will regularly be assessed in co-operation with the parents. This evaluation typically implies half-yearly meetings involving the parents, their therapist, the child psychotherapist, and maybe also the child himself, depending on his age and level of maturity.

Some children (for instance, children who were referred because of separation anxiety and a clinging, ambivalent attachment relationship) might not be able to let go of their parents, especially during the first therapy session. The parents are usually aware of this problem, which they might already have mentioned during assessment consultations. If that is the case, the problem needs to be discussed during the first session with the parents to help them consider, first, how the anxious child is best prepared for the task of letting go of his parents and entering the therapy room on his own with the therapist and, second, what to do if the child is unable to do this. In that situation, it is very important that the parent therapist explains to the parents that this is their task, not the task of the child psychotherapist, to help the child to let go.

The first therapy session with the child

All children and adolescents approach the therapist in a uniquely personal way, modelled on their subjective template of unconscious object relationships. One child might, for instance, present as a jaunty, unruly, but also artificially funny little boy, bringing to mind the fictional character "Emil of Lönneberga", created by the famous Swedish author of children's books, Astrid Lindgren. Another child could impress the therapist with his worried and serious facial expression, behaving like an anxious little adult burdened by far too many responsibilities. Yet another child might rigidly try to dominate the situation, behaving as if he is in full control of the situation, with no need for therapy.

The therapist's first meeting with a child can be compared to the first meeting between a mother and her new-born baby, as the mother engages from the first moment in a process of getting to know her baby. Similarly, the therapist relates in an emotionally open way and registers her own feelings for the child, staying with the immediacy of her subjective impressions based on the way she perceives the child in the present moment of the session. As mentioned earlier, she seeks to bracket her preconceptions: for instance, pushing to the back of her consciousness the reason for the referral and her knowledge of the child's family background and early development. Hence, from the outset and staying in the here and now, the therapist focuses on observing the child's movements in the therapeutic space, noticing how he initiates and breaks off contact, and how he relates to his toy box. Dividing her attention, she simultaneously notices not only the child's expectations of her and the therapy, but also her own emotional–cognitive reactions to the child.

Based on her receptivity, the therapist does her best to create space within the relationship for those dimensions of the child's inner world that relate to his early experiences of contact and parental care—that is, she aims at connecting to the new-born baby as represented subjectively in the mind of the older child. This process is facilitated by her attentive, non-directive, and non-judgemental attitude and underlined as something that stands apart from everyday life in the special setting of therapy. This encourages the child to bring his fundamental, subjective assumptions about emotional relationships into the therapy process, especially with regard to parental figures. Thus, even from the initial sessions, unconscious transferences are at play in the therapeutic relationship, mostly—through parallel parental countertransference—conveying to the therapist the child's early emotional experiences and needs (see also Chapter Five). Hence, at the beginning of therapy, a key task for the therapist is to unravel the child's transference-related assumptions by scanning through the entire sum of episodes occurring in the sessions, asking herself, "What kind of person does this child believe me to be? What kind of object am I to him?" (Hunter, 2001, p. 13).

The child's first movements in the therapy room often reflect a desire to explore what this new and, as yet, unfamiliar thing is, what it can be used for, and what kind of demands and frustrations one will confront here. Generally, in such a novel situation, most children react with mixed feelings, evidencing, on the one hand, anxious distrust and, on the other, a hopeful and explorative attitude. The child's behaviour often seems to pose entire series of questions to the therapist, which are sometimes also articulated in words, such as, what is this, what can you be used for, what may I do in here, can you stand me and my problems? Can I leave the therapy room? Can I do this? Why not? Some children hurriedly scan the entire playroom, moving from item to item, perhaps making criticisms that might cause the therapist to feel that she is at fault, that she is insufficiently prepared for this child, and that she does not have what it takes to help him. As discussed in Chapter Five, the key thing for the therapist is to hold on to her feelings, regardless of what they are, drawing on her private countertransference reflections to discern how the child experiences and tries to make use of her (for an example, see four-year-old Joseph, Chapter Five).

With most children, even the first session contains moments of genuine contact, in which the therapist, in short glimpses, can become aware of the child's specific anxieties and mental anguish: for example, as related to obsessions, frustrations, longing, and loss. Such present-moment encounters might last only seconds, the vulnerable self instantly buffered by defensive attitudes such as mute withdrawal, manic play activity with cars, or neat drawings of abstract patterns. However, the fact that both child and therapist are now aware that a moment of understanding occurred is important, as this could plant the seed for a genuine treatment alliance between the two.

Starting the session, psychodynamic therapists typically make space and wait for the child's own initiative. If, as is sometimes the case, a child has difficulties getting started—for instance, becoming anxious, remaining passive, and/or staying silent—the therapist interprets his reluctance and anxiety in face of the unknown situation. Such an early interpretation must include the therapist's observation of the child's reactions, described and particularised in literal terms; for example, by referring to the child's negative expectations of the therapist as yet another complete stranger and the child wondering, what is therapy anyway, what am I supposed to do here, and to whom will she disclose my problems. Sometimes, it might help if the therapist talks a little about the background to the decision to have the child go into therapy, which weekdays the child is supposed to come, the contents of the toy box, what one can do in therapy, etc. However, once the child calms down a little, the therapist then again leans back and waits for the child to take the lead. By analogy, the very beginning of the first therapy session might bring to mind the sensitive dance of turn-taking between a new-born infant and his attentive mother in a state of reverie, observing and adapting her emotional communication to his capacity and needs. Later in the session, or maybe during the second session, it might be appropriate to investigate with the child his ideas about why he is in therapy. Simply bringing these thoughts into the open can, in itself, relieve any negative phantasies he might have that contribute to his anxiety. In this connection, it could be appropriate for the therapist to mention what the parents told her about the child's issues, in this way reminding the child that his parents vouch for the therapy and the therapist.

Throughout the early sessions, it might be helpful to observe how the child deals with his personal toy box, as this can often communicate key aspects of his unconscious inner world: for instance, his phantasies about the therapy and the therapist and about his objects in general. It is important for the therapist to secure the necessary time and space before and after her sessions with the child to reflect on her own experiences from being with the child, especially to consider what feelings and ideas the relationship gives rise to in her mind.

* * *

Endings: a process shaped by experiences of absence

Ending is, in fact, a process that begins even before the beginning of therapy, since, regardless of the duration of a therapy course, the therapist needs to envisage and anticipate possible scenarios for the ending as early as during the assessment. Hence, assessment, beginning, and ending are related themes. Before the actual beginning of therapy, the therapist must, for instance, forecast the scope and aims of treatment to assess the possible span between optimal and necessary frequency and duration. Hence, typically, the more precise and adept our assessment and diagnosis, and the more realistic our regular evaluations, together with the parents and any referring agencies, of the child's developmental progress in therapy, the fewer premature endings of therapy will we experience.

Psychotherapy requires the mutual commitment of both participants in an emotionally intense relationship, which could be of prolonged duration. This is not least the case with children and adolescents, where the parents' commitment is also essential—the younger the child, the more so. The therapeutic relationship involves fundamental emotional issues which not only affect the client, but also the therapist, who applies her own emotionality, her own mind, as a necessary tool. Accordingly, questions of when and how to conclude a course of psychotherapy are complex and sensitive, and the ending requires a process of a certain duration.

As mentioned, a fundamental assumption of psychoanalytic developmental theory concerns the ability of the subject to symbolise/mentalize the temporary external absence of a parental figure. This emotional–cognitive achievement is considered an integral aspect of normal development that is especially connected to the development of thinking. Hence, on the one hand, the parental ability to provide tender emotional containment, mirroring, and attunement to the infant is crucial to his healthy development. On the other hand, it is just as crucial and necessary to the infant's healthy personality development that the parents are willing and able to expose him to their temporary absence in appropriate doses (see Chapters Two and Ten).

Bion (1962a) argued that the child's development of a capacity to contain and symbolise the absence of the object depends on his frustration tolerance—that is, his ability to take ownership of his own painful feelings generated by the absence, such as mixed feelings of hate, longing, and desperation. Based on the principle that what may be thought may also be remembered and modified, in time this development will enable the child to use his memories of good parental objects actively to allay his own painful longing in their absence. Or, put another way, in the face of absence and separation, the child becomes able to regulate his own emotional states, soothing himself by thinking of, and recalling, good, tender interactions and reunions with a parental object whom he trusts will come back.

In 1964, O'Shaughnessy wrote, "The absent object has the character of offering a 'critical' choice, in Dr. Bion's words 'between procedures designed to evade frustration and those designed to modify it'" (Bion 1962b, p. 29; O'Shaughnessy, 2004[1964], p. 21). She held that, in normal development, children are pushed by an innate urge towards tolerance and mastery of the absence of parental objects. She considered this a developmental necessity because, if absence (and distance) are not possible or cannot be endured, the relationship becomes symbiotic and, consequently, destructive to the child's experience of separateness and separate identity. Relating to Bion's complex theory of thinking, she lucidly phrased the issue as "how the absent object can cease to be a bad object" (p. 22) and suggested that this development revolved around three organising principles:

1. The child may experience the absent object as "a bad breast present"—"breast" here referring to object, parental figure, or therapist.
2 The child may experience the absent object as a bad aspect of an otherwise good object.
3. In a mental state where he is able to own his frustration (the child recognising this experience as his own painful longing for a missing good object), the child also comes to remember that the object can be trusted to return. Eventually, he will recognise that time away from the object is needed, not only to get an emotional perspective on his experiences with the object but also to get to know his own self as differentiated from the object.

O'Shaughnessy's model does not denote a literal, temporal order of distinct, fixed developmental phases, but should, rather, be understood as related to mental positions *vis-à-vis* an object. These organising principles can be perceived as stepping stones from which the child can view himself and his objects, moving now closer, now further away from acknowledging his own dependency or separateness, altering his perspectives with his varying vantage points. Consequently, his present stand will colour his perception of the ending to come. In relation to Klein's positions, this is yet another example of the continuous shifting between paranoid and depressive ways of experiencing and functioning that occurs throughout life. Thus, no human being, whether child, adolescent, or adult, is immune to pain and setbacks in the face of trauma, loss, illness, and other hardships (Klein, 1959).

In a therapy process that is approaching its conclusion, feelings formerly aroused by holidays and other breaks tend to resurface with a powerful intensity, once again taking centre stage and, accordingly, colouring the child's experience of the approaching end of therapy. The actual manifestations of these emotions are closely linked to the child's ability—now, one hopes, strengthened—to contain and cope with absence. The process of parting is, however, a bumpy road, which needs time to be worked through, and, accordingly, sufficient time must be set aside for the ending. It goes without saying that endings are especially difficult and painful to children, adolescents, and adults (as well as therapists) who have suffered early and/or prolonged or recurrent neglect, loss, and trauma. For clients with these types of experiences, the therapist must carefully plan and monitor the end of therapy with particular reflective consideration and empathy, paying close attention to the child's reactions during the period of termination and—if necessary—preparing the parents for possible emotional fallout between sessions.

How to know when to conclude therapy

If nothing else was explicitly agreed upon, most people think that therapy should end once the child's symptoms are gone or, at least, appreciably reduced. That is, in fact, typically the way it is, for instance, when the treatment of choice is cognitive therapy. However, for many children (for example, children suffering from emotional or behavioural disturbance as sequelae of early relationship disturbances, complex traumatisation, and other problems related to personality development), symptomatic improvement might not be sustainable unless it occurs in combination with certain changes in the child's personality structure. As a golden rule, this possibility should be discussed with the parents and the child himself even before therapy begins.

> Fifteen-year-old Maia was referred to psychotherapy because of recurrent anxious thoughts that she might be lesbian and because of painful compulsive thoughts of a sexual nature, which she felt compelled to share daily with her mother, who, understandably, became worried. Maia also suffered other forms of anxiety; for example, she would panic during thunderstorms and found it difficult to go to sleep alone at night and often demanded her mother's presence. When she was younger, she had suffered from other compulsive anxieties in the form of obsessive tidiness. Earlier on, as a child, she had wished that she were a boy. Generally, she felt insecure, depending, in a submissive way, on other people and their points of view. Lately, she had been speaking about suicide and said that she felt life to be meaningless.
>
> She was seen in individual once-weekly psychotherapy, while her parents engaged in concurrent consultations. After a year, the girl no longer felt haunted by sexual thoughts, she was able to sleep on her own, and she had applied for a spare-time job in a local shop. She also generally appeared much happier and said that she felt good. She no longer depended on her mother's help with homework, and her tendency to

avoid eye contact had improved considerably. Consequently, at this point, she wanted to end therapy.

I felt, however, that Maia needed more time, and when we discussed the issue, she admitted that she still felt anxious about doing something wrong, she worried a lot, and felt severely pressured by her homework. She agreed to continue therapy, which resulted in considerable improvement.

The above can be seen as an example that some children and adolescents (and adults) have never experienced a truly satisfying and fulfilling life and might, consequently, be too modest in their expectations of life. Feeling that life has improved a great deal, they cannot, on their own, imagine that they might come to feel even better. Moreover, more often than not, they, and perhaps also their parents, are likely to overestimate the effect of the psychotherapy, not aware that thriving on one's own is not the same as thriving while the continuous support from the therapist is still available.

Conversely, therapists also need to take precautions against what might be termed therapist omnipotence—that is, being too ambitious on behalf of the client. Sometimes, even experienced therapists overestimate what therapy can, in fact, achieve, not giving due and detailed consideration to the limitations imposed by the intensity and duration of therapy, the personality structure and resources of the client, and, in work with children or adolescents, not least, the quality and resources of the client's present relationships and living conditions.

From the outset, psychoanalysis and psychodynamic psychotherapy have been preoccupied by the question of what to expect from therapy and when to end it. Freud linked the aims of psychoanalysis to a reinstatement of sufficient abilities to enjoy and perform in life or, as it is often phrased, the ability to partake in meaningful love and work relationships. He also recognised increased reality testing as an important result of the therapeutic processes of mourning and working through (1916–1917, 1917e, 1937c). Concerning children and adolescents, Anna Freud linked the appropriate time for ending the therapy to the restoration of the child to a healthy course of development, relevant to his inborn resources and age appropriate mastery. She felt that as soon as impediments to this natural developmental course were removed, the therapy should be concluded. However, she did acknowledge that a realistic evaluation of the sustainability of this result might be difficult (Sandler et al., 1980). Klein emphasised the balance, proportions, and movements between, on the one hand, the split processes of the paranoid–schizoid position and, on the other hand, the increased integration of defensive splitting in the depressive position. She added that another important result was increased depth of the ego, facilitating improved access to phantasy and creativity (1950).

In an ordinary child and adolescent psychotherapy practice, one problem is how to evaluate whether and when such aims have been sufficiently attained. If part of the initial assessment of the child's personality included standardised, psychometric instruments assessing the child's wellbeing, these may, of course, be repeated. However, a comprehensive, in-depth evaluation requires something more. It goes without saying that a possible ending should be discussed with the parents, giving consideration to their opinion and evaluation of their child's improvement and remaining problems. In our experience, the five criteria mentioned below are helpful in ensuring a thorough evaluation of whether significant changes inside and outside psychotherapy have taken place. Thus, the five criteria could serve as guidelines for a discussion with the parents about when the child or adolescent is ready to end the therapy.

1. The child's or adolescent's symptoms (as described at referral) are reliably gone or, at least, significantly diminished.
2. His ability to partake in, contribute to, and learn from, his social relationships is reliably improved.
3. His ability to mentalize his impulses and feelings is reliably improved.
4. He is able to cope appropriately with the developmental tasks of his age level, considering his mental resources.
5. An indicator that is rarely mentioned is the child's ability during breaks in the therapy not only to retain the progress made, but also achieve new developments. In ordinary practice, this is quite easy to observe and evaluate. This indicator might be of special importance in the treatment of children and adolescents suffering from massive early neglect, complex traumatisation, or autism (Grünbaum, 2014; Houzel, 2004).

Four additional criteria are often mentioned in textbooks on child psychotherapy (Lanyado, 1999; Sandler et al., 1980). These might, however, best be understood as implicit preconditions for the realisation of the conditions mentioned above:

1. Diminished anxiety and stabilisation of the defence; hence, a reduction of the need for primitive, manic, or rigid defence mechanisms.
2. Stabilisation of reality orientation and testing.
3. Sufficient inner healing of trauma and deprivation.
4. Improvement of the capacity for constructive, creative, enjoyable play.

Emotional themes characteristic of endings

Parting ways with the therapist—thinking about taking leave, separating, and maybe never meeting again—reactivates the child's earliest experiences with absences and reunions in relation to parental figures. This sets in motion deeply ambivalent and split, subjective feelings and phantasies related to intimacy at all levels, and, consequently, themes related to dependence–separateness, especially remnants of earlier loss, trauma, and disillusionments, will often resurface. Thus, ending a therapy is a personal loss on a par with other personal losses. Hence, the period of the ending should be clearly demarcated and of sufficient duration to allow the child to work through mourning, anger, split feelings, anxiety, and doubt related to his ability to stand on his own two feet. The child should be helped to articulate these feelings inside the therapeutic space, since, otherwise, there is a considerable risk that mourning, anger, and anxiety are vented outside therapy in his close relationships.

Even if the symptoms that originally motivated the referral for psychotherapy have long since disappeared, towards the end of therapy some of the former problems will often recur, albeit typically in a milder form. For some children, this partial and often rather short setback might be rooted in the child's anxiety about having to cope without the support of the therapist; for other children it might, for instance, pop up as a form of testing whether the therapist's decision of ending the therapy is for real.

It is important to remember that what is at stake to the child is a dual loss, not only of the therapist as a transference figure, but also as a real-life figure in a personally important, new object relationship. Thus, themes related to earlier, in some ways comparable, losses, for instance, of grandparents, favourite teachers, playmates, and even pets, might surface in the sessions, directly and indirectly. At this stage, an important task for the therapist concerns the parallel processes of working through at both levels, that is, working with these memories and feelings as related both to the past (reactivated, older losses) and to the future (the forthcoming loss of the therapist). Sometimes, the child may find it easy to verbalise feelings related to the loss of the therapist directly, while the original experiences of separation and loss can only be communicated through the transference or in actions. Sometimes, the reverse is the case. In either situation, it is necessary—in order to achieve a non-traumatic ending that contributes to the child's future development—to ensure a parallel working through that addresses both levels.

Generally, as one might expect, throughout the period of ending, the emotional themes of any child or adolescent will fluctuate, coloured by paranoid–schizoid or depressive feelings according to the child's momentary emotional position and defensive organisation *vis-à-vis* the objects and, in the transference relationship, the therapist.

When depressive feelings are in ascendancy, the child could be concerned that he might have somehow caused the therapist to abandon him, maybe because of his deficiencies or misbehaving, making her choose other children as her favourites. A common theme concerns the child's feelings of guilt in case the therapist discovers that he actually feels quite ready to let go of her to manage on his own. This reaction is often characteristic in children with parents who have problems of autonomous functioning, sometimes due to chronic somatic or mental illness, sometimes because the parents unconsciously need the dependence of the child in order to maintain their own self-confidence.

As suggested above, when dominated by persecutory feelings, the same child might feel that the parting to come is yet another proof of the therapist's complete lack of value, perceiving her as completely incompetent and useless. As if he is ignorant of his own earlier gains, in this state of mind, the devaluation might even attain a retroactive force, the present situation altering memories of the past and the child coming to feel that, throughout, the therapist and the therapy were so deficient that he did not benefit from it at all. A child or young patient in this position could, thus, be prone to articulating anger and criticism rather than sadness at thoughts about the forthcoming parting (Klein, 1940; 1950).

Especially in adolescence, the parting might often give rise to some form of enactment; for example, absenting oneself from therapy is quite common. In this way, the adolescent radically avoids confronting painful emotions of parting that are difficult to evade in sessions. Furthermore, he might experience himself as being in control, in his phantasy switching roles with the therapist and, thus, through his actions, letting her know how it feels to be abandoned.

It is important to remember that despite the sadness of parting, endings also contain hopes and possibilities of joyful new beginnings and developments. Some children are able directly to address the pros and cons of ending—for instance, by discussing, on the one hand, the joy of more spare time with peers, and, on the other hand, the sadness and apprehension of letting go of the safety implied by therapy.

The balance between holding on to, and letting go of, the other is a lifelong, but difficult theme. Therapists also become emotionally involved in the development of their clients, whether children, adolescents, or adults. In this sense, the therapeutic relationship possesses an allegorical similarity to parental care, which, likewise, demands that the parents let go, allowing their child to separate, eventually becoming an autonomous person, leaving home, and making his own decisions. This ability to transcend one's original close family attachments and commit emotionally to new relationships, explorations, and developments presupposes a sufficient process of mourning. Thus, in general, in the relationships of real life, and in the therapeutic relationship, parting requires a proper process for saying goodbye in order to be able to welcome new close relationships.

The framework of endings

The setting of the ending should be framed in accordance with the frequency and duration of the therapy, a lengthy, intensive course demanding more time than a relatively brief course of once-weekly sessions. For an intensive and lengthy course of therapy, an agreement about the date of the final session should preferably be reached several months before, maybe six to twelve months before the actual end. For shorter therapies, three to six months (or sometimes even shorter) will be more appropriate.

Quite a few therapies end unexpectedly, without a prearranged agreement (see below). In this situation, it might often not be possible to achieve the best framework for a benign ending. Anyhow, as far as possible, the therapist should arrange sufficient time for a benign process of parting, even if this is—from a therapeutic point of view—part of a premature ending. Most often, but not necessarily always, the longer a period of ending one can negotiate, the better. If this is not possible, the therapist should insist on at least three sessions for the ending, one session for letting the child know, one for containment, working with his feelings and thoughts about the parting to come, and one session to help him reorientate himself in face of the final farewell.

In fact, gaps between model endings and possible endings are frequently encountered; however, an orderly, planned ending to an open-ended psychodynamic child or adolescent therapy would typically require a consideration of the following steps:

1. A mutually binding commitment between the parents, the therapist, and maybe the child himself, stating that (a) the child is ready to enter a period of ending, and (b) therapy will end at an exact date.
2. An agreement about the framework of ending, including decisions about whether to maintain or reduce the present frequency of sessions. On the one hand, the pain of parting may be alleviated by spacing out the sessions; on the other hand, this could mean that the feelings related to mourning, separation, and loss are avoided, which might prevent the child from benefiting in full from the work of ending. There are, however, certain circumstances in which thinning out the sessions might be the best choice: for example, if the child's present carers cannot offer sufficient emotional support for working through the pain of parting. In fact, however, this is much more rarely the case than often imagined by therapists. Thus, when the therapeutic work approaches the stage where the ending is considered, the therapist might need to seek supervision to discuss how best to approach it.
3. During the period of ending, one or more concluding parent and teamwork sessions should be arranged for mutual reflection

about (a) the effect of therapy, (b) what (if any) difficulties might arise in the child's future development, and (c) what (if any) future treatment or support will be needed.

4. Informing the parents and/or referring agency whether or not the ending is absolute, that is, whether the child and the parents may come back to the same therapists, or if not, where future help for the child can be obtained.

It is important to remember that even if the therapist mostly invites the child or young person to take the initiative with regard to bringing up the themes of therapy, during the ending, children and adolescents usually tend to avoid this difficult topic. Hence, the therapist might need to take a more active lead in initiating interpretations that reflect on feelings and phantasies related to the end of therapy.

Concerning short-term therapy with a fixed ending, the therapist knows beforehand that therapy lasts only for a limited time and, accordingly, right from the beginning she needs to consider how to handle the ending. Thus, in time-limited therapy, it is particularly important to be attentive to themes of parting from the outset, and as early as during the first few therapy sessions, the therapist should observe whether and how separation anxiety and loss are addressed. Furthermore, it is important to address these issues directly, especially during the final months of therapy.

Finally, therapists should always remember that the pain of parting is mutual, since both participants have been emotionally engaged with the therapy process. Thus, in line with the development of transference, the child is also constituted as a part of the therapist's inner world of objects. For many hours, the therapist has engaged her own emotionality in intense and demanding events, and, hence, she cannot let go of the child before she has worked through processes of mourning in her own mind. The more so since, during the therapy process, the child probably came much more to life to her as a person who is able to reach out to others.

Unanticipated endings

Unanticipated endings of child and adolescent therapy are, unfortunately, quite common, and probably all child and adolescent psychotherapists will have experienced premature termination of psychotherapy. Thus, Midgley and Navridi (2006) found that, from 1999 to 2003, forty to sixty per cent of psychotherapy cases at the Anna Freud Centre came to a premature ending. A further qualitative analysis of a small number of cases pointed to a connection between a restricted parental capacity to mentalize and their likelihood of terminating their child's therapy prematurely.

Generally, a host of practical and administrative–organisational reasons can be behind premature endings. Among these are, for instance, the parents moving house, getting divorced, or finding the practical and financial burdens of their child's therapy too heavy, keeping in mind that troubled children often have siblings who also need to get their fair share of family resources. If public services pay for the therapy, contributing factors behind unplanned endings might include staff turnover, changing municipal practices, budget cuts, shortage of qualified child psychotherapists, etc. However, the most important cause is probably that while adults normally decide for themselves how long to continue therapy, many external agents decide on behalf of the child how long his therapy may continue. It probably also plays a role that adults tend to overlook their children's difficulties related to separation and loss, underestimating their mental pain in connection with parting and, consequently, attaching less importance to the stability of persons in their child's support network. This could be of particular importance to children who have suffered comprehensive early neglect and loss, because these children are especially difficult to read and, moreover, likely to deny sadness and anxiety related to separation and loss.

In the event of a premature ending caused by decisions outside the therapist's control and contrary to her advice, she might find the ending period especially challenging to work with. When that is the case, she needs to contain not only the child's mourning and feelings of abandonment, but also her own countertransference feelings of sadness, anger, and disappointment. In this event, to ensure that the child is able to benefit from the preceding therapy, however short, the therapist must be aware of the huge emotional difference between unplanned endings and planned, albeit premature, endings.

Sometimes, the parents might wish to end the therapy even if the therapist finds this somewhat premature, based on the above criteria. All the same, a wise therapist may follow the parents' wishes in order to secure a planned ending. Thus, a prime concern is to end a therapy in a way that does not preclude or hamper future possibilities of therapy or other kinds of treatment. For the same reason, it is a central responsibility of the therapist never to inflate the achieved results of the therapy, but, rather, to provide the parents or those in custody of the child with a realistic assessment of the kind of difficulties he is at risk of encountering in his future development and what kind of future support or treatment he might need. Here, it is of no consequence whether the therapist herself will be able to provide this treatment.

If the premature ending is caused by limitations of the therapist or her institution, a possible referral to another child or adolescent psychotherapist should be considered. If that is possible, the therapist or the institution might be tempted to introduce this possibility quickly, maybe even at the same time as the parents and the child are informed of the ending. It is, however, important to delay this recommendation slightly to allow the child and his parents time and space to work through the feelings related to the loss of the therapist. It is important to give the child (and his parents) an opportunity to mourn before bringing up the possibility of continuing the work with another therapist. In fact, it is much better if the first mention of this possibility does not come from the therapist, but, rather, from the child or young client himself, his parents, or other carers.

After such a change of therapists, the new therapist needs to remember that one of her first tasks is to broach the subject that the child lost his former therapist, if possible initiating a dialogue about the feelings related to this loss. This can feel quite heavy, especially for an eager, new therapist who looks forward to working with the child. Nevertheless, listening to him mourning the loss of the former therapist, including his potentially idealised descriptions of her qualities and attributes, is an essential part of the process of rebuilding the therapeutic relationship and, thus, cannot be skipped.

A checklist at the conclusion of therapy

To sum up the above, at the conclusion of child and adolescent psychotherapy, certain topics might be helpful to discuss in sessions with the child or young person and his parents, whether with each parent individually or in joint sessions.

- How did the child or young person benefit from the therapy, and in what respects do the child and the parents feel that something (if anything) has changed?
- How does the therapist believe that the child or young person, the parents, and the family as a whole will develop in the future?
- In the therapist's opinion, are there problems or areas that the parents need continue to work on, either on their own or with the help of another therapist?
- In the future, what aspects of the child's or young person's future development might, in particular, require parental attention and possibly intervention?
- In the future, under what circumstances will the parents again need to request professional help for the child or themselves?

CHAPTER TEN

Breaks: a window to fundamental relationship themes

There is no such thing as psychotherapy without breaks in the form of shorter or longer (scheduled or unscheduled) interruptions in the planned time structure due to either the therapist's or the client's temporary absence. Accordingly, through their training, most psychodynamic psychotherapists become aware of the significance of breaks. However, even experienced psychotherapists typically assume that breaks induce separation anxiety, especially in the client, although the psychology of breaks is, in fact, much more complex. This is especially so because gaps in the therapeutic process affect both participants, bringing out feelings in the client as well as in the therapist, as a relational event that takes place in the transference relationship.

The key message in this chapter is that breaks in a child's psychotherapy can be regarded as an open window offering access to central, unconscious relationship themes that are unique to the child in question. Hence, an important and easily observable indicator of changes taking place—or not—in the inner world of the child is comparison over time aimed at mapping the child's reactions before and after breaks.

Fundamental relationship themes in child and adolescent psychotherapy

As mentioned above, the infant's earliest relational experiences give rise to unconscious structures in the child's inner world—the so-called object relationships—that can be understood as organising, unconscious phantasies about relationships with significant others. These object relationships are imbued with certain fundamental, uniquely subjective relationship themes or conflicts, the formulation of which depend upon the person's ability to work through and integrate personal relationship experiences into his or her personality.

These subjective relationship themes are unconsciously repeated in the child's and, later, the adult's interactions with others. They might, for example, be manifest as a piercing need for affectionate parental care paired with an equally strong, painful expectation of rejection and humiliation. Contingent on the unconscious identifications of the self, this inner conflict might, for example, catalyse repetitions of a relational pattern in which the self repeatedly acts in a way that provokes rejections in close relationships or, on the contrary, withdraws when a close relationship seems about to develop. Commensurate with the assumptions of Hinshelwood (1991), such uniquely specific relationship themes in the person's inner world are probably structured as phantasy imagery, appearing in the clinical material as pictures of certain relationships between self and objects. Furthermore, repetitions of a specific relational response pattern indicate that the person's psyche is organised around a painful "core object relationship", comprising unconscious phantasies of the relationship between the self and significant others (objects). The related phantasies most likely form a basis for this person's unique, subjective ideas about worst-case scenarios in relationships with others or, as stated by Hinshelwood, become "the point of maximum pain" (p. 172). This painful core of phantasies brings anxiety and related defence in its wake or, in other words, produces a deadlock of defensive phantasy formations of relationships, the function of which can, thus, be understood as an attempt to endure, regulate, and contain one's most fundamental relational hurts and conflicts.

To find a specific psychodynamic formulation suited for describing, in meaningful details, a certain client's fundamental relational problems, one must look for repetitions of certain specific relational themes or patterns that are observable in each of three separate object relationship domains. As a whole, the three domains have been labelled the relationship triad (Luborsky, 1997; Luborsky et al., 1992; Popp et al., 1990).

1. The therapeutic relationship and process will, from the very beginning of therapy, manifest certain relationship themes, unique to this therapy, that are repeated more often than other themes.
2. Similar themes can be observed as repeatedly occurring relational patterns in the person's concurrent relationships outside therapy.
3. Similar relational patterns can be recaptured in descriptions of infantile relationships with primary carers, for example, in the parents' description of the child's infancy or in the adult client's childhood memories.

Such close connections between a painful core of relationship themes and specific events in the therapeutic process are meticulously substantiated by research into psychoanalytic psychotherapy with adults (Albani et al., 2003; Eels, 2013; Glasser, 1994; Luborsky & Luborsky, 2006). However, research relating to core relationship themes in psychodynamic psychotherapy with children and adolescents is sparse, as only a few works explicitly address this issue.

Psychodynamic core object relationship themes in child psychotherapy

A quantitative empirical investigation performed by Luborsky et al. (1996) showed core object relationship themes to be present and consistent over time in story stem narratives told by a healthy, non-client sample of North American children when they were three years old and again at five years. Compared to results from psychotherapy research with adults, these children's persistent relational wishes/expectations of others and themselves appeared surprisingly positive, especially concerning the desire to be "loved and understood" or "feel good and comfortable", both desires in relation to supportive and understanding others (p. 303). The findings have limited clinical applicability, both because this healthy group of children was in no need of psychotherapy, and because their responses were produced by story stem narratives in a non-clinical setting rather than through comparison of actual relational patterns in daily life with observations from therapy.

By systematic application of the principles of interpretative phenomenological analysis, as formulated by Smith and colleagues (2009), in a case study analysis of assembled case file material from therapy with a six- to ten-year-old child, Grünbaum (2014) found similar core conflictual relationship themes to be present in process notes from the therapy and in independent descriptions by birth parents, residential staff, adoptive parents, and teachers of (a) the child's concurrent relationships outside therapy, (b) the earliest relationships, as described in case files by birth parents, the case worker, and residential staff, and (c) to a lesser degree, two and a half years after the end of therapy, in interviews with birth and adoptive parents, who described the child's reactions to relational stress.

> Early in her life, Samantha had suffered severely traumatising and neglectful care relationships. At one and a half years of age, she was removed from her home and placed in an institution for infants and young children. At this point, an assessment showed her to be passively withdrawn, severely malnourished, and well behind her age norms in all developmental areas. At three and a half years, she was adopted as the youngest child in a stable and loving family. At five years, she was referred to therapy because her cognitive–emotional development had come to a standstill.
>
> In the first two–three years of therapy, the therapy sessions were completely dominated by Samantha's focus on hostile parental and sibling figures. In these imaginings and phantasies, parental and sibling figures appeared in a host of different, more or less fantastic shapes, with few exceptions disconcertingly malignant and violent. It made no difference whether the depicted relationships concerned phantasy figures, for example, as represented in dolls' play or drawings, her concurrent or past personal life outside therapy, or her imaginations of the therapist's family, colleagues, or other child clients. With few variations, Samantha thus repeated a few, fundamentally similar play scenarios, in which starving, freezing cold infants and/or expansively explorative baby sisters get in the way of cruelly sadistic parental and sibling figures and are locked in deadly dangerous, confined spaces: for example, ice-cold, burning hot, suffocating, unstable, or, at the opposite end of the spectrum, more or less arbitrarily abandoned, excluded from the fun, denied sweets, isolated, kicked out, left to fend for themselves on a glacier or in a desert,

reduced to appealing to casual strangers to pick them up. In parallel, in the transference, I felt Samantha's reactions to be unusually unpredictable; this created a situation in which it seemed impossible to get the mental and geographical distance to Samantha right. I struggled to find a position from which I could maintain a workable therapeutic neutrality, neither too obtrusive nor too withdrawn.

Another characteristic feature, the evil-minded parental and sibling figures were so closely allied that, at times, it was hardly possible to tell them apart. In parallel, an independent psychological testing when Samantha was five years old found her ability to differentiate between parental and sibling figures deficient and uncertain. In therapy, the persecuting sibling figures practically never appeared alone, but only together with equally hostile parental figures. A sequential analysis accordingly showed that the emotional quality of the parental figures was decisive for the emotional quality of sibling figures; it was never the other way round.

As a third characteristic feature, Samantha's motivation and courage for cognitive–emotional exploration and ability to differentiate inner–outer and self–other seemed completely dependent on her feeling securely connected to good, protective parental figures. This characteristic (i.e., a close connection between, on the one hand, her ability for exploration and learning and, on the other hand, her experience of basic security/insecurity and good/bad parental care) had been described by the residential institution when she was only one and a half years old. Later, it was repeatedly described and exemplified, both in process notes from the therapy and by Samantha's adoptive parents and teachers.

Breaks: a window to central object relationships

Leaving aside Klein's (1945, 1961), O'Shaughnessy's (1964, 1989), and Pick's (1967) classic studies, few systematic studies have focused directly on the psychology of breaks in psychotherapy with children and adolescents. More recent works include a multiple case study by Labastida (1976) and the above-mentioned qualitative single-case study by Grünbaum (2014).

By contrast, numerous single-case studies indirectly reveal that, concomitant with a break in therapy, complications arose either in the therapeutic transference relationship or in external relations with concerned parents or members of the professional network. Thus, even if the author did not intend the impact of breaks to be centre stage, the reviewed case studies more often than not left the impression that the break did indeed leave an impact that was difficult for the child and the therapist to negotiate (e.g., Azarian et al., 1997; Canham, 1999; Kronengold, 2010; Mikardo, 1995; Thomson-Salo, 2004; Silverman, 2004; Sussman, 2001).

A commonality in these and similar case studies is descriptions of the periods before and after the break that highlight, on behalf of the child, intensified core relationship themes, behavioural repetitions related to former trauma, and related defensive patterns and, on behalf of the therapist, difficulties in predicting and containing the child's reactions to the break. Assuming the child's reactions depend on his mental ability to process and symbolise the therapist's absence, as detailed above, this ability, in turn, probably depends on the reliability and durability of good inner objects with the capacity to remain whole and alive, even under conditions of frustrated longing.

Inspired by O'Shaugnessy's three organising principles (1964, see Chapter Nine), breaks in therapy (i.e., an absent therapist) can be experienced in three different ways.

1. The therapist's absence is experienced as the presence of a persecuting therapist. From this position, the child can experience a therapist whose human and professional limitations are grossly magnified and distorted in accordance with the child's pre-existing inner template of persecuting objects and related identifications. Before or after a break, the therapist might, for example, be experienced as sadistic, profoundly lacking in empathy, intrusive, in conspiracy with the child's perceived enemies, or a weakling, fit only for abuse. In more severe distortions, the distinction between the therapist and former abusers might break down, or the child might suspect the therapist has been swapped, during the break, for another, altogether bad person.
2. The therapist's absence is experienced as a fatal change of mind in a previously helpful therapist. For a child oscillating between a paranoid–schizoid and a depressive point of view, breaks might spark an experience of being let down in a more partial way, as the therapist unpredictably changed from good to bad, for example, in a suspected betrayal of confidentiality, a loss of genuine interest in the child's wellbeing, a greater interest in other child clients, or an intention of keeping the child in therapy for much

too long, simply for profit. Phantasies like these might be part of the reason why an otherwise productive therapy is suddenly broken off after a break; an event described, for example, by Kronengold (2010).

3. The therapist's absence is experienced as a longing for a therapist recollected as predominantly helpful. From this depressive perspective, the child is able to keep the supportive qualities of the absent therapist in mind and becomes aware that feelings of anger, loss, and longing are related to this absence. This relates to the child's ability to keep in memory, and identify with, the therapist's ability, through empathic understanding and interpretation, to contain and ease anxiety and pain. The ability to keep good memories alive during a break requires the ability to own and mentalize one's own pain, ambivalence, jealousy, and hatred, for example, in relation to the realisation of the separateness of self and therapist.

In accordance with Klein's theory of positions (1959) and Bion's theory of thinking (1962a), this model should not be thought of as discrete developmental stages, but, rather, as mentally organising perspectives—that is, like steps on a flight of stairs, from where the child may look upon the therapist's past or upcoming absence, the shifting positions of the self in relation to the ability to process, rather than evade, mental pain. Thus, a reliable and durable mental connection to good inner objects should not mistakenly be perceived as a smooth or idyllic link, but, rather, as stable inner links to mindful figures who remain attentive, realistic, and alive, even when the going gets rough. As implied by the depressive position, this is not about the absence of conflict, but, rather, about the ability for reparation; in other words, the child's ability during breaks, and the related frustration/aggression, to remember and repair good inner images of a stable, separate self in a dependent relationship with caring inner parental figures and a viable parental couple in the transference image of an empathic and resilient therapist. If the child lacks this ability, his psyche could be flooded by persecutory anxiety and fragmented (dissociated)—often sensory-based—subjective traces of traumatic memory and related phantasy. In that case, the child might be prone to reliving and repeating certain aspects of past traumatising relationships on a bodily and behavioural level:

> Around breaks in Samantha's therapy, I often felt trapped in an unstoppable, vicious circle. The sequence might begin with Samantha becoming completely obsessed, frantically trying to hammer and kick her way into a locked cupboard because she suspected that I had provided other children with much better playthings. Once in a while, pausing, she would calm down by drawing serenely beautiful, cold figures preoccupied with secret activities and excluding other, smaller and more disjointed figures. Samantha was normally skilled at drawing, but, especially before breaks in the therapy, she might rapidly fill sheet after sheet with incoherent, incomplete faces and human beings with body parts placed more or less at random. In a split second, her state of mind might change to a dissociated state of total identification with an intoxicated, omnipotent–-sadistic paternal figure, mercilessly persecuting his victims, shouting and kicking. In this scenario, through her behaviour, Samantha seemed to assign to me the reverse role as the helpless victim of arbitrary punishment and rejection. Eventually, I felt compelled to put a stop to Samantha's frenzied actions by taking hold of her, at which point the girl might fall apart mentally like a traumatically overwhelmed infant, shutting down her consciousness. When that happened, her face might go blank and expressionless, entering an apparently mindless state as she rhythmically rocked her body, bumping her head into whatever happened to be nearby. In my mind, this behaviour kindled a faint echo of case file descriptions by Samantha's visiting nurse and nursery group teachers of a nine-month-old Samantha in a state of mental and bodily shutdown.

Samantha's reactions indicate that the therapist's forthcoming or past absence activated a fundamental fear of dying—in Bion's words, nameless dread—and associated relational core conflicts or themes: for example, hunger for vital nutrition and tender care *vs.* defiant rage and expectations of violence, misunderstandings of emotional and bodily expression, relational persecution, loss, and despair (Bion, 1962b, p. 96). Hence, the unique reactions to breaks of children in psychotherapy can be understood as more or less mentalized statements about how the subjective infant within the older child's inner world experiences the therapist's absence. As in Samantha's case, it is not unusual for breaks to have severe reverberations for traumatised children or adolescents, bringing to life echoes of early catastrophic reactions to traumatising events and related somato-psychic memory fragments (Grünbaum, 2010b). Hence, the break might cause memory traces of earlier trauma, loss, and abandonment to come to life and be communicated by the child, through projective identification, as memories-in-feelings related to the present event of the break (Klein, 1957). Thus, breaks could transform past trauma to an emotionally vivid experience that exists in the here-and-now of the transference relationship, rather than as narrated recollections of the past. Through this communicative and defensive *modus operandi,* the child turns passive suffering into active revenge, thus partly or completely liberating the self from unbearable feelings and memories, as these are, henceforth, identified as belonging to the therapist, who is correspondingly placed at the receiving end of unbearable feelings. Thus, attentiveness to the child's reactions around breaks and the related transference processes of projective and introjective identifications can, accordingly, offer the therapist special insights into deeply embedded traces of painful core object relationship experiences that can only be communicated through action.

Breaks that occur at the beginning of a therapy process might tend to become especially chaotic and painful. Most children do not spontaneously attribute their own painful reactions to the break, and this linkage needs to be gradually worked through. In less intensive courses or stages of therapy, as well as with children whose personality is less affected by early trauma and neglect, children and adolescents might be generally inclined to minimise the importance of a break, perhaps accompanied by a flight into omnipotent–narcissistic phantasies of self-sufficiency. In such situations, with the ordinary ambivalence towards the therapy gone, the child maintains that cancellations are of absolutely no importance or, even, a treat, since therapy is so boring anyway. This attitude carries the risk that the child might convince the parents that something else is far more important than therapy, and they might, therefore, choose to cancel the last session before, or the first session after, the break. Correspondingly, after longer breaks, the child and/or the parents might feel that the problems have disappeared and wish to end the therapy immediately. This rush reflects an anxiety that resuming therapy will only cause the problems to reappear. As described in the previous chapter, the child's or adolescent's ability to maintain progression through a break indicates real change, meaning that therapy is having an impact. This, however, usually takes place as a gradual change, not as a suddenly acquired ability, and, furthermore, before the therapy can be concluded, there is a final farewell to be worked through.

Psychodynamic psychotherapy is a relational endeavour, and, of course, one must always consider the therapist's contribution to difficulties occurring around breaks. The therapist's personal feelings and her way of introducing and generally coping with a forthcoming break—especially her ability to mentalize feelings related to separation anxiety and loss—play an important role for the child's reactions. According to our own experience as psychotherapists and supervisors, the therapist's self-knowledge could pose a problem in this area, because it is painful and often difficult to acknowledge that one's own need for relaxation and the temporary inaccessibility this necessitates are, in fact, responsible for sparking off the child's painful feelings and reactions.

It is important to bear this in mind by giving sufficient notice to prepare the child for a forthcoming break; for example, by announcing the break three or four sessions ahead of time. The therapist should keep an open mind on the individual child's possible phantasies about the upcoming break; for example, in relation to jealousy and envy related to the therapist's family life. Especially with younger children, it might be useful to prepare a calendar together with the child to count the days between the final session before the break and the first session after. As part of the therapeutic relationship, this calendar is not for the child to take home; between sessions and during the break it belongs in the child's personal folder/box. Finally, especially with mentally ill or disturbed children, it is important to prepare the parents regarding the risk of setbacks and increased acting out at home and in school.

Before or after the break: does it make a difference?

Breaks call for the child's mental ability to bridge mental and literal distance and separateness in phantasy, mobilising stable and viable links to good inner objects and resources. A precondition for this ability is a certain recognition and acceptance of separateness in relation to important others, including the transference relationship to the therapist. For some—probably most—children, there seem to be important differences in their experience of the period before and after the break, a distinction that can also be found, in a less clear-cut form, in the child's characteristic way of starting and ending the individual sessions. It is, therefore, important to remember that, in an ordinary course of psychodynamic psychotherapy, for example, with twice-weekly sessions, regular breaks between sessions will occur. Of these, the impact of the weekend break might be especially crucial.

The pain associated with a parting to come differs from the pain of seeing the therapist again after the break, eye to eye. It is, however, a wise therapist who takes no child's reaction for granted, but stays true to a dictum of observation before interpretation. Thus, the individual child will have his own personal way of dealing with, and relating to, the break to come and the break that was (as will the therapist). In the transference relationship, to one child, the metaphorical meaning of a forthcoming break might involve abandonment, like standing on the edge of a terrifying and dangerous abyss. By contrast, another child could, based on the template of early experience, be prone to expect and perceive close contact to be smothering and oppressive; this child might, instead, perceive the prospect of a break as standing at the gateway to freedom. Paradoxically, any given child might simultaneously experience both in a toxic mix, or the experience might change during therapy from one to the other. Correspondingly, reuniting with the therapist after a break can, at times, feel like returning to a safe base after a grand tour of exploration, reassuring the self that the therapist, even if she was left behind, still is safe and sound, and, at other times, it might, conversely, feel like returning from a painful separation only to find that the therapist has changed in the meantime, perhaps into a suffocating, empty, or inattentive, preoccupied therapist. In the latter case, the child might feel as if the therapist is still absent, despite the reunion; the therapist might seem different, and the child might even believe that she is somebody else.

In the final sessions before a break, some children might manifest separation anxiety, but far more common seem to be decreasing abilities for symbolic representation and communication, accompanied by increasing tendencies towards splitting and projective identification. More often than not, this is followed by a more or less comprehensive regression in cognitive–emotional functioning, for example, as related to thinking, learning, concepts of time and space, identity, social skills, and so on. These tendencies were described in therapy with children with autism (Houzel, 2004, 2008) and with children who had suffered profound early trauma and neglect (Grünbaum, 2014). In these sessions, therapists often encounter difficulties in establishing and maintaining a working relationship as well as problems related to neutrality and positioning, as the polarity between closeness and distance suddenly seems impossible to reconcile. The relationship might feel disastrous and painful, since the child rejects everything the therapist says, perhaps subjecting her to harsh rejection and ridicule. With some children, this can escalate into a triumphantly manic and gleeful state of mind, loud and incessant talking, shouting, or moving around. Especially with children who suffered early severe abuse and neglect, this can lead to explosive irritability and sudden ferocious attacks on the setting or the therapist. With other children, the therapist might feel both guilty and annoyed at a child's clinginess; she could even feel invaded by a despairing child, who more or less aggressively seeks to evade frustration, separateness, and separation. Painful episodes of confusion might be experienced in the transference relationship, as the child's inner cohesiveness falls apart, allowing for utterly confused, split, and dissociated states of mind, maybe alternating with an empty, grey, and heavily depressive atmosphere.

In the final two sessions before a break, Samantha appeared more vulnerable than usual. For example, she was likely to become flooded by psychosomatic pain or confusion, and her ability to differentiate between inner–outer and self–other came across as more than usually brittle. The narrative content of her play became more repetitive and fragmented, and the play scenarios of hostile alliances between aggressive parental and sibling figures disappeared completely from the sessions. Intriguingly, however, the singularly few, purely good parental and sibling figures in this therapy course only appeared shortly before breaks and at session ends, not at any other time. Furthermore, sessions before breaks were overlaid with quiescence, sensory activities, and a perpetual production of drawings, which she concealed from the therapist and often destroyed at the end of the session. I managed to reconstruct one of these drawings, depicting a serene-looking woman dropping, or deliberately throwing, a swaddled infant into streaming waters, thus literally communicating a feeling of being thrown into the depths by a careless and cruel parental figure: in the transference, by me. Similarly communicating through enactment, towards the end of such sessions, Samantha kept circling near the door, triumphantly threatening to leave before time, but when the time was actually up, she refused to leave and hid underneath the sandbox or the couch.

In some case descriptions, the authors mention that events occurring during the break erode or destroy the therapeutic alliance and setting. On closer inspection, this seems to be related to the ability of parents and professional network to contain the anxiety and related enactment of a mentally flooded child, who relapses into former states of mind and related behaviour, such as antisocial acts, straying, casting aspersions on the therapist, attacks of wildly confused, paranoid rage, or fragmented re-enactments of former traumatic experiences (Ironside, 1995; Rustin, 1989, 1998). During such episodes, some children literally came to more or less serious grief, actually hurting, endangering, or harming themselves, whether by accident or by intent (Alvarez, 1992; Dale, 1984; Watson, 1990).

> In the middle of therapy—with the transference relationship at its most intense—Samantha's parents and teachers described how, during a planned break, the girl had regressed to earlier behavioural problems, such as mindless rage and violent attacks on classmates, straying from school, and jeopardising her own safety by climbing so high that she was unable to get down again unaided. Furthermore, she went astray, uncritically and ingratiatingly approaching strangers, a behaviour last described by nursery teachers and carers at her residential institution when she was one to three years of age.

During the first few sessions after a break, though more varied, reactions often echo certain aspects of early tendencies of splitting and ambivalence in reuniting with primary carers. Especially children and adolescents who suffered early, complex trauma as well as children and adolescents with autism or psychosis might return after a break in a more or less confused state of mind, a brittle façade keeping together a fragmented self, as they feel they have lost not only their link to the therapist, but also vital parts of the self (O'Shaughnessy, 1989; Tustin, 1966).

During periods of especially intense transference feelings, the first encounter with the therapist after the break might be especially painful. Thus, especially for children who suffered early abuse and neglect, this can initially give rise to raw conflicts, as they are torn between unbearable longings for tender closeness and dependency and fiery, vengeful hatred against the therapist, who is still experienced as unreliable. Hence, after a break, these children desperately seek to fortify their well-known defensive positions, for example, pointedly maintaining an exaggerated physical and mental distance to the therapist, avoiding eye contact, claiming, with feigned or felt indifference, to have forgotten the therapist's name, or, in phantasy, via evocative projective identification, forcefully assigning the therapist the identity of an unwanted, worthless, excluded child, for whom nobody cares (Grünbaum, 2014; Labastida, 1976: Rustin, 1989).

> In the middle of therapy, at the start of the first session after a break, Samantha regularly suffered intense approach–avoidance conflicts. When she first entered the clinic and caught sight of me, for example, she would light up, smiling happily, but then she immediately panicked, turned her back, and rejected any contact. At this point, she might literally get stuck at the threshold to the therapy room, apparently unable to move, in a droning voice shouting confused threats of leaving me, never coming back, and, at the opposite end of the spectrum, threatening to force her way in to destroy everything in the therapy room, including me. (In my countertransference, the sight of Samantha stuck at the threshold evoked painful inner imagery of an alarmingly violent family life. Furthermore, during this period, I developed a certain hypersensitivity to noise, both in and outside the therapy room.)

For children like Samantha, breaks might bring out an experience of being caught in a dilemma relating to an overwhelmingly dreadful double anxiety: a fear of confinement inside and/or together with aggressive objects and the no less painful fear of isolation and exclusion from tenderly protective and nourishing objects. This core object relationship conflict seems comparable to claustro-agoraphobic borderline dilemmas in adults, as elucidated by Rey (1986), Green (1974), and Steiner (1993). In narrative terms, this phantasy seems to involve a helpless, terrorised infant-self, who passionately longs for an object providing tenderness–care–exploration but who is, instead, compulsively driven back and forth between two equally terrifying options: confinement inside a bad parental object, whose mental and bodily space is preoccupied by a crowd of murderously aggressive (sibling) rivals *vs.* exclusion from a protective, caring object, the self deprived of even the tiniest crumbs of nourishment, while other more privileged rivals feast on plenty.

Containing the ordeal of breaks: a prerequisite for change

Mental development and health are preconditioned by early parental care relationships capable of meeting and balancing the infant's fundamental needs for dependent personal relationships as well as possibilities for exploration, differentiation, and separateness (Blass & Blatt, 1992; Blatt & Luyten, 2009). Thus, breaks are more than just a stressful nuisance. Given a sufficiently intensive and stable structuring of appointments, with few unexpected breaks, the regular cycle of seasonal bank holidays (e.g., Easter, summer, autumn, and Christmas holidays) will establish the experience of a reliable, recurrent rhythm. This experience might be reminiscent of the infant's development of a circular concept of time, as related to the expectation of a limited, bearable time space between saying goodbye and hello again to parental figures leaving and coming back. Hence, working in and with a pre-settled structure of breaks can be a precondition both for the mental health of the therapist and for the therapy leading to real change in the child's inner world.

Children and adolescents tend to oscillate between moments of self-knowledge, including awareness of their own needs, feelings, and mental states, and defensive states of mind that more or less suspend their ability to differentiate and mentalize. As the transference relationship develops and deepens, such fluctuations (e.g., in the ability to differentiate own feelings from those of others) can gather and intensify around breaks, making them especially difficult. Like breaks, session endings and beginnings confront the child with awareness of the difference between phantasies about relationships inside the therapeutic space and the concurrent real-life relationships, and, hence, they might give rise to similar difficulties.

However, the self-same confrontation could provide an important impetus for mental growth, stimulating a wish to know about the self, its objects, and its personal history. Hence, in the midst of turmoil, breaks can inspire moments of working through central issues of personal identity, attachments, and family roots, such as, who am I? Why did my birth parents allow these things to happen? Why was I taken into care? How do I resemble or not resemble my birth or adoptive parents? Who is to blame for my problems? What are my problems, anyhow? What will my future be like?

This mental exploration of individual identity and psychosocial roots often takes place in a parallel process to a similar exploration of the transference relationship, as the child ponders such questions as, what is therapy? Why am I in therapy? What is a therapist? What is my therapist like, compared to others? What is the real nature of the relationship between me and my therapist? For adopted or fostered children, this search forms a particularly important part of the necessary process of mourning trauma and loss.

As a third, often parallel, development during the break, at home, the child might show new capacities for tender longing and love, allowing himself to receive and seek care and dependency. For example, traumatised children can withdraw into a frozen, defensive state as a reaction to the uncompensated, traumatic loss of parental care. During therapy, as this frozen self begins to thaw out, it might be precisely during a break that the child allows himself to receive tender love and caring from his parents and might even engage in a meaningful conversation about earlier loss and trauma. Allowing parental closeness during the break can, thus, mark an important turning point in the reparation of the relationship between parents and child. In other words, the break might bring the child into contact with denied but necessary feelings of sadness and longing, creating an opening for parental tenderness, child and parent mourning earlier loss and hardship together (Gaensbauer, 1995; Grünbaum, 2010b).

For most children and adolescents, breaks in the therapeutic process stimulate and accentuate fundamental relational themes related to conflicts and dilemmas of dependency–separateness, separation anxiety, jealousy, and envy. In the last few sessions before the break, the child's capacity for symbolic and mental representation of these dilemmas might weaken or even break down completely. The first few sessions after the break will bear the mark of the way in which the child experienced, processed, and defended against early (or earlier) devastating loss and trauma.

In an efficient psychodynamic therapy process, the child's increasing capacity not only to contain breaks without relapse but even to develop positively during breaks signifies real change and indicates that it can be realistic to prepare for the ending of the therapy. Thus, some case studies suggest that an increasing capacity to develop during breaks, without relapse, might even be used as a convenient and systematic assessment criterion for change (Houzel, 2008; Grünbaum, 2014).

Conclusion and summary

In relation to breaks, therapists working with children and adolescents should pay attention to at least four key factors.

1. There is a unique, subjective link between the individual child's central unconscious object relationship themes and the way the child experiences breaks.
2. Children's and adolescents' reactions to breaks will often be linked to inner dilemmas of dependency–separateness, for example, as a result of disturbed early relationships, loss, neglect, abuse, and trauma. The breaks, thus, facilitate the direct working through in the transference relationship of the evoked traumatic memories-in-feelings.
3. Breaks can cause relapse or, on the contrary, stimulate progressive development.
4. The individual child's experience of breaks might be a convenient and reliable indicator of change and, thus, signify that it is appropriate to begin planning for an end to an open-ended therapy course.

PART IV

PSYCHOTHERAPY WITH CHILDREN WHO HAVE SUFFERED MALTREATMENT AND COMPLEX TRAUMA

CHAPTER ELEVEN

Psychotherapy in the aftermath of early neglect and abuse

This chapter reviews some issues that could complicate psychotherapy with children who have suffered severe psychosocial deprivation, neglect, and/or abuse early in life. According to experience, and documented in a host of case studies, therapy on this background often demands the careful monitoring of both the setting and the applied psychotherapeutic technique. Thus, states of overwhelming panic and aggression and related phantasies of persecuting parental and sibling figures frequently cause difficulties with containment and self-regulation. Accordingly, at the end of the chapter, we outline certain adaptations of psychodynamic techniques that, in our experience, can ease the work and accommodate the special needs of this group of children.

In this book, the terms "early psychosocial deprivation", "early privation", and "early neglect" are synonymously applied, defined as a relationship between one or more care persons and a child up to two years of age, in which the child's fundamental needs of emotional and bodily wellbeing are neglected, and the child is actively or passively exposed to recurrent traumatic stress.

In retrospect: the historical context

Early deprivation, neglect, and abuse are heterogeneous concepts, which cover a wide range of disturbances of early relationships. As such, this information about the past relationships of a (now older) child is neither a description of his personality development nor a psychiatric diagnosis. It simply tells us that during his first few years of life, this child experienced severe deficiencies and disturbances in parental care. All the same, it is an important pointer, indicating to the child and adolescent psychotherapist that in a possible future psychotherapy, the transference relationship might come to contain painful subjective traces of early relational experience and maybe also certain weaknesses in or special features of relatedness, frustration tolerance, ability of affect regulation, empathy, and self-knowledge.

For many years, developmental psychology has known that early neglect and abuse—historically designated early maternal deprivation or privation—can have profound developmental consequences for many, but far from all, children. This was already concluded in what is by now a classical research review, initiated by the World Health Organization, based on systematic observations of infants raised without personal care and stimulation in huge, inhumane, residential institutions (Ainsworth, 1962). It took time for this research to become generally accepted, and especially the adjective in "maternal deprivation" gave rise to fierce controversies related to women's rights, but also to fruitful, ground-breaking research into the effects and quality of early care and attachment relationships. In particular, a series of carefully performed prospective studies should be mentioned, which followed a group of children who had been institutionalised during infancy, assessing their development at regular intervals throughout their childhood until adolescence, in some cases even until they themselves became parents (Hodges & Tizard, 1989).

By now, it has been carefully documented and is universally recognised that unstable or absent empathic relationships with a few, specific carers and/or recurrent exposure to traumatic stress during the first years of life carry a seriously increased risk of comprehensive disturbances of emotionality, behaviour, and personality (Fox & Rutter, 2010). In general, these disturbances concern attachment formation, affect regulation, mentalization, social adaptation, and peer relationships. Special mention should, however, be made of a related risk of a range of behavioural and attentional disturbances as well as a damaged capacity for adult parenting. Lengthy psychosocial and cognitive deprivation in residential institutions and/or multiple, acute stress factors reoccurring in a family context of chronic psychosocial strain might cause general impoverishment and retardation of cognitive–social development. In addition, massive global deprivation occurring in residential institutions seems related to the development of autism-like behavioural patterns and reactions (Downey et al., 1985; Zeanah & Gleason, 2010).

In *ICD-10* and *DSM-V*, attachment disorders of early childhood are classified up to five years of age and denote the emotional consequences of extremely insufficient parental care. *ICD-10* differentiates between two different forms of attachment disorder: (1) reactive attachment disorder, characterised by persistent abnormalities in the child's pattern of social relationships, for instance, fearfulness, hypervigilance, and poor social interactions with peers. The syndrome is presumably caused by severe parental neglect, abuse, or serious maltreatment. The existence of this behavioural pattern is well recognised and known to be associated with emotional disturbance. It is reactive to changes in environmental circumstances. (2) Disinhibited attachment disorder, characterised by diffuse attachments and prolonged immature attachment behaviours, for instance, attention-seeking, indiscriminately friendly behaviour, and poorly modulated peer interactions. This syndrome has a relatively specific association with severe institutional deprivation, but can also be caused by other environmental circumstances persistently failing to provide opportunities for the infant to develop selective attachments, for instance, because of extremely frequent replacements of the child's carers.

In *DC:0–3R*, the term deprivation/maltreatment disorder is employed up to four years of age, describing three different patterns caused by deprivation and maltreatment: (1) a pattern marked by emotional withdrawal and inhibition, (2) a disinhibited pattern marked by lack of discrimination, and (3) a mixture of (1) and (2). In addition, *DC:0–3R* includes a classification of relationship patterns between the children and their primary carers. Among other valuable descriptions of early relationship disturbances, this provides detailed descriptions of care relationships marked by hostility, neglect, and abuse (ZERO TO THREE, 2005).

The past twenty years of neuroscientific research has greatly developed our knowledge of the critical importance of the quality and timing of early experiences for psychological development. Thus, extremely severe early neglect and abuse presumably have certain harmful repercussions for the early development of brain functioning and the perceptual–sensory apparatus (Fox et al., 2010; Music, 2009). We shall not give a more detailed description of this, since, although the existing evidence is impressive in highlighting the adverse consequences of extreme sensory, cognitive, and emotional deprivation, it seems to offer an insufficient base for more far-reaching conclusions. In addition, bearing in mind the different conceptual levels of mind and brain, we consider it improbable that this specific field of research will be able to contribute directly to the development of child and adolescent psychotherapy (see Chapter One).

In general, while the scope and persistence of harmful after-effects presumably depend on the duration and degree of deprivation and maltreatment, the possibilities for the child's recovery seem to depend in particular on the quality of later care relationships, the child's age, and, to some degree, his innate resources (Rutter, 2002; Zeanah & Boris, 2000). Improved care relationships and environmental conditions can often cause an otherwise normally endowed child to catch up even with pronounced delays of general cognitive development. Similarly, a considerable improvement of emotional and social functions may take place; however, in these developmental areas there seems to be a more noticeable risk of lasting difficulties. Children suffering harmful after-effects of early neglect and abuse are most commonly referred to psychotherapy because of disturbed (i.e., disturbing), aggressive, or, conversely, anxious, passive, and maybe odd, behavioural patterns. These problems often appear in combination with conspicuous difficulties in social adaptation, disturbances of concentration and attention, manic (hyperactive) behaviour, and related learning difficulties. Hence, the developmental background of referrals that lists these kinds of problems frequently (but not always) involves massive early neglect and abuse.

Neglect, deprivation, and abuse can occur across societal contexts, as listed below.

1. Comprehensive institutional deprivation is, even today, experienced by some, but far from all, internationally adopted children,

who spent their early years in large, impersonal, residential institutions without sufficient opportunity for personal attention, affectionate care, and, consequently, the development of attachment relationships with a few adult parental figures. Depending on the length of the stay and the degree of emotional, social, sensory, cognitive, and nutritional privation, institutional deprivation can cause profound delays as well as lasting disturbance and damage to the child's emotional, social, and cognitive development.

2. Deficient and traumatising early care relationships in the family might be the result of combinations of extremely insufficient, erratic, and abusive parental patterns of care. This is often associated with the parents' personal problems, for instance, mental or somatic illness, domestic violence and abuse, and/or substance abuse. From their earliest years, the children might have been exposed to a combination of, for instance, intrusive, deficient, and/or unpredictable care for basic bodily needs, unreliable, disturbed, unempathic, and/or detached emotional care relationships, recurrent loss of attachment figures, multiple, unpredictably changing carers, loss of trust and related disillusionment; violence and other forms of personal abuse, and witnessing violence against siblings and/or between parental figures.
3. Discontinuity in the early care relationships is an easily overlooked but frequent characteristic of the early childhood of psychosocially disadvantaged children living in difficult family circumstances. It is a sad reality that both older and more recent reviews show how insufficient quality and lack of continuity in early interventions and child protection interventions in themselves can compromise the needs of infants and small children for continuity of care and attachments. Factors that contribute to this risk include, for instance, the professional team's insufficient consideration of a previous family history of parental neglect and abuse, a failure to assess the emotional needs and developmental status of the at-risk child, and a failure to assess the impact of interventions on the child's actual bodily and emotional–cognitive health. In addition, the impact of interventions aimed at improving parental skills is seldom assessed. Before the crucial importance of permanence of care was established, an unintended side-effect of child protection safety interventions in

many cases was that young children were exposed to a great number of caseworkers and support teachers, several moves, back and forth, between the family home of mentally unstable and abusive parents and short-time placements in the birth family network and other short-time foster or residential care arrangements, multiple hospitalisations, and multiple workers in day-care or residential parent–child programmes (Bunn, 2013; Grünbaum & Gammeltoft, 1993; Munro, 2011; Ofsted, 2015).

Preconditions of psychotherapeutic effect

Psychotherapy with children and adolescents, who have suffered severe psychosocial deprivation, neglect, and/or abuse early in life is a difficult and challenging task that requires the therapist or the therapist's supervisor to have sufficient experience with this very work. As mentioned, these children often are referred because people around them find their behaviour difficult to contain and endure, often due to combinations of disruptive and/or odd behaviour, hyperactivity, difficulties of social adaption and learning, as well as dissociative episodes. An additional difficulty could be alarmingly sudden mood swings with frequent temper outbreaks and/or passive, blank states of mind. Often, the child might show blatantly defiant or more disguised, passive resistance against the therapy. In the therapy, the transference relationship could, in due course, engender a despairing hopelessness that most psychotherapists will feel difficult to contain and endure. Thus, for long stretches, the therapy places strenuous demands on the therapist's abilities for empathy, containment, resilience, patience, and personal authority. This is probably one of the reasons why many professionals formerly claimed that psychotherapy with this group of children had no chance of succeeding and might even be harmful to the child. However, as shown below, this belief has long since been disproved, as evidenced by numerous case studies as well as a growing body of quantitative effect studies (see below and Chapter Thirteen for details).

The first systematic study of these children's psychodynamic psychotherapies, with once- or twice-weekly sessions for up to two years, was conducted at the Tavistock Clinic, where, for a number of years, researchers and therapists gathered and analysed treatment experiences (Boston & Szur, 1983). According to reports from this study, the vast majority of the children showed substantial improvement, especially with regard to their social relations, mood, confidence in grown-ups, and abilities for learning and reflection. The reliability and validity of these tentative results were, unfortunately, hampered by a high attrition rate, unvalidated rating instruments, and the lack of a control group. Even so, an appreciable, pivotal result of this study was that, for the first time ever, it was systematically demonstrated that trained child psychotherapists can work meaningfully with these children. Another important qualitative result of this study was that it was the first to elucidate certain key features of the psychotherapeutic process that these therapies had in common. The findings subsequently gave rise to numerous qualitative single-case studies, which have led to essential new understandings, partly of the children's experiences of self and others, partly of the therapeutic process, and partly of the nature of the transference relationship (Moestrup, 2016).

In later childhood and adolescence, the repercussions of early neglect and abuse are complex and cannot be unambiguously delimited to specific diagnostic categories. This problem, as well as ethical considerations and insufficient sample sizes complicate the implementation of sufficiently well controlled statistical studies of the effectiveness and efficacy of psychotherapy with these children. Accordingly, the statistical power of quantitative studies is often weak (see Chapter Thirteen). In recent years, however, more rigorous quantitative studies have brought stronger evidence of a good effect of psychotherapy with this group and a partly overlapping group of children with disruptive behavioural disturbances.

A review of twenty-one controlled research projects on different kinds of psychotherapy with children who had suffered early neglect showed that seventy-one per cent of these children fared better than children who had received no psychotherapy, community intervention as usual (for instance, educational support only), or no support (Skowron & Reinemann, 2005). Apparently, the specific therapeutic modality applied made no difference to the result—for instance, whether individual, group, family, parent–child, or multi-modal forms of treatment. However, in contrast to the usual findings, the therapist's theoretical frame of reference did seem to have a bearing on therapeutic effect. The results showed that the psychodynamic psychotherapies (e.g., psychoanalytic, analytic, existential, interpersonal, etc.) showed somewhat better results than the cognitive behavioural methods. The fact that the psychodynamic therapies tend to focus on the therapeutic relationship rather than on the formulation of specific treatment goals and rated techniques might have played a role, since these children often are very difficult to motivate for task-orientated work. Probably, another contributing factor was a difference in the duration of treatment, since the cognitive behavioural therapies were typically of considerably shorter duration (up to three months) than psychodynamic therapy (at least a year).

More systematic research is needed; however, at this juncture, it seems safe to conclude that qualified individual, psychodynamic psychotherapy has the potential to make essential contributions to the recovery of children who suffer harmful after-effects of early neglect and abuse. The improvement achieved appears to include changes in emotionality and personality development that cannot be achieved solely by means of non-therapeutic forms of intervention. Today, a widely approved and increasingly common way of working is to combine individual child and adolescent psychotherapy with a range of other forms of intervention, for instance, special needs teaching, psychoeducative courses, and milieu therapy, and, no less important, always supplemented with different forms of concurrent parent and family work.

Four conditions seem to constitute necessary prerequisites for the feasibility and effect of psychodynamic psychotherapy with this group.

1. A complete termination of ongoing deprivation, neglect, and abuse must be ensured. If the child's living conditions are not improved in this regard, the effect and sustainability of therapeutic results will be undermined, leaving the child at risk not only of future difficulties and disturbances of his mental and bodily health and development, but of aggravated disillusionment.
2. The duration and frequency of the psychotherapy must correspond both to the degree and duration of earlier deprivation and abuse and to the severity and complexity of the child's current psychological disturbance and suffering. Thus, a sufficient amount of psychotherapy seems a prerequisite for a benign and sustainable effect, with a corresponding risk that therapy

that is too infrequent and brief might exacerbate the child's pathology. Based on our own experience, we typically recommend psychotherapy to last at least two years, with a frequency of at least two sessions a week.

3. Certain modifications of the therapeutic setting and way of working. Why and how are described below.
4. Continuing work with the adults currently responsible for daily parenting, at least for the duration of the child's psychotherapy and longer if possible. For children placed into care, it is necessary to embed the child psychotherapy and the parent work in a continuing professional teamwork that involves the child protective services responsible for the placement. Further, when possible, it can be beneficial to the child for one or both birth parents to be offered some reflective work or, at least, regular contact with child protective services.

The psychotherapeutic process and relationship

In general, the psychotherapeutic process with these children and young persons is characterised by a perpetual oscillation between three positions, whose relative contributions to the transference relationship vary in the following ways.

1. From the very beginning, open windows to the child's motivation for learning about himself, his relationships, his identity, and his existential issues briefly pop up. These opportunities are important to notice and think about, but, sadly, they are very easily lost in the difficulties of creating a working relationship with the child.
2. For extended periods, the child might relate to the therapist with grudging passivity, eagle-eyed vigilance, defiant dismissal, or, conversely, in an artificially ingratiating, honeyed manner. These and other defensive ways of relating prevent sincere emotional communication and can resonate in the therapist's countertransference as a despairing, hopeless feeling that genuine emotional contact is impossible.
3. With some children, sudden flooded and manic states of mind are frequent, completely overwhelming the child's self-control

and ability to reflect. In these states, despairing or sadistic aggressive impulses, feelings, and phantasies can swamp the child's consciousness and result in vehemently aggressive and often delusional attacks on the setting, the therapy, or the therapist. Repercussions of such episodes can resound in the therapist's countertransference, for instance, as feelings of helplessness, hypervigilance, and a counterproductive tendency to withdraw professional commitment.

Quite commonly, the child's motivation for the work emerges in moments that are so fleeting that the therapist might easily miss them.

Eight-year-old Barbara eagerly runs full pelt into the playroom. She quickly finds felt-tip pens and paper, meanwhile almost incomprehensibly saying something about having had "Something difficult . . .". She breaks off mid-sentence, and the next moment she triumphantly declares, "I paint myself, no, this is mum, no, this is you, you, you. Look, how ugly you are, all black, ho ho ho." She paints the picture over in black, knocks down her chair, throws the picture in the bin, and rushes over to the sandbox at the other end of the room. She turns her back to me, throwing handfuls of sand on the floor. (I am perplexed, do not understand what is going on. I feel rejected and really pessimistic about this therapy.)

(Only later on, through supervision, I become aware that, in my process notes from this session, I had meticulously described the promising start, Barbara's initial eagerness, her mention of difficult thoughts, and her subsequent sudden shift of feelings.)

The early, adverse relational experience might have left a fragile relatedness in the child's subjective, inner world, which seems painfully split and ambivalent, organised around object relations that regularly give rise to confusingly mixed, often predominantly negative, transference feelings. In a long beginning, many children cannot acknowledge ownership of aggressive feelings, disavowed longing, or mixed feelings aroused by recurrent experiences of loss and reunion in relationships with precariously shifty or disappointing parental figures. Accordingly, most of the time, the therapist has to maintain a delicate balance between, on the one hand, sensitively timed and phrased interpretations of deeply felt, subjective survival strategies and, on the other hand, firm containment of derisive and hostile attacks.

At times, in her countertransference the therapist might, for instance, find it nearly impossible to maintain a suitable geographical and mental distance from the child, whose motivation for the work and ability to differentiate between inner states of mind and outer external reality comes and goes in a confusing pattern. Furthermore, the therapist needs to be exceedingly attentive to a tendency for the implicit offer of emotional understanding and closeness in the therapeutic relationship to rekindle painful feelings of hurt, loss, and longing. For a long time, the child might not want to recognise or contain, not to mention take ownership of, these feelings as part of his inner world, but instead feels persecuted, perhaps even believing that the therapist intentionally wants to torment him by saying or doing things that bring up painful memories.

Omnipotent and flooded states of mind

As mentioned, the commitment to understanding that is an implicit aspect of the therapeutic relationship might, in time, thaw out long since frozen yearnings for tenderly loving parental care, bringing to the fore previously unfelt feelings, such as aching voids of loneliness, disillusionment, and related despair and anger. Painful emotions of this sort threaten to overthrow the child's brick wall solid defensive strategies (Henry, 1974). Accordingly, after a productive early beginning of therapy, some children quickly come to perceive therapy as a threat, in which case, the process becomes progressively more difficult.

Deficiencies and disturbances in the child's early introjection of stable, predominantly benign (sufficiently available, empathic, and containing) parental relationships mean that later, when the child enters therapy, he will typically relate to the therapist as an unreliable, dysregulating, abandoning, and abusive figure. Regardless of how reliable and sensitive the therapist is, she will inevitably misunderstand the child at times and let him down by going away for breaks and between sessions. The child might perceive this as confirmation that adults are not to be trusted, which, in his inner world, might kindle unbearable pain, anxious confusion, and traumatically flooded states of mind—states akin to what Bion termed "nameless dread" (1962b).

Recurrent, disturbed early relational experiences can profoundly shape development, causing a form of early developmental adaptation to trauma, in which the infant is left no other choice than to fall back on his own prematurely developed defensive reactions. Thus, the subjective intentions of inhibited, odd, and/or impulsive behavioural reactions could be related to early defensive patterns aimed at gaining at least some control over external events and the related inner traumatic chaos. In therapy, during moments of severe stress, some children might fall back and react in ways reminiscent of such early defensive strategies, for instance by a more or less radical tendency to mental—sometimes also bodily—shutdown: suddenly falling asleep, rhythmic rocking, going blank, stopping dead, or repetitive fragments of appeasing or clinging behaviour patterns (see also Chapter Twelve).

> Four-year-old Joseph (described in detail in Chapter Five) would, at times, in a manically excited state, turn on the water at full power, flooding the floor of the playroom, or hurl around buckets filled with sand. Frustrated by my refusal to let him carry on like this, he would crawl underneath a low, four-legged coffee table in the therapy room, where he would crouch on all fours, completely silent, rhythmically rocking back and forth for some time, sometimes banging his head into the wall. In this state, he did not react to words or touch. (In my countertransference, I felt helplessly pained by witnessing this behaviour and was carried back to lengthy observations of one to one and a half year-old children in their cribs, early in my professional life at a severely understaffed residential institution.)
>
> During the same period, Joseph's parents told me that they had taken Joseph by car to the residential institution, intending to visit his ward. However, as they drove into the car park, Joseph fell to pieces completely, screaming and banging his head against the interior of the car.

Whatever their problems, children of all ages can temporarily take flight from confusion and pain in omnipotent phantasies, as expressed in symbolic play and drawings. However, the children described here will often, simultaneously, replace symbolic play with coercive actions, more or less unconsciously aimed at reversing the roles of therapist and child. These children have often relied on a precocious mastery of certain skills to cope with neglect, abuse, and loss, caring for themselves as well as the adults, which could contribute to the tendency towards coercion. Understandably, they anxiously defend a pseudo-adult position, and, as a starting point for the therapeutic work, it is important for the therapist not to underestimate the value of these competences, which might have had survival-related connotations in the personal history of the children.

Containing and understanding aggressive behaviour

The child's need to feel in control of the therapist and the therapeutic relationship creates a delicate situation, which is easily thrown off balance by even minor failures and misunderstandings on the part of the therapist. This is linked to the above-mentioned issue of finding the right distance or position from which to build a rapport with the child's unacknowledged or disavowed longings for attention, understanding, and tender affection.

In order to pick up on, and prevent, mounting anxiety, explosive feelings, and related loss of self-control, the therapist needs to be minutely attentive to both her own countertransference and the child's less obvious reactions. She needs to position herself in such a manner that the child does not feel her communication to be too insistently intense and, thus, invading, or too impartially distant and, thus, out of reach and detached. In a concrete, geographical sense, the therapist needs to consider how to position herself in the playroom; in an emotional and symbolic sense, she needs to be aware of her own tone of voice, facial expressions, and choice of words. Concerning her verbal communication, it might be best—especially during moments of intense emotionality—to refrain from detailed "why" and "who" interpretations, which ascribe certain hidden meanings to actions, feelings, and motives and attribute these to the child. During these intense moments, it might be more helpful merely to describe what is being felt—to use an expression coined by Alvarez (2010): "the whatness" of the experience—and to give this precedence over why and by whom it is being felt.

Child and adolescent psychotherapists usually strive, to the best of their abilities, to maintain a sensitive and constructive balance between interpretations and such clarifying comments, but, even so, they might at times encounter entrenched impasses or overwhelming chaos. Thus, it is quite common for a child in a flooded and confused state of mind to subject his therapist to a torrent of accusations concerning acts with a certain resemblance to the child's earlier experience of neglect, lack of empathy, passivity, incongruent reactions, or even gross misconduct. Since the child is painfully engulfed by feelings in the present moment, it will usually not be helpful to mention this resemblance directly, but, at a later time, when the child actively questions and explores his identity and the therapeutic relationship, it could be productive to bring it up.

All the same, if a child should explode with anger in a direct attack on the therapy room or the therapist, hurling sand, water, or playthings around, it is usually important to ease the emotional strain and increase the therapeutic neutrality and distance. If that fails to resolve or delimit the child's flooded state, the key goal is to maintain a containing state of mind while firmly protecting the boundaries, the setting, and the safety of the child and oneself, making sure that no one is physically hurt. As mentioned above, it might occasionally be necessary to end the session prematurely (see Chapter Four).

In this work especially, therapists, as mentioned, need to pay particular attention to their own countertransference, which provides crucial input that is needed to prevent situations getting out of hand. They want to monitor their own wellbeing and states of mind, for instance, by being alert to their own, perhaps accumulating feelings of impoverishment and weakening of therapeutic competence. Thus, a child's recurrent meltdown into chaotic dissociation and despairing rage can wear down the resilience of any therapist, who might feel the continual exposure to aggressive avoidance, devaluation, and contempt as never-ending insults that she is powerless to influence. This behaviour is difficult to contain and might evoke fatalistic and moralistic attitudes in the therapist, along with tendencies towards idealising interventions that, in effect, subject the child to retaliation, social isolation, or expulsion. Thus, it is a sad part of reality that children and adolescents who have suffered severe early neglect and abuse, in later childhood and adolescence might be at risk of unconsciously restaging early depriving and abusive relationships, both in therapy and in their ordinary daily life. This phenomenon was named "double deprivation" by Henry (1974).

A common staging post before the child's ultimate loss of control can be desperate attacks on his own playthings and creative productions or outright self-destructive acts. This might include heart-breaking violence against the teddy bear or other favourite cuddly toy, which is cruelly attacked in more or less overt ways: for instance, cut open and disembowelled or having its fur or limbs cut off. In such situations, it is important that the therapist is neither passively numb nor feels compelled to intervene with a moralistic, prohibiting stance. What is needed is containment of a despair that is partly turned against the self and partly externalised. In these situations, from a neutral position, the therapist must calmly describe the feelings and phantasies that might be implied by the enacted roles of aggressor and helpless victim. As mentioned, it is essential to tactfully leave open the casting of roles and to avoid forcing the child to identify with one or the other of the two roles. Thus, if the therapist has the mental capacity to adopt a workable understanding, non-interfering distance, the child might be able, through play and actions, to impersonate—rather than violently enact—teddy as an abandoned, abused, unwanted infant *vis-à-vis* a harsh, unreliable, or fragile parental figure. When this happens, the child is often able to digest the therapist's carefully worded verbal description of teddy's feelings.

Hostile sibling figures in the child's inner world

Children who have suffered early neglect and abuse are generally acutely sensitive to traces of other children in the playroom. Correspondingly, a preponderant theme in their therapies is often the looming threat of fierce rivalry with hostile sibling figures. Sometimes, this has an early or even current experiential parallel in, for instance, violent sibling or peer relationships in a birth, adoptive, or foster family, or in a residential institution. Yet, it might, as well, concern the child's transference-related phantasies, in which emotional states of want and deficiency are unconsciously equated with dreadfully anxious and envious phantasies that the therapist is preoccupied with other, preferred children, who have snatched whatever crumbs of attention and affection are available, enjoying all the good things that were meant for the child.

In line with this, when a child suddenly despairs and, for example, claims that a specific doll from his personal toy box has gone missing, a favourite toy is broken, drawings and other creative productions are ugly or ruined, a common reason might be that the child has noticed, at a preconscious level (by Smith (1990) aptly named "at the perceptual edge of the transference"), that since the previous session, the furniture in the doll's house has been moved, or the sand in the sandbox has been soaked (see Chapter Five). If so, in a split second, a good working relationship could turn to chaotic and difficult rejection, demonstrated, for instance, by a turned back and the hidden, secretive play of a rejected, abused infant *vis-à-vis* uncaring parental figures in a hostile alliance with aggressively invasive sibling figures. Such intensely persecutory feelings and phantasies of hostile alliances between aggressive siblings and parental figures frequently turn up in these therapies as an underlying, subjective cause of the oft-described sudden states of mental flooding, somatic reactions, and aggressive attacks. Further, these states of mind can dominate for a considerable length of time and be quite difficult to ameliorate. Accordingly, one of the first indicators of real change in the child's emotional inner life—that is, in the balance between loving and hateful feelings—may be evidenced in an alteration from images of fiercely hostile sibling figures to ordinary mixed conceptions of other children as peers who contain both good and bad emotional qualities.

It is also important for the therapist to remember that, for these children, close attachments to real-life siblings or sibling-like peers during the early years might have provided lifesaving, parent-like qualities. For these children, the implicit invitation of individual psychotherapy to leave the cohesive unity of the sibling group in favour of an exclusive relationship with an adult could evoke severe feelings of guilt and survival-related anxiety. It could even be felt as a dangerous capitulation, in which case it might be necessary to begin the treatment with prolonged therapeutically supportive and explorative work with the sibling group. One of the aims of this approach is to support the children and (if possible) their parents or carers in a clarifying process that differentiates and describes the individual children's personal needs and characteristics (Grünbaum, 1998). Another aim of this work is to lessen the peer group pressure, creating space for the development of trust and attachment to caring adults. If this effort is successful, group processes related to sibling jealousy and envy are likely to become more salient, a development for which the children's current carers need to be emotionally prepared (A. Freud, 1955; A. Freud & Dann, 1951).

Especially with children who have experienced profound disillusionment, the therapist needs to be aware that a difficult split might develop when the child appears to be at the brink of recovery. Thus, while parents and teachers report that outside therapy, in everyday life, the child's social and emotional development progresses significantly, at the same time, the child's actions and attitudes towards the therapist in therapy are becoming increasingly sadistic and hostile. This marks a complex situation, since, even if the child's sadistic behaviour points to profound aggressive identification with antisocial, gang-like groupings, it can frequently function as unconscious protection against anxiety evoked by denied feelings of dependence in relation to a caring object in the transference to the therapist. If that is the case, manic moods and the idealisation of exclusive, antisocial gangs might, for a time, win out over depressive longings for the membership of an ordinary sibling-like group of peers (Grünbaum, 2014).

This particular combination of manic behaviour, devaluating rejection, and phantasies of conspiracy with equal-minded, hostile peers against adult authority in general—and the therapist in particular—has its origins in profound splitting and suspicion of adults and everything they stand for. Furthermore, this state of mind bespeaks the continued, hidden existence in the child's mind of dissociated pockets of secret fantasies of omnipotent identifications that serve to keep unspeakable dread at bay. As indicated above, this appears to be linked to unconscious phantasies of violently scary inner objects, who, in their appearance, combine and blur differences of age and sex, creating a subjective inner imagery of bizarrely combined siblings-cum-parental couples.

Children who have suffered early neglect and abuse face particular challenges in developing a stable identity. In working through, integrating, and detaching their personal identity from a burdensome past of family tragedies, the young person might, for some time, need to lean on somewhat omnipotent phantasies of peer group membership. Therefore, in the later stages of the therapy, working with identity issues often brings up issues related to memberships of peer groups or gangs. It might be difficult to differentiate between the pathological, defensive aspects of such phantasies and ordinary, developmental, healthy differentiation, where the child, to some extent, idealises peer groups as a means of detaching from infantile dependency on parental figures in order to gain more autonomy. Unfortunately, sometimes a young person succeeds in prematurely convincing his parents and/or the referring agency that he has recovered and has no further need of therapy. Yet, ending therapy at the peak of peer group idealisation is problematic, since the child—especially in late latency/early adolescence—needs to work through the fact that real and lasting change is not only a question of improved behaviour in the external world outside therapy, but also of internal development, which confronts the child with an existential choice between denied dependency and genuine autonomy. As these questions move centre stage, the therapist needs to relate to the child's choice between peer group or gang membership. At this point, the therapist needs to help the child understand that this is not a matter of fate, and that is not an either-or phenomenon. Rather, it is a developmental dilemma that the young person needs to confront as one of the ordinary dilemmas of life, and, like oedipal dilemmas, it has to be worked through in order for the child to find his own personal solution.

Psychotherapeutic strategies: working through early neglect and abuse

The following summary of recommended strategies was inspired by accumulated personal experience and recent reviews of case studies in child and adolescent psychotherapy (Grünbaum, 2014; Moestrup, 2016).

1. Active neutrality in a firmly defined, containing context. On the one hand, the therapist needs to be attentively observant of any flicker of the child's genuine feelings and motivation for change, ready to pick up and relate to them. On the other hand, she also needs to stay alert, ready to intervene quickly with firm authority in case of sudden impulsive, aggressive, or panic-stricken defensive attacks on the setting, the therapist, or the child himself.
2. Delicate observation of distance-related dilemmas. Based on her observations of the child and her own countertransference, the therapist should continuously monitor the geographical and mental distance between the child and herself, making an effort not to come too close, risking an overly intense and, hence, frightening relationship, or moving too far away, risking a shallow and lifeless relationship. An analogy would be a new-born, vulnerable infant, who needs the parents to stay fully receptive and attuned, not only to the infant's presently available sensory and

communicative channels, but also to his need for periods of repose.

3. Interpretation in a containing context. Before interpreting, the therapist needs to consider how the child might understand and react to the interpretation. In the long run, interpretations of feelings and unconscious phantasies aim at facilitating the child's self-insight, containment, and control, helping him to take ownership of his own feelings—whether pleasant or unpleasant. To achieve that, in a long beginning, the therapist must be aware that the child only slowly comes to build up trust, both in his own ability to endure an emotional experience without resorting to psychosomatic pain or impulsive, externalising, or self-harming behaviour, and in the therapist as a reliable helper.
4. Containment of countertransference feelings and phantasies. In order to intervene constructively, the therapist must at all times sustain a mindful consciousness of her own countertransference. Yet, she needs to be able to wait patiently and contain her own impressions, since finding the right moment to intervene depends on her observations of the child's ability to listen and contain.
5. Meticulous observation, timing, and wording of interpretations are crucial for the impact of the interpretations on the child. Especially when referring to painful feelings such as loss, longing, disappointment, disillusionment, despair, and related experiences, the therapist needs to build on her observations of the child, formulating her understanding in tentative and unsaturated ways that allow the child to maintain an emotional distance. This might, for instance, include interpretations that leave sufficient open space for the child himself to fill out, and which remind the child that feelings and actions are not the same, implying that the therapist and the therapy can survive whatever feelings the child might have.
6. Difficulties with symbolic thinking (mentalizing). Quite a few of these children might find it difficult to understand the as-if character of transference interpretations. Hence, when interpreting her own transference role, it could be appropriate for the therapist to add an explanation, worded in concrete terms, that clarifies her actual role in relation to the child. One could, for instance, mention that, of course, the therapist is not nearly as important

to the child as his parents in his everyday life, but that, nevertheless, most children will experience holidays and other breaks in the therapy as reminders of earlier loss and separation.

7. Awareness of the risk of double deprivation. The desperation, desolate and needy states, envy, and emotional impoverishment emanating from the child might not only resound in the therapist's countertransference but might also ripple through the teamwork, endangering the child's real-life relationships and the treatment alliance with parents and community workers responsible for the overall treatment organisation. Thus, an important task for the therapists working with the child and the parents is to prevent this accumulation of unbearable experiences and feelings by providing regular opportunities for the network to meet to air their feelings and points of views and discuss the impact of their collective efforts on the child's development.
8. Defensive pockets of dissociated, psychotic thinking can contain a kernel of real-life experiences leading to complex traumas. Early relationship disturbance, deprivation, and abuse often leave behind a certain fragile instability in the child's grip on reality. At certain times, therefore, the therapist will need to authenticate the child's differentiation between, on the one hand, the overwhelming real events of a traumatising past and, on the other hand, an inner reality flooded by needy states, helplessness, envy, and despairing rage and sorrow.
9. Working through the pain of loss, neglect, and abuse. Although a central part of the therapy revolves around working through painful, subjective memories of the child's personal past, this is not where the work begins. Initially, the child or adolescent will typically be unable to relate emotionally to these events and the related pain. A certain development of the therapeutic relationship is needed, particularly the transference-related aspects of the child's ability to contain and recognise his own depressive feelings towards the therapist, since this might reawaken and bring to life deeper, genuinely emotional resonance and related remembrance of early object experiences.

CHAPTER TWELVE

Psychotherapy with children who have suffered complex trauma

This chapter concerns psychotherapy with children and adolescents who experience extensive later ramifications of recurrent and prolonged, intentionally inflicted, and, therefore, complex traumatisation. Accordingly, included are neither preventative large-scale interventions and debriefing after acute trauma nor short-time individual interventions (including debriefing and preventative psychotherapy) aimed at dealing with traumatic stress reactions after a recent single traumatic experience.

A common denominator of the concepts of trauma, traumatisation, neglect, abuse, and deprivation, is the interaction between adverse, external events and the subjective reaction of the person experiencing these events. Consequently, there are certain overlaps between, on the one hand, children who suffer after-effects of *early* neglect and abuse—and related *early* traumatisation—and, on the other hand, children who suffer the repercussions of *complex* traumatisation. Thus, children suffering the effects of complex traumatisation might—but will not necessarily—also suffer after-effects of early neglect and abuse. This introductory proviso might seem unnecessarily cautious; however, it is included because, in our clinical experience, the therapeutic process with these two groups of children differs considerably.

What is traumatisation?

In a now classical overview of different types of traumatic exposure in childhood, Pynoos (1993, p. 208) distinguished between four main categories, based on the degree of deliberate and intentional assault.

1. Random catastrophes caused by natural and technological disasters, whether small- or large-scale: for instance, earthquake, fire, tsunami, nuclear reactor accident, etc.
2. Random accidents in which the child and his family are victimised by chance: for instance, by transportation calamities, burns, accidental shootings, etc.
3. Intra- and extrafamilial, intentional violence including:
   (a) kidnapping, hostage situations, community violence: for instance, related to criminal gangs;
   (b) political, ethnic, or religious persecution;
   (c) national and civil war, terrorism, torture;
   (d) internment in concentration camp;
   (e) physical and sexual abuse and witnessing violence against others (for instance, incest, rape, killing, interspousal violence, suicidal behaviour).
4. Life-threatening illness and consequent medical procedures, of course, are of another nature, since the medical procedures aim at cure or relief. All the same, both the illness in itself and the related medical practices might cause recurrent, comprehensive suffering affecting not only the stricken child, but also his siblings, parents, and grandparents, who are, thus, also exposed to a resultant risk of complex traumatisation.

As implied above and stressed by Cyrulnik (2001), traumatic events typically strike twice. The first blow comes from the external, potentially traumatising event in the form of immediate, disruptive consequences to the child's everyday life and attachment relationships. The second blow originates from the inner world, consisting of the person's psychological reaction to these outside events. Hence, regardless of how terrifying and prolonged the threatening, external events are, they imply a risk, but, in themselves, they are inconclusive as to whether a certain child or young person will develop lasting traumatisation. Thus, some children might be able, for instance, thanks to environmental support, to contain and mentalise the traumatising event and its consequences and get on with life, not entirely untroubled, of course, but without permanent injury to their personality development and mental health.

* * *

The World Health Organization's Classification of Mental and Behavioural Disorders, *ICD-10*, differentiates acute stress reaction—occurring immediately in connection with an exceptionally stressful life event—from post traumatic stress disorder (PTSD), which is a delayed, prolonged reaction to an exceptionally threatening or catastrophic event or situation (pp. 106–110). PTSD generally requires that certain symptoms develop within six months of the stressful event:

A. Exposure to a stressful event or situation (either short- or long-lasting) of an exceptionally threatening or catastrophic nature, which is likely to cause pervasive distress in almost anyone.
B. (1) Persistent remembering or "reliving" of the event (e.g., intrusive flashbacks, vivid memories, or recurring dreams), or
   (2) Experiencing distress when exposed to circumstances resembling or associated with the stressor (reminders).
C. Actual or preferred avoidance of circumstances resembling or associated with the stressor.
D. (1) Inability to recall, either partially or completely, some important aspects of the period of exposure to the stressor.
   (2) Persistent symptoms of heightened psychological sensitivity and physiological arousal (at least two of, e.g., sleep difficulties, irritability, difficulty in concentrating, hypervigilance, exaggerated startle response).
E. Criteria B, C, and D all occurring within six months of the stressful event or at the end of a period of stress.

This formulation of the PTSD diagnosis has, in general, been criticised as being too limited to capture the symptoms and developmental damage in children, adolescents, and even adults who have been exposed to prolonged man-made malevolence and cruelty in the form of recurrent, intrusive, often life-threatening assaults. In relation to adults, a description of such complex trauma has been labelled DESNOS: "disorders of extreme stress not otherwise specified"

(Luxenberg et al., 2001). Furthermore, for young children up to seven years of age, the World Health Organization's diagnostic criteria are not particularly suitable, even with regard to single trauma, and much less so for complex trauma. There is, however, a supplementary diagnostic classification system aimed especially at children: *DC:0–3R* (ZERO TO THREE, 2005). In this diagnostic system, the symptom pattern of PTSD is considered so important that it heads the list and is given priority over other diagnoses, provided that there is a relationship between the exposure of the child to a clear stress condition or traumatic event and the onset of symptoms.

According to *DC:0–3R*, a PTSD diagnosis requires that the symptoms have had a duration of at least a month, and all four of the below-mentioned criteria must be met (pp. 15–17):

1. The child has been exposed to a traumatic experience, whether a single event, a series of connected events, or a permanently recurrent stress situation.
2. The child shows evidence of re-experiencing the traumatic event(s) by displaying at least one of the following symptoms:
   (a) posttraumatic play—that is, play that re-enacts aspects of the trauma, is compulsively driven, fails to relieve anxiety, and is more literal and less elaborate and imaginative than usual;
   (b) recurrent and intrusive recollections of the traumatic event(s) outside play, for instance, represented by persistent questions;
   (c) recurring nightmares, the content of which may not necessarily be about the traumatic event(s);
   (d) physiological distress, expressed in language or behaviour, when exposed to reminders of the traumatic event(s);
   (e) Recurrent intrusive flashbacks or episodes of dissociation—that is, the child repeatedly re-enacts the event(s) without awareness of the source of these ideas and behaviours. The symptom may also present as repeated states of staring or freezing.
3. Numbing of responsiveness or interference with developmental momentum appears or intensifies after the traumatic event(s) and is revealed by at least one of the following symptoms:
   (a) increased social withdrawal;

   (b) restricted range of affect;
   (c) markedly diminished interest or participation in significant activities, including play, social interactions, and daily routines;
   (d) efforts to avoid activities, places, or people that arouse recollection of the trauma, including efforts to avoid thoughts, feelings, and conversations associated with the trauma. Tendencies of avoidance are particularly common in childhood.
4. Symptoms of increased arousal are generally frequent in traumatised children and present in similar ways to the above description of adult symptoms. According to this system, at least two of the following symptoms must be present:
   (a) difficulties going to sleep, for instance, bedtime protests, difficulties falling asleep, repeated night waking;
   (b) difficulties concentrating;
   (c) hypervigilance;
   (d) exaggerated startle response;
   (e) increased irritability, outbursts of anger, extreme fussiness, or temper tantrums.

The risk of developing childhood PTSD depends on a number of factors, among which the nature and duration of the traumatic event(s) seem important. Prolonged, recurrent, man-made trauma appears to increase the risk considerably. Further contributing factors include parental attitudes, the quality of caring relationships in the recovery milieu, the age and sex of the child, and probably also the quality of early attachments and the child's innate resources. Comorbidity, especially depression, conduct disorder, mixed disorders of conduct and emotions, anxiety disorders, and psychosomatic complaints, is common.

The prevalence of PTSD in children and adolescents (the rate of PTSD after the experience of one or more traumatic event(s)) and the life-time incidence of PTSD (how many children of a certain age will have displayed symptoms of PTSD at some point in the course of their life) varies considerably across studies, depending in part on the kind of trauma involved, what social and cultural groups the study included, and how and when the PTSD symptoms were assessed (Perrin et al., 2000). Evidence from recent systematic reviews suggests that among refugee children and adolescents, the prevalence of PTSD could range between seven and seventeen per cent, with an average of eleven per cent (Fazel et al., 2005). This seems in accordance with a Danish study, which found that up to sixteen per cent of a group of primary and secondary school children exposed to a huge fireworks disaster were still suffering from PTSD proper sixteen months after the event, while twenty-two per cent displayed PTSD symptoms at a subclinical level. The youngest children and the girls were most affected. Further, the results showed that somatic complaints were frequent, and that the parents often underestimated the suffering of their children (Duch & Elklit, 2008).

Immediately after direct exposure to a collective disaster, such as the atrocities of war, the prevalence of PTSD among the affected children and adolescents is likely to be considerably higher than at some point later in time, since most of the affected children and adolescents (but not all) will show a decline in the presence of symptoms. A survey of eighteen studies suggested a particularly high incidence of PTSD among directly exposed children one month after the event, with figures up to thirty-eight per cent (Neria et al., 2008). A longitudinal study of two hundred and seventeen young adults who had survived a shipwreck as adolescents found even a higher rate, with PTSD being present in up to fifty-one per cent, a third of whom had still not recovered five to eight years after the accident (Yule et al., 2000). A Danish study of adolescents in secondary school found that as many as eighty-seven per cent of the girls and seventy-eight per cent of the boys had experienced at least one potentially traumatic event, with a life-time prevalence of PTSD in nine per cent and subclinical PTSD symptoms in fourteen per cent of the included children (Elklit, 2002).

Developmental adaptation to complex traumatisation: a psychodynamic view

The term trauma originated as a medical term, derived from Greek, referring to a violent incident that led to physical injury by piercing the skin, thus causing a wound. In regard to acute mental trauma, the term implies a sudden, frightening, external event causing a violent shock and, thus, creating a psychic "wound" that affects the stricken individual's whole being and, *inter alia*, acutely disturbing ordinary mental equilibrium, poise, and adaptation. In the following, we distinguish between such an acute shock trauma and complex traumatisation.

An acute shock trauma is a sudden overwhelming experience in which the normal defensive and adaptive mental operations break down, resulting in a collapse of the ordinary barrier between the external and the inner world. Consequently, the affected person's consciousness is flooded by chaotic, confused impressions, in which the perception of external events can merge with fragments of normally unconscious, fundamental, anxiety-ridden phantasies. This leads to a painful mental state of paralysed helplessness, confusion, and a fundamental fear of dying.

Complex trauma refers to a more or less chronic condition stemming from a combination of recurrent, man-made shock trauma over extended periods—often over several developmental periods—against a background of persistently accumulating traumatic stress. In this context, the child, who is in a chronic state of hypervigilant alertness, is able, to a certain degree (consciously and unconsciously), to anticipate and do his best to avoid further traumatic blows. This persistent, complex situation might, in time, lead to developmental adaptation to continual traumatisation, in which case tendencies towards avoidance are constituted as a permanent personality disposition (see further explanation below).

This is the case for many children and adolescents growing up in traumatised refugee families, among others. They have often suffered repeated loss and violent personal assaults due to war, racially, religiously, or ethnically motivated cleansing, political persecution of their parents, or torture. A sad aspect of this reality is that complex traumatisation can be generationally transmitted, because persecution and torture affect and might reduce and distort parental capacities: for instance, by weakening the victims' self-control and capacity to provide empathic care to their children (Dalgaard & Montgomery, 2015; van Ee et al., 2016). In addition, both before and after immigration to a new country, children and adolescents are often, directly or indirectly, stressed by accumulating socioeconomic alienation, erosion of basic trust and feelings of safety, social isolation, lack of opportunities for playing with peers, learning difficulties, and health problems as a result of periodic deprivation of opportunities for schooling, education, and healthcare.

Other groups bearing increased risks of complex traumatisation are children and adolescents who have suffered psychosocial deprivation and/or sexual, physical, and mental abuse, as well as children who have witnessed violence between their parents and against their siblings. Further, a group that is often overlooked is older and younger siblings of children with life-threatening illnesses and disabilities, who run a double risk of complex traumatic exposure, sometimes stretching through their entire childhood. This is related, first, to their own feelings of loss, mourning, and guilt in relation to the chronically or terminally ill sibling. Second, they might experience prolonged deprivation of parental care and attention due to the parents' understandable difficulties in mustering the emotional and practical resources for attending to the needs of the afflicted child as well as his siblings, while, at the same time, struggling to contain their own mourning and despair. Third, the healthy child or children in the family might be traumatised by witnessing the sufferings of the parents and the afflicted sibling; thus, it is not unusual for the healthy child or children to be burdened by a semi-parental sense of responsibility.

The dynamics of developmental adaptation to complex traumatisation

Becoming accustomed to an everyday life steeped in threatening and overwhelming events and relationships posing a perceived threat to physical and/or mental survival forces the psyche of the child or young person to engage in a subjective adaptation to this chronic state of affairs.

Accordingly, developmental adaptation to complex traumatisation is understood as a lasting (re)structuring of strategies related to defence and adaptation to increase mental and bodily distance from potentially traumatic stimuli, whether the origin of these are to be found in recurrent exposure to threatening external events or in an inner world that is chronically stressed by anticipatory anxiety, humiliation, defeat, and despair. This kind of developmental adaptation implies the unconscious creation of a protective system aimed at minimising the risk of future traumatic reactions, primarily through avoidant defensive mechanisms with a dual focus:

1. A defensive strategy directed inwards aimed at decreasing the risk of further traumatic breakdowns by deleting, blunting, or, at

least, minimising the traces of shock trauma and related fear of dying.

2. An adaptive strategy directed towards the external world aimed at decreasing the risk of further assaults by means of certain alterations in social behaviour. These alterations might involve subjective variations of fundamentally defensive behavioural patterns related to survival, such as fight, flight, submissive dependency, or ganging up with stronger peers, which Bion (1961) described as characteristic behavioural patterns in unfamiliar, anxiety-provoking situations.

By adapting developmentally to complex trauma, the child buys some degree of inner peace; however, this relief comes at a high price in other developmental areas, including the resulting unconscious paralysis of the capacity for mentalizing personal experiences. Furthermore, the achieved peace of mind is fragile and bound to break down at regular intervals, giving way to compulsive repetitions. Thus, in action, the child communicates an ongoing inner catastrophic event that is no longer recognised as part of himself and, therefore, cannot be communicated in words. When this happens, an empathic observer might recognise behavioural fragments that could be said to contain the beginning of the child's subjective narration of his original experience of the relationship and context of the recurrent traumatisation (for an example, see Chapter Eleven, four-year-old Joseph). This constant tension between tendencies towards avoidance and re-experiencing is often called the dialectics of trauma.

In children and adolescents, traumatic repetition compulsion tends to appear especially during quiet moments or moments of acute stress, since, in both these situations, dissociated, fragmented forms of re-experiencing can intrude painfully into the conscious mind. Hence, due to momentary breaches of the normal barrier between conscious and unconscious thoughts, fragments of formerly repressed, forgotten, or uncomprehended traumatic experiences might cohere and momentarily flood the child's consciousness, like revolting flotsam, shattering his hopes of recovery and causing an inner catastrophe of disillusionment and heart-breaking loss of faith in the goodness of his objects. In metaphorical terms, the child's inner world could be compared to a terrifying abyss of unspeakable horrors that floods the child's mind, causing a state of "nameless dread", to borrow Bion's term (1962b). Children and adolescents will do just about anything to avoid becoming fully aware of these inner images and feelings, and, hence, in a split second, the flooded states of mind can be replaced by acute enactment of, for instance, separation anxiety, manic movement, paranoid panic-rage, empty states of mind, etc.

The developmental price to pay for this mental adaptation to permanent trauma includes a continual destabilisation of the child's sense of reality, increased risk of recurrent dissociative episodes, emotional and, sometimes, even cognitive inhibition, disturbance of self-insight and social skills, and a consequent risk of social isolation. These impairments interfere with the child's later personality development, as he might not only eschew the social interactions required for his further personality development, but might also miss out, entirely or partly, on learning from social and emotional experiences. Over time, this will cause comprehensive damage to his personality structure.

Psychotherapeutic insights and challenges

The most common reasons for referring children and adolescents to psychotherapy who have suffered complex trauma are difficulties in the parent–child relationship, social isolation, and/or bullying (with the child as victim or perpetrator) in relation to peers, learning difficulties, attacks of panic, anxiety, and/or peculiar behavioural patterns that emerge suddenly, and which parents and teachers describe as incomprehensible, without intent or meaning. Prevailing passivity or the reverse, manic/hyperactive behaviour, is often part of the description. The parents might be aware that, over a number of years, the child's personality has changed from an ordinary confident child with ordinary conflicts and concerns to a child or adolescent who remains socially aloof and is pained by sudden states of depression, anxiety, confusion, or rage, apparently appearing without warning, like a bolt of lightning from a clear sky.

Destabilised parental objects reverberate in the child's present relationships with his real parents

Complex traumatisation affects the child's basic trust in his parents and can cause permanent damage to the parent–child relationship.

This is even more pronounced if the parents themselves have suffered complex traumatisation. Thus, the feasibility and impact of child psychotherapy and the concurrent work with the parent(s) normally requires the completion of an adequate, family-orientated assessment that sorts out individual and family needs for treatment and support with a view to implementing relevant community interventions (Grünbaum, 1998).

Relating to adults who had been subjected to torture, Laub and Auerhahn (1993) described a tendency in phantasy to blame the parental figures of the inner world, assigning them a degree of responsibility in the complex chain of traumatising events. In our experience, the same applies to children and adolescents, who might have a general feeling that what happened was the result of a fundamental, unforgivable parental fault. Irrespective of the real parents' actual part in recurrent traumatic assaults, this feeling tends to blanket the child's subjective, inner world. Thus, whether the parents were the aggressors or were themselves the helpless victims of overpowering attacks, or whether, as adoptive parents, they might not even have met the child until after the event(s), in the child's unconscious phantasy, they can become the targets of blame. This might continue—even years after the actual traumatic assaults, when the child's family life has improved—as pervasively flooded and terrorised states of mind dominating his inner world, causing incessant traumatic despair, which, over and over again, reproduces the traumatic breakdown of the child's inner connection with good (supportive and reliable) parental objects. In this way, the complexly traumatised child's deep subjective conviction of betrayal can be compulsively repeated: for instance, in dissociative episodes, fragments of play, and, especially, nightmares with narrative scenarios of catastrophe, in which parental figures are allotted persecuting and selfish roles, perhaps even in supernatural ways. This unconscious inner destruction of good object relationships continually chips away at the child's fundamental trust in the benign omnipotence of his parental figures. The ongoing inner processes in the aftermath of complex trauma thus amplify the paranoid aspects of the ordinary ambivalence between children and their parents, which might profoundly undermine the real-life relationship between the child and his parents, especially during adolescence (Grünbaum, 2010b).

In this way, complex trauma not only adversely affects the child's personality and future development, but might also undermine his family relationships. Thus, concurrent parent work often needs to be supplemented with specific psychoeducation about acute traumatic reactions in children and adolescents and about the differences between, on the one hand, ordinary developmental crises and temporary developmental problems, and, on the other, sequelae of complex traumatic experience. Whether or not the parents themselves are complexly traumatised, as mentioned, they tend to underestimate the sufferings of their traumatised children and often find it difficult to discuss the calamitous family history. Accordingly, the parents often need to discuss with their therapist what their children know and what they need to know, and, if possible, it might be appropriate to supplement the work with family consultations.

Beginnings of psychotherapy: survival and avoidance

In later childhood and adulthood, the complexly traumatic events are not necessarily present in the mind as conscious, episodic memories, but might, instead, be evident in tendencies towards avoidance, muddled states, strange visions, bodily sensations, compulsive thoughts or acts, and, not least, petrified, painfully collapsed or empty states. Although the meaning of these states and behaviours is often obscure, and the child typically tends to deny their existence, descriptions offered by parents and teachers clearly suggest that when they occur, something experienced as ego-alien has possessed the child (Kaplan, 2006; Terr, 1991).

At the time of referral, what preoccupies the parents most is often an anxious and sad realisation that certain traumatising events appear to have changed their child; for instance:

"He changed completely during those terrible three years when we lived together with X."

"She has not been herself since they took her from me at the prison, back in X-land. For several weeks, none of us knew where she was kept; in fact, we still don't know."

"The agonising ordeal was his sister's illness. Since she passed away, he has been completely out of sorts. We were crushed by her illness and death, that's why we didn't realise until several years later. But now, he's nothing like the happy boy we knew when he was little."

The parents' experience that their child has a "changed" personality after being exposed to severe recurrent and/or prolonged trauma, strain, and loss is, in itself, a valid reason for an offer of child or adolescent psychotherapy and concurrent support for the parents. However, once the child's actual psychotherapy begins, the therapist must bracket this and other causal explanations and base her work on the issues revealed by the child's own subjective narrative.

Children who have suffered complex trauma often are unable to speak directly and in details about past abuse and hardship. Instead, they often go to great pains to avoid thinking of these experiences. Their motivation for the therapeutic work can, rather, be found in their personal experience of present-day problems, often derived from compulsive repetition and strategies of avoidance and survival, or, for instance, glimpsed in nightmares or sudden flashbacks, states of alarm, inability to tolerate certain sounds, painful feelings of inner emptiness and stress, a fear of falling apart, and problematic relationships with peers, teachers, and parents. The initial therapeutic contact with the child or young person is often characterised by silence, separation anxiety, and passivity, or, conversely, with manic activity. These states of mind, therefore, need to be contained before the process can move forward.

> Adel (seven-and-a-half years old at referral) was an only child who had spent his first five years of life in an ordinary caring and secure extended family, closely attached to his paternal grandparents. The outbreak of an atrocious civil war forced the parents to flee their country with Adel on short notice, separating from the rest of the family. They fled to an equally dangerous neighbouring country, where they were captured with false identity papers and imprisoned under brutal and depriving conditions, the mother and Adel together, the father in another prison. During the following eight months, Adel, now five to six years old, witnessed the violent mental and physical abuse of his mother and other female prisoners. During an especially scary and chaotic series of events, he was separated from his mother, who found him hours later in a state of shock, literally scared stiff. After they were released, the family was granted asylum in Denmark, where, six months later, Adel was referred for psychotherapy because of panicky separation anxiety, general irritability with frenzied breakdowns, and unprovoked, violent attacks on other children. He could not handle being on his own, even for short periods, and seemed constantly on guard, expecting new disasters. In

particular, he constantly had to keep an eye on his parents, anxious that they might disappear. In class, he was distressed, constantly crying, and unable to learn. According to the parents, he had developed into a very different child from the Adel they knew before the flight. Since Adel and the therapist did not speak the same language, an interpreter was present during the sessions. The following is an excerpt from the first session of his twice-weekly therapy.

Adel lines soldiers up against each other. A ferocious battle ensues; many soldiers are stabbed in the stomach, and only a few survive. As this unfolds, he remains silent, moving the soldiers around on the table without any facial expression, while they fight and drop dead without a sound. The distinction between the fighting parties is chaotic; it is almost impossible to tell friend from enemy, and it is unclear which party Adel favours. (I am struck by the contrast between his violent experiences and the highly controlled, unemotional mood of his play. After some time, I suggest that it is scary to be caught in the middle of a war; so scary, in fact, that one might become all stiff and frozen inside, as if one were dead). Adel appears to ignore my comment, but he stops his activity, blinks intensely and rubs his eyes. He comments on this, saying that when he looks at something for too long, his eyes always tear up. He takes more soldiers and other playthings, then sits quite still for some time, appearing to be a million miles away, as he silently claws into the toys with his fingernails. Later, he plays at the table, building a fenced-in area, which holds a cow and a dog. Still silent and with an expressionless face, he adds dolls, a mother and two grandparents, positioned as far away from the fighting soldiers as possible. He adds more and more dolls, apparently without any system, randomly scattering child dolls of both sexes and different ages. He picks up an infant doll, intends to place it in the arms of a mummy doll, but the mummy doll keels over and drops the baby, who falls to the floor. Adel stops, again vigorously rubbing his eyes, saying, "They always tear up when I look at something for too long." (I suggest that his eyes might want to cry because mummy dropped the baby on the floor.) "No, no," he says, irritated, "they just do that." He removes a doll from the fenced-in area "to go to school". Then he loses interest in the play. The rest of the session he sits on the floor beside his toy box, pulling and clawing at different objects until they fall apart, which, apparently, he does not seem to notice. From time to time, he asks what time it is.

During the following months, Adel oscillated between short sequences of play, which he suddenly disrupted, quiet passivity, and the destruction of toys and other materials, which he silently, and apparently without emotion, clawed and pulled to shreds. Towards me, he remained silent and aloof. (I found his silent destruction so sad and nearly unbearable to witness.) At other times, he targeted a woman figure standing at a platform, coldly aiming bricks at her until she fell down. (This activity resembled someone being stoned to death; it echoed in my mind as deeply disturbing, bringing anxious thoughts that before the flight, Adel might have witnessed such public executions in the family's country of origin.)

The stonings went on for months, but disappeared after an interpretation of Adel's present transference feelings (my suggestion that this doll had to be stoned when he felt really angry with me).

Repetition compulsion and inhibition of symbol formation

In therapy with these children and young persons, a tendency to bog down typically occurs sooner or later. At first, it seems to emerge almost imperceptibly, perhaps as parallel inhibitions in the child's play and the therapist's thinking. As is often the case with wordless impasses, the therapist's countertransference is an important source of information, and sometimes it is the only one. Gradually, the child's ability to play might falter, ultimately coming to a complete standstill and being displaced by a frozen position of hypervigilance. This mental state could transition into mind-numbing sensory activities, such as the child stroking or grinding the sand with his fingers, monotonously fingering a plaything, compulsively sucking and biting his fingers, the inside of his cheeks, other body parts, or his jersey, rhythmically swaying back and forth, or maybe banging bricks, his hand, or even his head against things.

At the same time, the therapist might notice an increasing absence of symbolic meaning as a resonant silence seems to spread, not only in the external reality of the therapy room, but also inside her own mind. Parallel with this, she might experience difficulties in her ability to contain the child's silent, edgy, or manic states of mind. The manic states might present as bursts of loud activity; for instance, monotonously scraping a car or other plaything hard against the bottom of the sandbox, producing a metallic, tinny sound which the therapist perceives as intensely invasive. At other times, as the silence spreads both in the therapist's mind and in the therapy room; the therapist might feel engulfed by half bodily, half mental discomfort, sleepiness, confusion, or even paranoid feelings and phantasies.

Symbolic play, repetition compulsion, and re-enactment of trauma in the transference relationship

As eloquently described by, among others, Winnicott (1971a) and Caper (1996), play and other forms of creative activity presuppose the ability mentally to maintain an experimental space between inner, subjective phantasy and external reality. This ability is what enables ordinary healthy children to mentally process and contain acutely experienced, single trauma through short-term psychodynamic play psychotherapy and concurrent parent support (Ryan & Needham, 2001).

As described above, complex traumatisation often impairs the ability to differentiate between external and internal realities, for instance, between one's own and other peoples' feelings and states of mind. Thus, sometimes, playing loses its make-believe character, bringing past traumatic reality too close to conscious thought, so that it suddenly feels much too real and is abruptly interrupted. The sudden interruptions can be understood as the child's attempts to contain painfully traumatised states of mind, probably such moments when subjectively processed memory fragments of past traumatising episodes threaten to invade ordinarily unconscious, developmental phantasies about relationships. This tendency is most probably augmented by certain similarities between unconscious, developmental phantasy images and the bodily and mental maltreatment inherent in torture, sexual abuse, and other cruelties. Probably, the same unconscious mechanisms are involved in mental blocks of the ability to dream, leading to post-trauma nightmares (Grünbaum, 2010a).

Most complexly traumatised children might, accordingly, be able to engage in play briefly, but these short sequences of creative and symbolic play soon dwindle into monotonous activity, compulsively revolving around the sore spots: the traumatic source of inhibition. Hence, before and after the resulting empty states, it is essential that the therapist notices in detail what was going on, both in play and within the transference relationship between herself and the child. Thus, just before the interruption, meaningful and important symbolic work might have taken place, where the child related certain aspects, however tiny and diffuse, of traumatic memory to the therapist, whether by playing, talking, drawing, or in other ways.

Nevertheless, as described in Chapter Five, even when working with traumatised children, the psychodynamic psychotherapist's prime task is not to be concerned with the historical past but, rather, with the influence of the past on the present moment as a cognitive–emotional template shaping the child's present experiences in and of the therapeutic relationship. Focusing her attention on the way in which the traumatic memory colours the present relationship between herself and the child, she can gradually help the child to make the emotional connection between transference phantasies and repetition compulsion. This linking can often cause undigested memory fragments from past traumatising assaults to surface in the child's consciousness, causing strategies of survival and avoidance to intensify and become re-enacted in the therapeutic relationship. This is a crucial point in therapy, and, to the therapist, it is a particularly moving experience to be a part of. Thus, amid increasingly confusing combinations of symbolic play, concrete repetition–enactment, and empty periods, episodes with a certain resemblance to past traumatic experiences occur. Initially, so briefly that the therapist might be unsure and has to debate with herself whether her knowledge of the child's personal history and development disturbs her sense of reality—for instance, whether "crying" really was an appropriate word to use in relation to Adel's eyes. When working with children like Adel, such sudden doubts about one's own sense of reality are quite common and often signify that something important is being denied by the child. Relative to the phrase, "I didn't believe my eyes", one may assume that this particular countertransference phenomenon could reflect an echo of the multi-traumatised child's self-protective attempts at schizoid avoidance, creating a sense of unreality, depersonalisation, and loss of control.

Children and adolescents are likely to adapt to their own psychopathology. Initially, they might not realise that repetition compulsion is a symptom that occurs for a meaningful reason but will be much more inclined to dismiss it as an accidental, ego-alien habit occurring by chance. Ultimately, such a child might even flatly deny that a present-moment fragment of behaviour, as described by the therapist, occurred at all. In the experience of the child, these are meaningless chance occurrences, like Adel's belief that looking too long at something in itself caused him to tear up. At this point, it is important for the therapist to be able to remain silently empathic, neither giving up on nor putting pressure on the child, but, rather, persisting in her efforts to find a suitable, unsaturated verbal statement that the child can recognise and fill in with his own details.

Working through fragmented memories of complex trauma

A central, oft-discussed technical issue relates to the question of whether, and if so, when and how, the therapist should more actively introduce verbal references to the child's actual real-life traumatic history. Opinions range from therapists preferring a fairly early, direct introduction of what they feel are the emotionally salient aspects of the traumatising chain of events (Gaensbauer, 1994) to therapists who refrain completely from direct references (Lanyado, 2004).

In our experience, it is usually helpful if the therapist, at some point, directly describes her observations of the child's tendency towards repetition, linking this to related phantasy formations and tentatively suggesting certain links to specific aspects of his traumatic history. However, interventions of this sort should not come too early, because, to be able to digest them mentally, the child needs the framework of a rich transference relationship that supports a certain degree of risk-taking. Whether or not the child perceives such an interpretation as meaningful depends on whether the previous work has sufficiently clarified his tendencies in the transference relationship to repeat such anxious, aggressive–passive adaptations to a permanent situation of complex traumatisation. This stepping stone is a necessary precondition for interpretations of past traumatic events to achieve cognitive–emotional life in the present moment, thus becoming relevant to the child's present experience of himself and his relationships.

In these therapies, it might be necessary for the therapist to be slightly more actively explicit and literal than with most other children. Linking to past trauma can be done directly in a verbal interpretation, for instance, by describing the connections linking present reactions and symptoms to specific aspects of past traumatic events. It can also be done as an enacted intervention in the child's play activity, for instance, with the introduction of missing details and figures known to be central, both from the therapist's previous work with the child and from case files and interviews with the parents. Whichever way this gentle push is provided, it is important for the therapist to observe and sensitively follow the leads offered by the child, taking care not to introduce references to traumatic real-life events arbitrarily, but only in response to the child's subjective communication. This can facilitate a process—often initially perceived as unwanted by the child—in which further inner images and other kinds of memory fragments surface in the mind of the child. Therefore, meaningful work with fragmented memories proceeds in an uneven fashion, like travelling on a bumpy road, often interrupted by avoidance, as the child repeatedly returns to a not-knowing state, where previous therapeutic progress suddenly appears to be swept away. These reactions are indicative of a flooded state, in which severe anxiety sparks a self-protective schizoid splitting of the inner world, causing a state of total or partial traumatic amnesia.

In the course of time, as traumatic memories are gradually worked through, several, usually concurrent, developments are normally set in motion.

1. Genuinely symbolic representations of certain parts or aspects of traumatic chains of events come to stand out.
2. Tendencies towards identifying with the aggressor(s) might, at certain times, give rise to sadistic or masochistic enactments of traumatic object relationships, perhaps primarily represented in play scenarios and drawings or, perhaps, more or less openly fixed on the therapist and relived as transference phenomena.
3. The appearance of new glimpses of episodic memory are verbalised, retold, and shared in verbal dialogue with the therapist. In these dialogues, an important aspect of therapeutic intervention is to address and mobilise the child's anger over maltreatment and abuse. Thus, as described above, due to developmental adaptation to trauma, the child typically unconsciously blanks out this legitimate anger and needs help to retrieve the aggressive feelings and to direct them outwards rather than towards the self.

At a certain point in the therapeutic process, an important turning point might appear, stemming from a situation where the therapist, more or less intuitively, helps the child (re-)create links between traumatic experiences and fundamental, developmental phantasies, for instance, about dependence *vs.* separateness and the oedipal constellation. We understand this development as an indicator that the dissociative chasm is on its way to healing, connecting one compartment of the mind, in which eternal traumatic repetition compulsion resides, with another, healthy compartment, in which the creative potential of unconscious object related phantasies resides.

Complex traumatisation and psychotherapeutic strategies: a summary

The main methodical points brought forward in this chapter are recapitulated below.

1. At the referral of a child who has suffered complex traumatisation, the receiving agency needs to be aware that the adverse sequelae of complex traumatisation might affect the entire family; thus, an effective intervention often requires an extended, family-orientated assessment, which involves and assesses the needs of parents and siblings.
2. When she initiates the therapy process, the therapist has to bracket her knowledge of the child's traumatic personal history, instead focusing on the child's way of using the therapist and the therapeutic relationship. Thus, the therapist needs to focus on the child's subjective complaints, especially on the way in which strategies of survival, avoidance, and repetition are played out in relation to the therapist.
3. The therapist can facilitate the emergence of narrative memories by working in the present moment of the transference, doing her best to link the child's subjective experiences of painful symptoms with his tendencies towards the compulsive repetition of behavioural patterns, thematic play sequences, and nightmares.
4. Working through memories of traumatic chains of events requires a strong transference relationship, in which the therapist opens her mind to allow the child's catastrophic experiences, expectations of recurrent traumatisation, and related protective strategies to resonate in her own mind in a process of reverie,

containment, and mentalisation that gives rise to her own subjective understanding in the form of personal images, feelings, and thoughts.

5. At this point, the therapist's mentioning of key aspects of the child's traumatic past can have a vital catalytic effect, provided that the description also conveys her understanding of how the child has subjectively added personal meaning to these past experiences.
6. Working through traumatic memories is an uneven process, characterised by the dialectics of trauma: that is, by mostly unconscious (but sometimes conscious) movements towards and away from the traumatic memories and feelings.
7. An important part of working through past maltreatment, abuse, and alienation is to address the child's legitimate anger in an effort to deflect this anger from the self and direct it instead at the perpetrators.

PART V

RESEARCH IN PSYCHODYNAMIC CHILD AND ADOLESCENT PSYCHOTHERAPY

CHAPTER THIRTEEN

The present state of research in psychodynamic child and adolescent psychotherapy

Over the years, systematic empirical research in child and adolescent psychotherapy has been repeatedly described as lagging behind the corresponding research in adult psychotherapy (e.g., Boëthius & Berggren, 2000; Mortensen, 2010; Windaus, 2006). The lag has been particularly pronounced with regard to psychodynamic psychotherapy and psychoanalysis of children and adolescents (Kazdin, 2003). This might still be true; none the less, the field has undergone considerable development, and today we have fairly thorough knowledge of the results of child and adolescent psychotherapy, both in general and for special groups. We will return to this point later. First, however, it seems justified to take a closer look at special complications associated with research in psychotherapy with children and adolescents that contribute to a slower development in this field compared to adult psychotherapy.

Special complications in research involving children and adolescents

The greater difficulties associated with child and adolescent research in comparison with research involving adults stem partly from the complexity of child and adolescent psychotherapy, which has been described in the preceding chapters. We have emphasised (see Chapter Three) that children are not independent persons in physical, psychological, or legal terms, but are heavily dependent on their parents (or other carers). Therefore, parents have to be taken into consideration from the outset, in connection with planning and preparing a research project. Among other things, they have to consent to both their own and their children's participation, and they are involved at every stage of the assessment and treatment process, too.

Research has increasingly demonstrated the importance of a good working alliance between the therapist and the client for the outcome of psychotherapy. In child and adolescent psychotherapy, however, it is not only the alliance with the child that is important; to a large extent, the alliance with the parents is also essential for both the implementation and the maintenance of the psychotherapy process.

At every stage of a treatment, from the very first contact until the end, the parents' participation increases the cost, the necessary allocation of time, the complexity of the research design, the number of variables, and the range of possible interpretations of the findings.

Another complication is the fact that children have only a limited capacity for verbalising their problems. That is, of course, especially true for younger children, but even adolescents can have difficulties describing their feelings and ideas in words. Thus, a number of common assessment instruments, such as questionnaires and interviews, are of limited value. Often, more indirect methods are necessary, such as tests, observation, or information from parents and teachers. Through projective tests and play, the child reveals information about himself in symbolic form—that is, in a language that has to be interpreted by the examiner in order to be understood. That requires clinical experience on the part of the researcher and also makes it more difficult to validate the results.

Information from parents and teachers often differs substantially from the information children and adolescents provide about themselves (e.g., Achenbach & Rescorla, 2007; Cantwell & Rutter, 1994; Fonagy & Target, 1996). This further complicates the issues of reliability and validity.

Yet another factor that contributes to the complexity of research in child and adolescent psychotherapy is the fact that children continuously develop. Under any circumstances, the child will change during the course of psychotherapy, and it can be difficult to determine whether the changes are due to the therapy or simply reflect the child's general age development and maturation. All these factors have a consequence that research with children and adolescents makes greater demands on both time and economic resources than research with adult subjects. Also, as already mentioned, there are special problems regarding reliability and validity.

The relationship between practice and science

The ideal of the scientist–practitioner in the field of psychotherapy is old and well founded (Shakow et al., 1947). Researchers who do not have a practice background and who lack personal experience with the field they are studying run the risk of conducting research that fails to address the complicated conditions characteristic of practice, not least when it comes to psychodynamic child and adolescent psychotherapy.

This ideal has always been difficult to live up to, and, often, a bigger or smaller gap has existed between practitioners and scientists. Historically, the culture of clinical practice has differed significantly from the culture of science, and the two have been difficult to reconcile. Even today, it is not easy to be the only researcher in a treatment culture. One is easily seen as an intruder, as someone who is wasting the limited time of the practitioners, who does not produce anything of value, and who works much too slowly. Conversely, a practitioner in a research culture might be seen as something of a quack, who acts without proper validated knowledge. As Midgley (2008) commented, even if things have improved in recent years, the actual relationship between researchers and psychotherapists has long been characterised by mutual distrust and even, at times, contempt.

Practising psychotherapists have often been blamed for their lack of interest in incorporating research findings into their practice. In return, they have often felt the results of the research to be dull and irrelevant. The criticism aimed at practitioners is well known and widely accepted; it is, perhaps, less known and acknowledged that some aspects of the criticism of the research field have also been justified.

When it comes to the evaluation of the effect of psychotherapy, randomised controlled trials (RCTs) are generally regarded as the highest standard of research, and this format is often used to justify that a treatment can be regarded as evidence-based. RCTs require the inclusion of a control group and a random distribution of the subjects to a treatment and a control group. This type of research is, however, not easily applied to child and adolescent psychotherapy. That kind of research generally requires the involvement of relatively large groups of subjects, matched with regard to a specific diagnosis or symptomatology, and excluding patients with comorbidity. This makes for a very unnatural population, however, as the vast majority of the children and adolescents seen in practice have several diagnoses. It is, for example, known that only twenty per cent of all children referred to treatment have no complicating factors (Kennedy, 2004).

Most of the RCT research in child and adolescent psychotherapy did not include clinic populations, but only selected children in a laboratory setting. Often, the subjects have been schoolchildren, but not children referred for treatment. Their problems have, consequently, rarely been as serious as those found in clinical practice, and the children's family backgrounds have often been better. In addition, the duration of treatment has often been short, eight to ten weeks, whereas ordinary clinical treatment usually lasts one to two years; the treatment has often taken place in groups, and the therapists have not always been well trained. Often, the parents have not been included either. The criteria for improvement have often been simple, such as cessation of symptoms (e.g., Kazdin, 2002).

The present diagnostic systems, *ICD* (*International Classification of Diseases*) and *DSM* (*Diagnostic and Statistical Manual of Mental Disorders*), constitute a special problem in research. At a time when we know more than ever before about the significance of the early relationships between the child and his carers, it is paradoxical that we use diagnostic systems which rely exclusively on descriptions of symptoms and almost completely exclude relational circumstances. As it is only possible to operate with a limited number of variables at a time in empirical outcome research, the use of simple symptom-based diagnoses is quite suitable there, but it has resulted in much greater knowledge about treatment of simple disturbances without comorbidity and without serious complications than about treatment of more extensive and complicated states; also, it has told us more about the short-term effect of treatment than about the long-term effect (Kennedy, 2004).

However, most psychological disturbances in children are chronic or recurrent, different psychological disturbances often occur together, comorbidity is common, and both symptoms and disorders often change in the course of the child's development (Carlberg, 2009). Often, family and other environmental problems also play a part. All this has as its consequence that outcome research, which only takes the diagnoses into consideration, must be regarded as insufficient. In psychodynamic child and adolescent psychotherapy, the diagnosis is not necessarily the factor of greatest importance; rather, the focus is on the child's total personality and his interactions with his environment. The aim is not primarily to remedy the obvious symptoms but, rather, to try to understand and influence the child's understanding of his inner world. External factors that influence the child's life circumstances are, of course, no less important to take into consideration and seek to modify, if necessary. In relation to research, it means that it is not sufficient to measure the outcome of treatment on the potential cessation of symptoms, but that other characteristics of the child need to be examined as well. It is, however, not always easy to know which are the best measures of the outcome, and it might prove necessary to develop new outcome measures.

Neither the question of control groups nor that of randomisation is simple when it comes to research in psychotherapy. For ethical reasons, it cannot be justified to have control groups that do not receive any kind of treatment. This problem is often solved through a comparison of groups of clients referred to different kinds of treatment. However, a random distribution of clients to different forms of treatments, which would be the most appropriate method from an empirical research point of view, is not a good solution. Clients often have an opinion about what type of treatment they prefer, and they could withdraw from the treatment if they are offered a form they do not like.

Regardless of how important quantitative research is, it is necessary to acknowledge that studying the outcome of psychodynamic child and adolescent psychotherapy alone is not enough. As mentioned, quantitative research can only operate with a limited number of variables at a time, and—even more important—it is not suitable for describing, for example, inner states or more complicated psychological patterns. When that is the intended target, it is necessary to use qualitative methods as well and to base the research on a phenomenological and interpretative foundation.

To yield results that are perceived as relevant by practitioners, research, thus, requires personal acquaintance with the issues that are actually found in practice. Consequently, not only must clinicians have some knowledge of research and research methods, researchers also need training in, and experience with, clinical practice. Both types of training are, however, time-consuming and expensive, and to enable this dual awareness will require institutions to offer combined training in both fields.

During the past ten to fifteen years, however, a mutual rapprochement between practitioners and researchers has taken place. Some of the larger training institutes for psychotherapists, such as the Tavistock Institute in London and the Erica Foundation in Stockholm, now combine training in child and adolescent psychotherapy with training in research. Over the past twenty years, a programme of practice-based research has been developed at the Tavistock Institute, where all future psychotherapists will receive basic training in research methodology with the possibility of advanced PhD training.

It has also been necessary to develop and use systematic qualitative methods, often originally developed for use in sociology or psychology. This has led to a considerable increase in and renewal of research designs and methods, which allows for other forms of research than the traditional RCT format and still offers valid results.

The problem of how to enlist sufficiently large populations can, for example, be solved through co-operation among several treatment institutions (e.g., several treatment schools). This approach is organisationally demanding and increases the vulnerability to changes in the participating institutions, but, as has been shown in several studies, it is feasible (e.g., Nissen & Hansen, 2006; Trowell et al., 2007).

Research in child and adolescent psychotherapy is more important than ever, and the growing awareness of the usefulness and effectiveness of psychotherapy in society at large is justified. It is, therefore, essential that we, as psychotherapists, are able to demonstrate the effectiveness of our work.

It may be debated which concept of evidence should form the basis of the evaluation of research studies, but the requirement that treatment must be evidence-based is probably here to stay.

Historical development

In the following, we describe some main features of the development of research and some of the findings. According to McLeod (2001), research in psychodynamic child and adolescent psychotherapy has progressed in three stages: until about 1950, the emphasis was on description and exploration, and the primary research approach was single-case studies. During the second phase, from about 1950 on, there has been growing political pressure to examine the effectiveness of child and adolescent psychotherapy. The pressure has further increased with the spread of evidence-based medicine and psychiatry, where it is claimed that no treatment should be offered (particularly not paid for by public means) unless there is sufficient scientific evidence for its effect. Most of the above-mentioned outcome research was conducted during this phase, but, as described, it has been of somewhat limited value for psychodynamic child and adolescent psychotherapy. Kazdin (2002) mentions that almost 1,500 studies of child and adolescent psychotherapy have shown its effectiveness, but, for the above-mentioned reasons, there is growing awareness that many of the results from this research cannot be generalised to ordinary clinical practice.

During the third, present phase there are still efforts to establish an evidence base by means of "scientific" empirical methods, but there are also new sophisticated qualitative methods available for elucidating psychodynamic questions.

As also pointed out by Michael Rustin (2009), research in psychodynamic psychotherapy has existed since the beginning, originally in the form of single-case descriptions, conceptual analyses, discussions in clinical workshops, etc. The significance of all this work, which led to a rapid development of child and adolescent psychotherapy in regard to both new theoretical concepts and changing methods, should not be underestimated. This kind of research still exists and will probably continue to be as important as ever. No matter how valuable, as mentioned, qualitative studies are not sufficient to meet present-day requirements of evidence-based results.

Over the past almost twenty years, a number of reviews have been published that describe both the problems characterising the research in this field and the new findings of the research.

The first of these works was Boëthius and Berggren's book *Forskning om barn-och ungdomspsykoterapi* (2000). It offers a thorough description of the state of the child and adolescent research field until the turn of the century as well as a detailed description of the methodological difficulties inherent in research in child and adolescent psychotherapy.

Later, two reviews were published of the research conducted in the UK, one by Kennedy (2004) and one by Kennedy and Midgley (2007). These are the first systematic reviews of the evidence base for child and adolescent psychotherapy in the UK. They are based on very thorough database searches and also include studies from other countries. Kennedy's review from 2004 describes thirty studies, almost all conducted on clinic populations of children with multiple and severe disorders and a high degree of comorbidity. The studies are categorised into four groups according to the quality of the research design.

The other review, by Kennedy and Midgley (2007), differs from the first by including research from across the field, covering child, adolescent, and parent–infant psychotherapy. The latter field lies outside the scope of the present text. This review also differs from the first by not only containing outcome studies, but also a considerable amount of process research.

Process research is the empirical study of what actually happens during treatment—a systematic study of why and how changes take place as a result of a therapeutic intervention (Midgley et al., 2009). Thus, the assessment of the effect of psychotherapy is one thing, another, and more demanding, issue is to try to understand the processes that cause the changes. Kennedy and Midgley (2007) mention that the lack of, and need for, process research have been pointed out by many over the past decade or more (e.g., Russell, 1999; Rutter, 2005). Kazdin (2002) has justly emphasised that psychoanalytic psychotherapy is well suited for this kind of research, because it has always taken an interest in, and has developed theories about, therapeutic change and the mechanisms of change.

Also to be mentioned is an overview of the research on individual child and adolescent psychodynamic psychotherapy from a workshop for clinicians and researchers at the Erica Foundation (Carlberg et al., 2008). These three reports are all found on EFPP's home page (www.efpp.org). It is interesting to see the development that has taken place during the relatively few years from the publication of Berggren and Boëthius's book in 2000 to the publication of these reviews.

Finally, several recent books about research in child and adolescent psychotherapy have been published, including works by Fonagy and colleagues (2002b), Carr (2009), Midgley et al. (2009), and Tsiantis and Trowell (2011).

In the following, we describe some of the most important findings of both outcome and process research and offer a summary of our current knowledge.

Results of outcome research

The main conclusion from the above-mentioned literature is that psychodynamic child and adolescent psychotherapy has a good effect on children and adolescents with a variety of psychic disorders. Many different outcome measures have been applied in the studies. One study used only physiological tools, while other studies have assessed, for example, social function and school performance, behaviour, symptomatology, family function, and psychiatric and psychological disturbances, and improvement has been found within all these areas. A number of studies also found that the improvement continues and is even increased on long-term follow-up.

One of the general findings of the research is that children with less extensive disturbances can be helped by short-term treatment, while children with more extensive disorders require both longer term and more intensive work. It has also been found in several studies (e.g., Baruch et al., 1998; Muratori et al., 2002) that children with behaviour disorders are more difficult to treat than children with emotional disorders and require more intensive treatment.

It is, perhaps, not very surprising that psychodynamic psychotherapy seems effective for emotional problems and behaviour disorders, but it might be worth calling attention to certain studies that assessed the effect of psychotherapy on more complicated disorders, disorders that have sometimes been regarded as being beyond therapeutic reach. This is, for example, the case with Boston and Lush's (1994) study of severely deprived children, Trowell and colleagues' (2002) study of sexually abused children, and Boston and colleagues' (2009) study of fostered, adopted, and in-care children. Psychodynamic psychotherapy has also been found to be effective for learning problems (Heinicke & Ramsey-Klee, 1986), autism (Reid et al., 2001), and anorexia (Robin et al., 1999; Vilsvik & Vaglum, 1990).

Kennedy (2004) emphasises the importance of long-term follow-up, as this is better suited for showing the benefits of long-term therapy. Among the described studies, seven followed the children for one to one-and-a-half years, seven followed them for two years, four for four years, one for five years, and one followed the children's subsequent development all the way into adulthood.

Likewise, several studies emphasise the importance of involving the family. Trowell and colleagues (2007), who investigated treatment of children with depression, described how the family dynamics change when the children begin to improve, as the parents are then compelled, to a greater degree, to face their own problems and work with themselves. In one case, a reduced family function was found when the children had received individual treatment, while the parents were not offered any treatment (Szapocznik et al., 1989).

The Anna Freud study

A study that deserves special mention, although it is retrospective and does not include control groups, is Fonagy and Target's (1996) comprehensive study of 763 previous child psychotherapies from the Anna Freud Centre in London during the time from 1952 to 1991. As mentioned, the study had certain limitations, but it does include a very large material of different psychotherapies and rests on the very thorough case notes made at the Centre. Seventy-six per cent of the children had received intensive analysis four to five times weekly, while twenty-four per cent received non-intensive psychotherapy one to two times weekly. The study showed considerable improvement for both groups, slightly better for the group receiving intensive analysis. Particularly the younger children profited from a more intensive treatment, while it seemed to make less of a difference for the adolescents. On the whole, younger children achieved greater improvement than adolescents. Generally, greater improvement was seen for children with emotional disturbances than for children with behaviour disorders, who were also more likely to drop out prematurely. The difference disappeared, however, if the latter group received longer therapy, a minimum of three years.

A key finding of this study was that while children with less extensive disturbances improved with both intensive and non-intensive treatment, the frequency of the treatment made a big difference for the more severely disturbed children. Among them, seventy-nine per cent of those in intensive treatment improved, compared to only twenty-six per cent of those in non-intensive treatment. This result may be compared with the fact that children who have received insufficient treatment during childhood might show greater problems in adulthood than a control group, which has received no treatment at all (Target & Fonagy, 2002). This gives cause for emphasising the importance of not offering inadequate treatment to children with severe problems, as that risks exacerbating their situation. This is, perhaps, not surprising. A child who has experienced many disruptions and losses and who already distrusts the adults around him will easily have this distrust further reinforced by entering a treatment that holds out the promise of help, only to be broken off, perhaps when the child has just begun to feel hope and trust.

A follow-up study was conducted with some of the original participants in this study who had now reached adulthood and were between twenty-five and fifty years old (Schachter, 2004; Schachter & Target, 2009). The participants were thoroughly assessed, but, unfortunately, the limited number of subjects involved in the follow-up study, thirty-four in total, rather limits what we can conclude from it. With some caution, however, we may conclude that childhood treatment does seem to have inferred a protective effect.

Our present knowledge

Carlberg and colleagues (2008) summarise the current state of research-based knowledge about therapeutic effect.

1. Psychodynamic psychotherapy helps. The magnitude of the effect is similar to that of other kinds of psychotherapy with adults. About three quarters of the children who receive psychotherapy improve significantly more than children who receive no treatment.
2. The positive process of change continues after the termination of treatment. In the cases where it has been examined, the effect has continued into adulthood.

3. Young children and teenagers seem to profit more from psychotherapy than the age group in between.
4. Less disturbed children seem to benefit from once-weekly psychotherapy.
5. More disturbed children seem to require longer and more intensive treatment.
6. Children with internalised problems seem to profit more from psychotherapy than children with externalised symptoms. However, if children with externalised problems do not drop out, which often happens, they, too, benefit, particularly if they also have anxiety symptoms.
7. Psychotherapy might, occasionally, be harmful for severely disturbed children if the therapy, for example, is too short or not intensive enough, or if no parallel work is offered to the parents.

The authors further describe that psychotherapy has had a demonstrably beneficial effect on children with the following specific disorders or challenges:

- depression;
- poorly managed diabetes;
- anxiety disorders;
- behaviour disorders;
- personality disorders;
- specific learning difficulties;
- pervasive developmental disorders;
- eating disorders;
- severely deprived children and children in foster care;
- sexually abused girls.

Process research

Process research has gradually grown both more widespread and more sophisticated. It raises many questions about how psychotherapy processes are best studied: through the psychotherapist's observations, through video recordings, through in-depth analyses of single cases, or through the use of more comprehensive materials? Is it best studied through quantitative or qualitative methods? The use of multiple methods of assessment is characteristic of process research; that provides the opportunity of both confirming and disproving links and of obtaining a more comprehensive material.

Llewellyn and Hardy (2001) distinguish among three types of process research that have developed during the past twenty years:

1. Descriptive studies (which develop measurement methods for important aspects of therapy, such as the quality of play or the therapeutic alliance, and that study what distinguishes psychodynamic psychotherapy from other child therapies).
2. Hypothesis-testing studies (which study the links between specific psychotherapy processes and treatment outcome).
3. Theory development studies (which generate theories about change).

Kennedy and Midgley (2007) write that most of the studies in their review are in the first of these categories, but it contains studies of the other two kinds also. As examples of hypothesis-testing studies, they mention Traux and Wittmer's (1973) and Gorin's (1993) studies. Studies belonging to the third category include Philps' (2003, 2009), Carlberg's (1997), and several others.

Their review not only emphasises the results of the research, but also some of the measures that may be used to describe the process, as well as many instruments of measurement. The review is, thus, also intended as a useful manual for researchers.

It would go too far to mention all the described studies or research instruments here. Only a few of the most important studies will be given as examples, but the review can be recommended for anyone who is interested in either clinical practice or clinical research.

The authors asked three main questions:

1. How does child and adolescent psychotherapy work?
2. For whom does it work?
3. Which children and adolescents profit from which kind of treatment?

A number of studies have intended to describe what children actually do during their therapy sessions, for example, how they play. For that purpose, a number of observation instruments have been developed: for example, "play therapy observation instrument" (Howe & Silvern, 1981) and "child psychoanalytic play interview" (Marans et al., 1991). Instruments are also developed to describe the defences used by the children, for instance, "defense mechanism inventory" (Cramer, 1991) and "comprehensive assessment of defence style" (Laor et al., 2001). Also the quality of the child's object relations may be assessed, for example, using the "child attachment interview" (Target et al., 2003) or the "object relations inventory" (Blatt et al., 1998).

Some research, in particular, assesses the interaction between the child and the therapist. Other studies have focused on assessing the therapeutic alliance and the overall process of therapies where both the child's and the therapist's acts and attitudes, as well as their mutual interaction, are assessed and classified according to a number of previously determined categories. This uncovers meaningful patterns that can be used to describe the therapeutic process. Researchers have also developed a number of instruments for this purpose.

Some researchers have chosen to examine so-called "turning points" in child psychotherapy, among them Carlberg (1997, 2009) and Terr et al. (2005). It might, for instance, be a turning point when a child who has been unable to play begins to do so, or when a child who has avoided contact begins to interact with his therapist.

An example of a study that combined results from multiple institutions is Trowell and colleagues' (2009) outcome study of the treatment of childhood depression. The multi-site study was conducted in London, Helsinki, and Athens and combined the use of quantitative and qualitative methods. In total, forty-two children participated in the study. The children were randomly distributed to family therapy or individual therapy. The study showed positive results for both psychotherapeutic modalities and further progress after a follow-up period. The qualitative part of the study showed, among other things, that identity problems seemed to play an important role. In most of the cases, it turned out to be important to work with aggression management.

EPOS (Erica Process and Outcome Study) (Carlberg, 2009) also includes projects covering a total of nineteen psychotherapies in different institutions. The study found that all the children improved during therapy, and that the comorbidity that most of them displayed had disappeared. The study offers examples of the way in which changes might appear in the child or in his relation with his therapist.

Often, a gradual process of development was found, rather than specific turning points. In some cases, the work with the parents was described as resulting in positive changes.

Finally, in a very recent example of qualitative research, a new treatment manual (Catty, 2016) for short-term psychoanalytic psychotherapy for adolescents with depression has been tested in a multi-site randomised controlled trial in the UK, "Improving mood with psychoanalytic and cognitive therapies" (IMPACT) and around the world. Findings from these research projects have been presented by, among others, Midgley and colleagues (2015, 2016), and Stapley and colleagues (2016).

It can be concluded from Kennedy and Midgley's (2007) review that a considerable amount of research now exists that has studied the process in psychodynamic child and adolescent psychotherapy and explored how the process is related to the results and to the therapy process in other kinds of psychotherapy.

As Llewellyn and Hardy (2001) have emphasised, process research has still not been able to attract the same degree of attention or funding as outcome research, because it is assumed by many to offer less clear answers as to which therapy is most effective with which clients. It is, however, an underestimation of the potential of process research to help therapists understand what is at play when psychotherapy goes well, and when it does not. Process research offers a way of increasing the effectiveness of psychotherapy by analysing the specific factors in therapy and highlighting individual differences.

Conclusions

From the beginning, intensive research has been carried out in psychodynamic psychotherapy in the form of case studies, conferences, discussions, and study groups. As valuable as this has been, it has not been able to offset the lack of quantitative research that has characterised the field for so many years. The quantitative research that did exist was, furthermore, rarely of such a character that it reflected the complicated conditions in the actual practice of psychodynamic child and adolescent psychotherapy. Furthermore, for many years, the relationship between scientists and practitioners was characterised by a lack of contact and insufficient mutual knowledge about each other.

In recent years, this has changed. The demand for evidence related to psychotherapeutic work has gradually led to a rather comprehensive body of empirical research in child and adolescent psychotherapy. In addition, this research is of higher quality and to a higher degree based on clinical work than much of the older research. The narrow positivistic scientific ideal has had to yield to a broader understanding of what constitutes high-quality research and, thus, led to the inclusion of qualitative methods and process research. Among other things, this has resulted in the development of instruments designed to measure a number of process variables. The most important point, however, is perhaps the understanding of the need for practitioners and scientists to acquire knowledge of both clinical practice and research through their basic training.

As a consequence of this development, we are now in a situation where we know, and are able to document, that psychodynamic psychotherapy is effective for a wide range of psychological disorders and rests on a solid evidence base. It is, perhaps, particularly important to mention that not only does it work for children with simple and relatively mild disorders and a limited range of symptoms, it also works for children with severe early disturbances, such as maltreated, sexually abused, or in-care children. Finally, it has been demonstrated how crucially important it is for children with severe disorders to receive sufficiently long and intensive psychotherapy and for parents and other carers to be involved in the treatment as well.

REFERENCES

Achenbach, T. M., & Rescorla, L. A. (2007). *Multicultural Understanding of Child and Adolescence Psychopathology*. New York: Guilford Press.

Ackerman, N. (1958). *Psychodynamics of Family Life*. New York: Basic Books.

Ainsworth, M. D. (1962). The effects of maternal deprivation: a review of findings and controversy in the context of research strategy. In: M. D. Ainsworth, R. G. Andry, R. G Harlow, S. Lebovici, M. Mead, D. G. Prugh, & B. Wootton (1962). *Deprivation of Maternal Care: A Reassessment of its Effects* (pp. 97–165). Geneva: World Health Organisation.

Ainsworth, M. D. S., Blehar, M. C., Waters, E., & Wall, C. (1978). *Patterns of Attachment: Assessed in the Strange Situation and at Home*. Hillsdale, NJ: Lawrence Erlbaum.

Albani, C., Blaser, G., König, S., Thomä, H., & Kächele, H. (2003). Study of a psychoanalytic process using the Core Conflictual Relationship Theme (CCRT) method according to the Ulm Process Model. *European Journal of Psychotherapy and Counselling*, 4: 11–32.

Alpert, A. (1959). Reversibility of pathological fixations associated with maternal deprivation in infancy. *Psychoanalytic Study of the Child, 14*: 169–185.

Altman, N., Briggs, R., Frankel, J., Gensler, D., & Pasqual, P. (2002). *Relational Child Psychotherapy*. New York: Other Press.

Alvarez, A. (1992). *Live Company: Psychoanalytic Psychotherapy with Autistic, Borderline, Deprived and Abused Children*. London & New York: Routledge [reprinted London: Routledge, 1999].

Alvarez, A. (2010). Levels of analytic work and levels of pathology: the work of calibration. *International Journal of Psychoanalysis, 91*: 859–878.

Axline, V. M. (1969). *Play Therapy*. New York: Ballantine Books.

Azarian, A., Miller, T. W., Palumbo, A. J., & Skriptchenko-Gregorian, V. (1997). Anniversary reactions in a five-year-old boy. *Psychoanalytic Study of the Child, 52*: 214–226.

Bailey, T. (2006). There is no such thing as an adolescent. In: M. Lanyado & A. Horne (Eds.), *A Question of Technique* (pp. 180–199). London: Routledge.

Baldwin, E. N. (2014). Recognizing guilt and shame: therapeutic ruptures with parents of children in psychotherapy. *Psychoanalytic Social Work, 21*: 2–18.

Baruch, G., Fearon, P., & Gerber, A. (1998). Evaluating the outcome of community-based psychoanalytic psychotherapy service for young people: one year repeated follow up. In: F. Davenhill & M. Patrick (Eds.), *Rethinking Clinical Audit* (pp. 157–182). London: Routledge.

Bentzen, M., & Hart, S. (2015). *Through Windows of Opportunity: A Neuroaffective Approach to Child Psychotherapy*. London: Karnac.

Berk, L. E. (2009). *Child Development*. Boston, MA: Pearson Education.

Bernstein, I., & Sax, A. M. (1978). Indications and contraindications for child analysis. In: J. Glenn (Ed.), *Child Analysis and Therapy* (pp. 67–108). New York: Jason Aronson.

Bion, W. R. (1961). *Experiences in Groups*. London: Tavistock [reprinted in: *Experiences in Groups, and Other Papers* (pp. 24–103). London: Routledge, 2013].

Bion, W. R. (1962a). A theory of thinking. *International Journal of Psychoanalysis, 43*: 306–310 [reprinted in: E. B. Spillius (Ed.), *Melanie Klein Today: Developments in Theory and Practice. Volume 1: Mainly Theory* (pp. 178–186). London: Routledge, 1988].

Bion, W. R. (1962b). *Learning from Experience*. London: Heinemann [reprinted London: Karnac, 1991].

Bion, W. R. (1963). *Elements of Psychoanalysis*. London: Heinemann [reprinted London: Karnac, 1989].

Bion, W. R. (1967). Notes on memory and desire. *Psychoanalytic Forum, 2*: 272–273, 279–280 [reprinted in: E. B. Spillius (Ed.), *Melanie Klein Today: Developments in Theory and Practice. Volume 2: Mainly Practice* (pp. 17–21). London: Routledge, 1988].

Bion, W. R. (1970). *Attention and Interpretation.* London: Tavistock [reprinted London: Karnac, 1984].

Bjorklund, D. F., & Blasi, C. H. (2012). *Child and Adolescent Development. An Integrated Approach.* Belmont, CA: Wadsworth.

Björn, G. J., Bodén, C., Sydsjö, G., & Gustafson, P. A. (2011). Psychological evaluation of refugee children: contrasting results from play diagnosis and parental interviews. *Clinical Child Psychology and Psychiatry, 16*(4): 517–534.

Blass, R. B., & Blatt, S. J. (1992). Attachment and separateness: a theoretical context for the integration of object relations theory with self psychology. *Psychoanalytic Study of the Child, 47*: 189–204.

Blatt, S. J., & Luyten, P. (2009). A structural–developmental psychodynamic approach to psychopathology: two polarities of experience across the life span. *Development and Psychopathology, 21*: 793–814.

Blatt, S. J., Auerbach, J. S., & Aryan, M. (1998). Representational structures and the therapeutic process. In: R. Bornstein & J. Masling (Eds.), *Empirical Studies of the Therapeutic Hour* (pp. 63–107). Washington, DC: American Psychological Association.

Blos, P. (1962). *On Adolescence.* New York: Free Press of Glencoe.

Boëthius, S. B., & Berggren, G. (2000). *Forskning om barn-och ungdomspsykoterapi. En kunskapsöversikt*. Stockholm: Ericastiftelsen.

Boston, M., & Lush, D. (1994). Further considerations of methodology for evaluating psychoanalytic psychotherapy: reflection in the light of research experience. *Journal of Child Psychotherapy, 20*: 205–229.

Boston, M., & Szur, R. (Eds.) (1983). *Psychotherapy with Severely Deprived Children.* London: Routledge & Kegan Paul.

Boston, M., Lush, D., & Grainger. E. (2009). Evaluation of psychoanalytic psychotherapy with fostered, adopted and "in-care" children. In: N. Midgley, J. Anderson, E. Grainger, T. Nesic-Vuckovic, & C. Urwin (Eds.), *Child Psychotherapy and Research* (pp. 117–128). London: Routledge.

Bowlby, J. (1951). *Maternal Care and Mental Health.* Geneva: World Health Organization.

Bowlby, J. (1969). *Attachment.* London: Hogarth Press.

Bowlby, J. (1973). *Separation: Anxiety and Anger.* London: Hogarth Press.

Bowlby, J. (1980). *Loss: Sadness and Depression.* London: Hogarth Press.

Bowlby, J. (1988). *A Secure Base. Clinical Applications of Attachment Theory.* London: Routledge.

Bradley, S. (2003). *Affect Regulation and the Development of Psychopathology.* New York: Guilford Press.

Brafman, A. H. (2012). *The Language of Drawings: A New Finding in Psychodynamic Work.* London: Karnac.

Bronstein, C. (2001). *Kleinian Theory. A Contemporary Perspective.* London: Whurr.

Bunn, A. (2013). *SIGNS OF SAFETY® IN ENGLAND: An NSPCC Commissioned Report on the Signs of Safety Model in Child Protection.* Available at: www.nspcc.org.uk (accessed 30 July 2016).

Canham, H. (1999). The development of the concept of time in fostered and adopted children. *Psychoanalytic Inquiry, 19*(2): 160–171.

Cantwell, D. P., & Rutter, M. (1994). Classification: conceptual issues and substantive findings. In: M. Rutter, E. Taylor, & L. Hersov (Eds.), *Child and Adolescent Psychiatry: Modern Approaches* (pp. 3–21). Oxford: Blackwell.

Caper, R. (1996). Play, experimentation and creativity. *International Journal of Psychoanalysis, 77*: 859–869.

Carlberg, G. (1997). Laughter opens the door: turning points in child psychotherapy. *Journal of Child Psychotherapy, 23*: 331–349.

Carlberg, G. (1999). Vändpunkter i barnpsykoterapi. Doctoral dissertation. Stockholm: Universitetets Pedagogiska Institution.

Carlberg, G. (2009). Exploring change processes in psychodynamic child psychotherapy: the therapist's perspective. In: N. Midgley, J. Anderson, E. Grainger, T. Nesic-Vuckovic, & C. Urwin (Eds.), *Child Psychotherapy and Research—New Approaches, Emergent Findings* (pp. 100–112). London: Routledge.

Carlberg, G., Eresund, P., & Boëthius, S. B. (2008). *Child and Adolescent Psychotherapy Research. Workshops for Clinicians and Researchers at the Erica Foundation.* Stockholm: The Erica Foundation.

Carr, A. (2009). *What Works with Children, Adolescents, and Adults?* London: Routledge.

Catty, J. (Ed.) (2016). *Short-term Psychoanalytic Psychotherapy for Adolescents with Depression: A Treatment Manual.* London: Karnac.

Chang, C. Y., Ritter, K. B., & Hays, D. G. (2005). Multicultural trends and toys in play therapy. *International Journal of Play Therapy, 14*(2): 69–85.

Chethik, M. (1989). *Techniques of Child Therapy. Psychodynamic Strategies.* New York: Guilford Press.

Cleve, E. (2004). *From Chaos to Coherence. Psychotherapy with a Little Boy with ADHD.* London. Karnac.

Cohen, P. M., & Solnit, A. J. (1993). Play and therapeutic action. *Psychoanalytic Study of the Child, 48*: 49–63.

Cramer, P. (1991). *The Development of Defence Mechanisms: Theory, Research and Assessment.* New York: Springer.

Cyrulnik, B. (2001). *Les Vilains Petits Canards*. Paris: Odile Jacob [reprinted as *The Whispering of Ghosts: Trauma and Resilience*. New York: Other Press, 2005].

Dale, F. (1984). The reunification of Sundip: the bringing together split-off parts of the personality in a boy with psychotic features. *Journal of Child Psychotherapy, 10*(2): 217–232.

Dalgaard, N. T., & Montgomery, E. (2015). Disclosure and silencing: a systematic review of the literature on patterns of trauma communication in refugee families. *Transcultural Psychiatry, 52*(5): 579–593.

Downey, L., Shuse, D., Rutter, M., Quinton, D., & Mrazek, D. (1985). The nature and qualities of parenting provided by women raised in institutions. *Journal of Child Psychology & Psychiatry & Allied Disciplines, 26*(4): 599–625.

Duch, C., & Elklit, A. (2008). Børneperspektiv på en katastrofe. *Psykolog Nyt, 4*: 8–12.

Edgcumbe, R. (2000). *Anna Freud: A View of Development, Disturbance and Therapeutic Techniques*. London: Routledge.

Eels, T. D. (2013). The case formulation approach to psychotherapy research revisited. *Pragmatic Case Studies in Psychotherapy, 9*(4): 426–447.

Elklit, A. (2002). Victimization and PTSD in a Danish national youth probability sample. *Journal of the American Academy of Child and Adolescent Psychiatry, 41*(2): 174–181.

Elvins, R., & Green, J. (2008). The conceptualization and measure of therapeutic alliance: an empirical review. *Clinical Psychology Review, 28*: 1167–1187.

Erikson, E. (1968). *Identity. Youth and Crisis*. New York: Norton.

Fazel, M., Wheeler, J., & Danesh, J. (2005). Prevalence of serious mental disorder in 7000 refugees resettled in western countries: a systematic review. *The Lancet, 365*: 1309–1314.

Ferro, A. (1999). *The Bi-Personal Field: Experiences in Child Analysis*. London: Routledge.

Fonagy, P., & Allison, E. (2012). What is mentalization? The concept and its foundations in developmental research. In: N. Midgley & I. Vrouva (Eds.), *Minding the Child. Mentalization-Based Interventions with Children, Young People and their Families* (pp. 11–34). London: Routledge.

Fonagy, P., & Target, M. (1996). Predictors of outcome in child psychoanalysis: a retrospective study of 793 cases at the Anna Freud Centre. *Journal of the American Psychoanalytic Association, 44*(1): 27–77.

Fonagy, P., Gergely G., Jurist, E. L., & Target, M. (2002a). *Affect Regulation, Mentalization, and the Development of the Self*. New York: Other Press.

Fonagy, P., Target, M., Cottrell, D., Phillips, J., & Kurtz, Z. (2002b). *What Works for Whom? A Critical Review of Treatments for Children and Adolescents.* London: The Guilford Press.

Fox, N. A., & Rutter, M. (2010). Introduction to the special section on the effects of early experience on development. *Child Development, 81*: 23–27.

Fox, S., Levitt, P., & Nelson, C. A. (2010). How the timing and quality of early experiences influence the development of brain architecture. *Child Development, 81*: 306–325.

Freud, A. (1937). *The Ego and the Mechanisms of Defence.* London: Hogarth.

Freud, A. (1946). *The Psycho-Analytical Treatment of Children.* New York: International Universities Press.

Freud, A. (1955). Special experiences of young children, particularly in times of social disturbance. In: K. Soddy (Ed.), *Mental Health and Infant Development. Proceedings of the International Seminar held by the World Federation for Mental Health at Chichester, England* (pp. 141–159). London: Routledge and Kegan Paul.

Freud, A. (1958). Adolescence. *Psychoanalytic Study of the Child, 13*: 255–278.

Freud, A. (1965). *Normality and Pathology in Childhood.* New York: International Universities Press [reprinted: London: Hogarth Press, 1966].

Freud, A. (1966a). A short history of child analysis. *Psychoanalytic Study of the Child, 21*: 7–14.

Freud, A. (1966b). *Normality and Pathology in Childhood.* London: Hogarth Press.

Freud, A., & Burlingham, D. (1944). *Infants without Families. The Case for and against Residential Nurseries.* London: Allen and Unwin.

Freud, A., & Dann, S. (1951). An experiment in group upbringing. *Psychoanalytic Study of the Child, 6*: 127–168.

Freud, S. (1895). *Project for a Scientific Psychology. S. E., 1*: 283–391. London: Hogarth.

Freud, S. (1900a). *The Interpretation of Dreams. S. E., 4–5.* London: Hogarth.

Freud, S. (1909b). *Analysis of a Phobia in a Five-Year-Old Boy. S. E., 10*: 5–150. London: Hogarth.

Freud, S. (1910d). The future prospects of psycho-analytic therapy. *S. E., 11*: 141–151. London: Hogarth.

Freud, S. (1914g). Remembering, repeating and working-through. *S. E., 12*: 147–156. London: Hogarth.

Freud, S. (1916–1917). *Introductory Lectures on Psycho-Analysis. S. E., 16*: 431–447. London: Hogarth.

Freud, S. (1917e). Mourning and melancholia. *S. E., 14*: 239–258. London: Hogarth.

Freud, S. (1937c). Analysis terminable and interminable. *S. E., 23*: 211–254. London: Hogarth.

Furman, E. (1992). On feeling and being felt with. *Psychoanalytic Study of the Child, 47*: 67–84.

Gaensbauer, T. J. (1994). Therapeutic work with a traumatized toddler. *Psychoanalytic Study of the Child, 49*: 412–433.

Gaensbauer, T. J. (1995). Trauma in the preverbal period: symptoms, memories and developmental impact. *Psychoanalytic Study of the Child, 50*: 123–149.

Geissman, C., & Geissman, P. (1998). *A History of Child Psychoanalysis*. London: Routledge.

Glasser, M. (1994). Violence: a psychoanalytical research project. *Journal of Forensic Psychiatry, 5*(2): 311–320.

Gorin, S. (1993). The prediction of child psychotherapy outcome: factors specific to treatment. *Psychotherapy, 30*(1): 152–158.

Green, A. (1974). The analyst, symbolization and absence in the analytic setting (on changes in analytic practice and analytic experience). In memory of D. W. Winnicott. *International Journal of Psychoanalysis, 56*(1): 1–22 [reprinted in: *On Private Madness* (pp. 30–59). London: Hogarth, 1986].

Grønseth, R. (1969). Egostøttende psykoterapi. *Nordisk Psykologi, 18*(5): 365–374.

Grünbaum, L. (1989). Om psykoanalytisk børneterapi og udviklingsstandsning på baggrund af mangelfuld selv-objekt differentiering. *Agrippa, 11*(1): 5–28.

Grünbaum, L. (1998). Children in torture-surviving families: child psychotherapy within a family-orientated context. In: J. Pestalozzi (Ed.), *Psychoanalytic Psychotherapy in Institutional Settings* (pp. 119–140). London: Karnac.

Grünbaum, L. (1999–2000). Psykoanalytisk børneterapi—hvordan virker hvad? *Matrix, 16*(3): 245–268.

Grünbaum, L. (2010a). The post-traumatic nightmare: the via regia to unconscious integration? In: A. Gautier & A. Sabatini (Eds.), *Bearing Witness: Psychoanalytic Work with People Traumatised by Torture and State Violence* (pp. 65–89). London: Karnac.

Grünbaum, L. (2010b). Survival and helplessness in empty space. In: K. V. Mortensen & L. Grünbaum (Eds.), *Play and Power* (pp. 69–94). London: Karnac.

Grünbaum, L. (2014). Anxieties and dilemmas relating to breaks in the therapeutic relationship with children whose relationships in early infancy were reported to have been emotionally unstable and traumatised—a systematic study of child psychotherapy with a young child who had suffered early abuse and neglect. PhD dissertation, University of East London, in conjunction with the Tavistock Clinic.

Grünbaum, L., & Gammeltoft, M. (1993). Young children of schizophrenic mothers: difficulties of intervention. *American Journal Orthopsychiatry, 63*(1): 16–27.

Hart, S. (2008). *Brain, Attachment, Personality. An Introduction to Neuro-affective Development*. London: Karnac.

Hart, S., & Bentzen, M. (2013). Jagten på de nonspecifikke faktorer i psykoterapi med børn. Copenhagen: Hans Reitzel [reprinted as: Bentzen, M., & Hart, S. *Through Windows of Opportunity: A Neuro-affective Approach to Child Psychotherapy*. London: Karnac, 2015].

Hartnup, T. (1999). The therapeutic setting: the people and the place. In: M. Lanyado & A. Horne (Eds.), *Child and Adolescent Psychotherapy—Psychoanalytic Approaches* (pp. 93–104). London: Routledge.

Heimann, P. (1950). On countertransference. *International Journal of Psychoanalysis, 31*: 81–84.

Heinicke, C. M., & Ramsey-Klee, D. M. (1986). Outcome of child psychotherapy as a function of frequency of session. *Journal of the American Academy of Child Psychiatry, 14*: 561–588.

Henry, G. (1974). Doubly deprived. *Journal of Child Psychotherapy, 4*(2): 29–43 [reprinted as "Double deprivation" in: G. Williams (1997). *Internal Landscapes and Foreign Bodies. Eating Disorders and Other Pathologies* (pp. 33–49). London: Duckworth 1997].

Hinshelwood, R. D. (1991). Psychodynamic formulation in assessment for psychotherapy. *British Journal of Psychotherapy, 8*(2): 166–174.

Hodges, J., & Tizard, B. (1989). Social and family relationships of ex-institutional adolescents. *Journal of Child Psychology & Psychiatry & Allied Disciplines, 30*(1): 77–97.

Horne, A. (2000). Keeping the child in mind: thoughts on work with parents of children in therapy. In: J. Tsiantis, S. B. Boetius, B. Hallerfors, A. Horne, & I. Tischler (Eds.), *Work with Parents: Psychoanalytic Psychotherapy with Children and Adolescents* (pp. 47–63). London: Karnac.

Horne, A. (2006). Brief communications from the edge: psychotherapy with challenging adolescents. In: M. Lanyado & A. Horne (Eds.), *A Question of Technique* (pp. 149–165). London: Routledge.

Houzel, D. (2004). The psychoanalysis of infantile autism. *Journal of Child Psychotherapy, 30*(2): 225–237.

Houzel, D. (2008). The creation of psychic space, the "nest of babies" fantasy and the emergence of the Oedipus complex. In: K. Barrows (Ed.),

Autism in Childhood and Autistic Features in Adults. A Psychoanalytic Perspective (pp. 119–145). London: Karnac.

Howe, P., & Silvern, L. (1981). Behavioural observations of children during play therapy: preliminary development of a research instrument. *Journal of Personality Development, 45*(2): 168–182.

Hug-Hellmuth, H. (1912). Analyse eines Traumes eines Fünfeinhalbjährigen. *Zentralblatt für Psychoanalyse und Psychotherapie, 2*(3): 122–127.

Hug–Hellmuth, H. (1921). On the technique of child analysis. *International Journal of Psychoanalysis, 2*: 287–305.

Hunter, M. (2001). *Psychotherapy with Young People in Care: Lost and Found.* Hove: Brunner-Routledge.

Ironside, L. (1995). Beyond the boundaries: a patient, a therapist and an allegation of sexual abuse. *Journal of Child Psychotherapy, 21*(2): 183–207.

Jarvis, C. (2005). Parenting problems: research and clinical perspectives on parenting adolescents. *Journal of Child Psychotherapy, 31*: 209–220.

Jolley, R. P. (2010). *Children and Pictures: Drawing and Understanding.* Hong Kong: Wiley-Blackwell.

Joseph, B. (1985). Transference: the total situation. *International Journal of Psychoanalysis, 66*: 447–454 [reprinted in: E. B. Spillius (Ed.), *Melanie Klein Today. Developments in Theory and Practice. Volume 2: Mainly Practice* (pp. 61–72). London: Routledge, 1988].

Kaplan, S. (2006). Children in genocide—extreme traumatization and the "affect propeller". *International Journal of Psychoanalysis, 87*: 725–746.

Kazdin, A. E. (2002). *Psychotherapy for Children and Adolescents: Directions for Research and Practice.* Oxford: Oxford University Press.

Kazdin, A. E. (2003). Psychotherapy for children and adolescents. *Annual Review of Psychology, 54*: 253–276.

Kazdin, A. E., Whitley, M., & Marciano, P. (2006). Child–therapist and parent–therapist alliance and therapeutic change in the treatment of children referred for oppositional, aggressive, and antisocial behavior. *Journal of Child Psychology and Psychiatry, 47*(5): 436–445.

Kennedy, E. (2004). *Child and Adolescent Psychotherapy: A Systematic Review of Psychoanalytic Approaches.* London: North Central London Strategic Health Authority.

Kennedy, E., & Midgley, N. (2007). *Process and Outcome Research in Child, Adolescent and Parent-Infant Psychotherapy: A Thematic Review.* London: North Central London Strategic Health Authority.

King, P., & Steiner, R. (1991). *The Freud–Klein Controversies, 1941–45.* London: Routledge.

Kjærgaard, C. B., & Westergaard, M. (2016). Den terapeutiske alliance med børn i psykodynamisk legeterapi. In: L. Grünbaum & K. V. Mortensen

(Eds.), *Psykodynamisk Psykoterapi med Børn og Unge. Bind 2. Et område i udvikling* (pp. 31–49). Copenhagen: Hans Reitzels.

Klein, M. (1921). Eine Kinderentwicklung. *Imago, 7*: 251–309 [reprinted as The development of a child in: *Love, Guilt and Reparation and Other Works 1921–1945* (pp. 1–53). London: Hogarth, 1975].

Klein, M. (1923). Zur Frühanalyse. *Imago, 9*: 222–259 [reprinted as Early analysis in: *Love, Guilt and Reparation and Other Works 1921–1945* (pp. 77–105). London: Hogarth, 1975].

Klein, M. (1927). Symposium on child-analysis. *International Journal of Psychoanalysis, 8* [reprinted in: *Love, Guilt and Reparation and Other Works 1921–1945* (pp. 139–169). London: Hogarth, 1975].

Klein, M. (1929). Personification in the play of children. *International Journal of Psychoanalysis, 19*: 193–204 [reprinted in: *Love, Guilt and Reparation and Other Works 1921–1945* (pp. 199–209). London: Hogarth, 1975].

Klein, M. (1930). The importance of symbol-formation in the development of the ego. *International Journal of Psychoanalysis, 11*: 24–39 [reprinted in: *Love, Guilt and Reparation and Other Works 1921–1945* (pp. 219–232). London: Hogarth, 1975].

Klein, M. (1932). *The Psychoanalysis of Children.* London: Hogarth [reprinted London: Vintage, 1997].

Klein, M. (1935). A contribution to the psychogenesis of manic-depressive states. *International Journal of Psychoanalysis, 16*: 145–174 [reprinted in: *Love, Guilt and Reparation and Other Works 1921–1945* (pp. 261–289). London: Hogarth, 1975].

Klein, M. (1940). Mourning and its relation to manic-depressive states. *International Journal of Psychoanalysis, 21*: 125–153 [reprinted in: *Love, Guilt and Reparation and Other Works 1921–1945* (pp. 344–369). London: Hogarth, 1975].

Klein, M. (1945). The Oedipus complex in the light of early anxieties. *International Journal of Psychoanalysis, 26*: 58–62 [reprinted in: *Love, Guilt and Reparation and Other Works 1921–1945* (pp. 370–419). London: Hogarth, 1975].

Klein, M. (1946). Notes on some schizoid mechanisms. *International Journal of Psychoanalysis, 27*: 99–110 [reprinted in: *Envy and Gratitude and Other Works 1946–1963* (pp. 1–24). London: Hogarth, 1975].

Klein, M. (1950). On the criteria for the termination of a psycho-analysis. *International Journal of Psychoanalysis, 31*: 78–80 [reprinted in: *Envy and Gratitude and Other Works 1946–1963* (pp. 43–47). London: Hogarth, 1975].

Klein, M. (1952). The origins of transference. *International Journal of Psychoanalysis, 33*: 433–438 [reprinted in: *Envy and Gratitude and Other Works 1946–1963* (pp. 48–56). London: Hogarth, 1975].

Klein, M. (1955). The psycho-analytic play technique: its history and significance. In: M. Klein, P. Heimann, & R. E. Money-Kyrle (Eds.), *New Directions in Psycho-Analysis. The Significance of Infant Conflict in the Pattern of Adult Behaviour* (pp. 3–22). London: Tavistock [reprinted in: *Envy and Gratitude and Other Works 1946–1963* (pp. 122–140). London: Hogarth, 1975].

Klein, M. (1957). Envy and gratitude. London: Tavistock [reprinted in: *Envy and Gratitude and Other Works 1946–1963* (pp. 176–235). London: Hogarth, 1975].

Klein, M. (1959). Our adult world and its roots in infancy. *Human Relations, 12*: 291–303 [reprinted in: *Envy and Gratitude and Other Works 1946–1963* (pp. 247–263). London: Hogarth, 1975].

Klein, M. (1961). *Narrative of a Child Analysis: The Conduct of the Psycho-analysis of Children as Seen in the Treatment of a Ten-Year-Old Boy.* London: Hogarth.

Klein, M. (1975a). *Love, Guilt and Reparation and Other Works 1921–1945.* London: Hogarth.

Klein, M. (1975b). *Envy and Gratitude and Other Works 1946–1963.* London: Hogarth.

Kramer, E. (1971). *Art as Therapy with Children.* New York: Schocken Books.

Kronengold, H. (2010). Hey toy man. *Journal of Infant, Child, and Adolescent Psychotherapy, 9*: 3–17.

Labastida, A. T. (1976). Ansiedades de separation y reunion en la transferencia en quatro ninos (Separation and reunion anxieties in the transference of four children). *Neurología, Neurocirugía, Psiquiatría, 17*(2): 95–101.

Lagerheim, B. (1988). *Utvecklas med handikapp.* Stockholm: Norstedt.

Lanyado, M. (1999). Holding and letting go: some thoughts about the process of ending therapy. *Journal of Child Psychotherapy, 25*(3): 357–378.

Lanyado, M. (2004). *The Presence of the Therapist: Treating Childhood Trauma.* Hove: Brunner-Routledge.

Lanyado, M., & Horne, A. (1999). The therapeutic relationship and process. In: M. Lanyado & A. Horne (Eds.), *The Handbook of Child & Adolescent Psychotherapy: Psychoanalytic Approaches* (pp. 55–71). London: Routledge.

Laor, N., Wolmer, L., & Cicchetti, D. (2001). The comprehensive assessment of defense style: measuring defense mechanisms in children and adolescents. *Journal of Nervous and Mental Disease, 189*(6): 360–368.

Laub, D., & Auerhahn, N. C. (1993). Knowing and not knowing. Massive psychic trauma: forms of traumatic memory. *International Journal of Psychoanalysis, 74*: 287–302.

Laufer, M. (1997). Developmental breakdown in adolescence: problems of understanding and helping. In: M. Laufer (Ed.), *Adolescent Breakdown and Beyond* (pp. 3–15). London: Karnac.

Levine, M., & Smolak, L. (2002). Body image development in adolescence. In: I. F. Cash & T. Pruzinsky (Eds.), *Body Image. A Handbook of Theory Research and Clinical Practice* (pp. 74–82). New York: Guilford Press.

Lindqvist, K. (April 2013). *Mentalisation Based Time-Limited Psychotherapy with Children and Parents*. Workshop at the Erica Foundation. Stockholm: Erica Foundation.

Llewellyn, S., & Hardy, G. (2001). Process research in understanding and applying psychological therapies. *British Journal of Clinical Psychology, 40*: 1–21.

Luborsky, L. (1997). The core conflictual relationship theme (CCRT): a basic case formulation method. In: T. Eels (Ed.), *Handbook of Psychotherapy Case Formulation* (pp. 58–83). New York: Guilford.

Luborsky, L., & Luborsky, E. (2006). *Research and Psychotherapy—The Vital Link*. Lanham, MD: Jason Aronson.

Luborsky, L., Barber, J. P., & Diguer, L. (1992). The meanings of narratives told during psychotherapy: the fruits of a new observational unit. *Psychotherapy Research, 2*: 277–290.

Luborsky, L., Luborsky, E., Diguer, L., Schmidt, K., Dengler, D., Schaffler, P., Faude, J., Morris, M., Buchsbaum, H., & Emde, R. (1996). Extending the core relationship theme into early childhood. In: G. G. Noam & K. W. Fischer (Eds.), *Development and Vulnerability in Close Relationships* (pp. 287–308). Hillsdale, NJ: Lawrence Erlbaum.

Luxenberg, T., Spinazzola, J., & van der Kolk, B. A. (2001). Complex trauma and disorders of extreme stress (DESNOS) diagnosis, part one: Assessment. *Directions in Psychiatry, 21*(25): 373–392.

Mahler, M., Pine, F., & Bergman, A. (1975). *The Psychological Birth of the Human Infant*. New York: Basic Books.

Main, M., & Hesse, E. (1990). Parents' unresolved traumatic experiences are related to infant disorganized attachment status: is frightened and/or frightening parent behavior the linking mechanism? In: M. T. Greenberg, D. Cicchetti, & E. M. Cummings (Eds.), *Attachment in the Preschool Years: Theory, Research and Intervention* (pp. 161–182). Chicago, IL: University of Chicago Press.

Main, M., & Solomon, J. (1986). Discovery of a disorganized/disoriented attachment pattern. In: T. B. Brazelton & M. W. Yogman (Eds.), *Affective Development in Infancy* (pp. 95–124). Norwood, NJ: Ablex.

Marans, S., Mayes, L., Cicchetti, D., Dahl, K., Marans, W., & Cohen, D. (1991). The child psychoanalytic play interview. *Journal of American Psychoanalytic Association, 39*: 1015–1036.

Marcia, J. (1980). Identity in adolescence. In: J. Adelson (Ed.), *Handbook of Adolescent Psychology* (pp. 159–187). New York: Wiley.

McLeod, J. (2001). *Qualitative Research in Psychotherapy and Counselling*. London: Sage.

Meeks, J., & Bernet, W. (2001). *The Fragile Alliance*. Melbourne: Krieger.

Meltzer, D. (1967). *The Psycho-analytical Process*. London: Heinemann [reprinted Strathtay, Perthshire: Clunie Press, 1979].

Micucci, J. A. (2009). *The Adolescent in Family Therapy: Harnessing the Power of Relationships* (2nd edn). New York: Guilford Press.

Midgley, N. (2008). Overview of the research on individual child and adolescent psychodynamic psychotherapy. In: G. Carlberg, P. Eresund, & S. B. Boëthius (Eds.), *Child and Adolescent Psychotherapy Research*. Workshop for Clinicians and Researchers at the Erica Foundation, October 2008. Available at: www-efpp/research.

Midgley, N., & Navridi, E. (2006). An exploratory study of premature termination in child analysis. *Journal of Infant, Child, and Adolescent Psychotherapy, 5*: 437–458.

Midgley, N., Anderson, J., Grainger, E., Nesic-Vuckovic, T., & Urwin, C. (2009). *Child Psychotherapy and Research*. London: Routledge.

Midgley, N., Isaacs, D., Weitkamp, K., & Target, M. (2016). The experience of adolescents participating in a randomised clinical trial in the field of mental health: a qualitative study. *Trials, 17*: 364.

Midgley, N., Parkinson, S., Holmes, J., Stapley, E., Eatough, V., & Target, M. (2015). Beyond a diagnosis: the experience of depression among clinically-referred adolescents. *Journal of Adolescence, 44*: 269–279.

Mikardo, J. (1995). Finding a voice: the treatment of a speech-impaired boy. *Journal of Child Psychotherapy, 21*(2): 225–252.

Moestrup, N. (2016). Psykoanalytisk legeterapi med omsorgssvigtede og anbragte børn. In: L. Grünbaum & K. V. Mortensen (Eds.), *Psykodynamisk Psykoterapi med Børn og Unge. Bind 2. Et område i udvikling* (pp. 109–126). Copenhagen: Hans Reitzel.

Mortensen, K. V. (2010). Research in psychoanalytic psychotherapy with children: an enterprise in need of power? In: K. V. Mortensen & L. Grünbaum (Eds.), *Play and Power* (pp. 145–159). London: Karnac.

Moses, R. H., & Moses, R. (1986). Steps in self development. *Psychoanalytic Study of the Child, 41*: 491–513.

Munro, E. (2011). *The Munro Review of Child Protection: Final Report, A Child-centred System*. London: The Stationery Office Limited on behalf of the Controller of Her Majesty's Stationery Office. Available at: www.education.gov.uk/publications (accessed 30 July 2016).

Muratori, F., Picchi, L., Casella, C., Tancredi, R., Millone, A., & Patarnello, M. G. (2002). Efficacy of brief dynamic psychotherapy for children with emotional disorders. *Psychotherapy and Psychosomatics, 71*: 28–38.

Music, G. (2009). Neuroscience and child psychotherapy. In: M. Lanyado & A. Horne (Eds.), *Child and Adolescent Psychotherapy: Psychoanalytic Approaches* (pp. 51–72). London: Routledge.

Neria, Y., Nandi, A., & Galea, S. (2008). Post-traumatic stress disorder following disasters: a systematic review. *Psychological Medicine, 38*(4): 467–480.

Nissen, P., & Hansen, K. G. (2006). *Effektundersøgelse af Psykodynamisk Miljøterapeutisk Døgnbehandling*. Copenhagen: Danmarks Pædagogiske Universitets.

Nordbo, A. (2004). Psykologi og neurovidenskab. *Psykolognyt, 58*: 8–11.

Novick, K., & Novick, J. (2005). *Working with Parents Makes Therapy Work*. New York: Jason Aronson.

Ofsted (March 2015). *Early Help: Whose Responsibility?* London: The Office for Standards in Education, Children's Services and Skills. Available at: www.gov.uk/government/organisations/ofsted (accessed 30 July 2016).

O'Shaughnessy, E. (1964). The absent object. *Journal of Child Psychotherapy, 1*(2): 134–143 [reprinted in: P. S. Barrows (Ed.), *Key Papers from the Journal of Child Psychotherapy* (pp. 13–23). Hove: Brunner-Routledge, 2004].

O'Shaughnessy, E. (1989). The invisible Oedipus complex. In: R. Britton, M. Feldman, & E. O'Shaughnessy (Eds.), *The Oedipus Complex Today: Clinical Implications* (pp. 129–150). London: Karnac.

Ottosen, M. H., Andersen, D., Dahl, K. M., Hansen, A. T., Lausten, M., & Østergaard, S. V. (2014). *Børn og unge i Danmark. Velfærd og Trivsel 2014*. Copenhagen: SFI—Det Nationale Forskningscenter for Velfærd.

Perrin, S., Smith, P., & Yule, W. (2000). Practitioner review: the assessment and treatment of post-traumatic stress disorder in children and adolescents. *Journal of Child Psychology and Psychiatry, 3*: 277–289.

Petot, J. M. (1990–1991). *Melanie Klein. Vol. I and Vol. II*. Madison, NY: International Universities Press.

Philps, J. F. (2003). Applications of child psychotherapy to work with children in temporary foster care. Psych. D. thesis, University of East London.

Philps, J. F. (2009). Mapping process in child psychotherapy: steps towards drafting a new method for evaluating psychoanalytic case studies. In: N. Midgley, J. Anderson, E. Grainger, T. Nesic-Vuckovic, & C. Urwin (Eds.), *Child Psychotherapy and Research—New Approaches, Emergent Findings* (pp. 56–71). London: Routledge.

Pick, I. B. (1967). On stealing: clinical notes on three adolescent boys. *Journal of Child Psychotherapy*, 2: 67–79.

Pick, I. B. (1985). Working through in the countertransference. *International Journal of Psychoanalysis*, 66: 57–166 [reprinted in: E. B. Spillius (Ed.), *Melanie Klein Today. Developments in Theory and Practice, Volume 2: Mainly Practice* (pp. 34–47). London: Routledge, 1988].

Popp, C., Luborsky, L., & Crits-Cristoph, P. (1990). The parallel of the CCRT based on waking narratives with the CCRT based on dreams. In: L. Luborsky & P. Crits-Cristoph (Eds.), *Understanding Transference: The CCRT Method* (pp. 158–172). New York: Basic Books.

Psychodynamic Diagnostic Manual Task Force (2006). *Psychodynamic Diagnostic Manual*. Silver Spring, MD: Alliance of Psychoanalytic Organizations.

Pynoos, R. (1993). Traumatic stress and developmental psychopathology in children and adolescents. In: J. M. Oldham, M. B. Riben, & A. Tasman (Eds.), *American Psychiatric Press Review of Psychiatry, vol. 12* (pp. 205–238). Washington, DC: American Psychiatric Press.

Reed, G. S. (1990). A reconsideration of the concept of transference neurosis. *International Journal of Psychoanalysis*, 71: 205–218.

Reich, W. (1928). On character analysis. In: R. Fliess (Ed.), *The Psychoanalytic Reader: An Anthology of Essential Papers with Critical Introductions* (pp. 129–147). New York: International University Press, 1948.

Reid, S., Alvarez, A., & Lee, A. (2001). The Tavistock autism workshop approach: assessment, treatment and research. In: J. Richter & S. Coates (Eds.), *Autism—the Search for Coherence* (pp. 182–192). London: Jessica Kingsley.

Rey, J. H. (1986). The schizoid mode of being and the space-time continuum (beyond metaphor). *Journal of The Melanie Klein Society*, 4(2): 12–52 [reprinted in: *Universals of Psychoanalysis in the Treatment of Psychotic and Borderline States—Factors of Space–Time and Language* (pp. 8–30). London: Free Association Books, 1994].

Riesenberg-Malcolm, R. (2001). Bion's theory of containment. In: C. Bronstein (Ed.), *Kleinian Theory: A Contemporary Perspective* (pp. 165–180). London: Whurr.

Robin, A., Siegel, P., Moye, A. Gilroy, M., Dennis, A. B., & Sikand, A. (1999). A controlled comparison of family versus individual psychotherapy for adolescents with anorexia nervosa. *Journal of the American Academy of Child and Adolescent Psychiatry, 38*: 1482–1489.

Rose, J. (1997). Distortions of time in the transference: some clinical and theoretical implications. *International Journal of Psychoanalysis, 78*: 453–468.

Rosenfeld, H. (1971). A clinical approach to the psychoanalytic theory of the life and death instincts: an investigation into the aggressive aspects of narcissism. *International Journal of Psychoanalysis, 52*: 169–178 [reprinted in: E. B. Spillius (Ed.), *Melanie Klein Today, Vol. 1: Mainly Theory* (pp. 239–255). London: Routledge and the Institute of Psycho-Analysis, 1988].

Russell, R. (1999). Child psychotherapy process research: suggestions for the new millennium. In: S. Russ & T. Ollendick, T. (Eds.), *Handbook of Psychotherapies with Children and Families* (pp. 541–552). New York: Kluwer Academic/Plenum.

Rustin, Margaret (1989). Identity: fragmentation and recovery in psychoanalytic psychotherapy. *Social Discourse, 2*: 311–319.

Rustin, Margaret (1998). Observation, understanding and interpretation: the story of a supervision. *Journal of Child Psychotherapy, 24*(3): 433–448.

Rustin, Margaret (2000). Dialogues with parents. In: J. Tsiantis, S. B. Boethius, B. Hallerfors, A. Horne, & L. Tischler (Eds.), *Work with Parents. Psychoanalytic Psychotherapy with Children and Adolescents* (pp. 1–23). London: Karnac.

Rustin, Margaret (2009). Work with parents. In: M. Lanyado & A. Horne (Eds.), *The Handbook of Child and Adolescent Psychotherapy. Psychoanalytic Approaches* (pp. 206–219). London: Routledge.

Rustin, Margaret, & Quagliata, E. (Eds.) (2000). *Assessment in Child Psychotherapy*. London: Duckworth.

Rustin, Michael (2009). What do child psychotherapists know? In: N. Midgley, J. Anderson, E. Grainger, T. Nesic-Vuckovic, & C. Urwin (Eds.), *Child Psychotherapy and Research* (pp. 35–49). London: Routledge.

Rutter, M. (2002). Maternal deprivation. In: M. H. Bornstein (Eds.), *Handbook of Parenting, Second Edition, Volume 4, Social Conditions and Applied Parenting* (pp. 181–202). London: Lawrence Erlbaum.

Rutter, M. (2005). CAMHS Research Priorities. Talk given at the first National CAMHS Conference, Birmingham.

Ryan, V., & Needham, C. (2001). Non-directive play therapy with children experiencing psychic trauma. *Clinical Child Psychology and Psychiatry, 6*(3): 437–453.

Sachs, B. (2009). *Family-centered Treatment with Struggling Young Adults: A Clinician's Guide to the Transformation from Adolescence to Autonomy.* New York: Guilford Press.

Sandell, A. (1997). Om tonårspsykoanalys—en introduktion till historiska och aktuella psykoanalytiska aspekter på adolescensen. Om psykoanalys för barn och ungdomar. *Svenska psykoanalytiska föreningens skriftserie, 1*: 20–29.

Sandler, A.-M., & Sandler, J. (1998). *Internal Objects Revisited.* London: Karnac.

Sandler, J. (1976). Countertransference and role-responsiveness. *International Review of Psycho-Analysis, 3*: 43–47.

Sandler, J., Kennedy, H., & Tyson, R. L. (1980). *The Technique of Child Psychoanalysis. Discussions with Anna Freud.* Cambridge, MA: Harvard University Press.

Schachter, A. (2004). The adult outcome of child psychoanalysis: a long-term follow-up study. PhD dissertation, University of London.

Schachter, A., & Target, M. (2009). The adult outcome of child psychoanalysis: the Anna Freud Centre long-term follow-up study. In: N. Midgley, J. Anderson, E. Grainger, T. Nesic-Vuckovic, & C. Urwin (Eds.), *Child Psychotherapy and Research: New Approaches, Emerging Findings* (pp. 144–156). London: Routledge.

Schaefer, C., Cormick, J., & Ohnogi, A. (Eds.) (2010). *International Handbook of Play Therapy: Advances in Assessment, Theory, Research and Practice.* New York: Jason Aronson.

Searles, H. F. (1975). Countertransference and theoretical model. *Psychotherapy of Schizophrenia*, 223–228 [reprinted in: *Countertransference and Related Subjects* (pp. 373–379). Madison-Connecticut: International Universities Press, 1979].

Segal, H. (1957). Notes on symbol formation. *International Journal of Psychoanalysis, 38*: 391–397 [reprinted in: *The Work of Hanna Segal. A Kleinian Approach to Clinical Practice: Delusion and Artistic Creativity & other Psycho-Analytic Essays* (pp. 49–65). London: Karnac, 1986].

Segal, H. (1977). Countertransference. *International Journal of Psychoanalytic Psychotherapy, 6*: 31–37 [reprinted in: *The Work of Hanna Segal. A Kleinian Approach to Clinical Practice: Delusions and Artistic Creativity & Other Psychoanalytic Essays* (pp. 81–87). London: Free Association Books, 1986].

Segal, H. (1979). *Klein.* Glasgow: Fontana/Collins.

Segal, H. (1992). *Melanie Klein*. London: Sage.

Shakow, D., Hilgard, E. R., Kelly, E. L., Luchey, B., Sanford, R. N., & Shaffer, L. F. (1947). Recommended Graduate Training Program in Clinical Psychology. *American Psychologist, 2*: 539–558.

Silverman, M. A. (2004). Insecurity and fear of attachment in a troubled adoption. A clinical example. *Journal of Infant, Child, and Adolescent Psychotherapy, 3*(3): 313–328.

Siskind, D. (1997). *Working with Parents. Establishing the Essential Alliance in Child Psychotherapy and Consultation*. Northvale, NJ: Jason Aronson.

Skowron, E., & Reinemann, D. (2005). Effectiveness of psychological interventions for child maltreatment: a meta-analysis. *Psychotherapy: Theory, Research, Practice, Training, 42*(1): 52–71.

Slijper, F. M. E. (2008). Treatment in practice. In: A. J. E. Verheugt-Pleiter, J. Zevalkink, & M. G. J. Schmeets (Eds.), *Mentalizing in Child Therapy. Guidelines for Clinical Practitioners* (pp. 179–192). London: Karnac.

Smith, H. F. (1990). Cues: the perceptual edge of the transference. *International Journal of Psychoanalysis, 71*(2): 219–228.

Smith, J. A., Flowers, P., & Larkin, M. (2009). *Interpretative Phenomenological Analysis – Theory, Method, and Research*. London: Sage [reprinted 2010].

Spillius, E. B. (1994). Developments in Kleinian thought: overview and personal view. *Psychoanalytic Inquiry, 14*(3): 324–364.

Spillius, E. B. (2001). Freud and Klein on the concept of phantasy. In: C. Bronstein (Ed.), *Kleinian Theory: A Contemporary Perspective* (pp. 17–31). London: Whurr.

Spillius, E. B. (2007). In Melanie Klein's archive. In: P. Roth & R. Rusbridger (Eds.), *Encounters with Melanie Klein. Selected Papers of Elisabeth Spillius* (pp. 63–126). London: Routledge.

Spillius, E. B., Milton, J., Garvey, P., Couve, C., & Steiner, D. (2011). *The New Dictionary of Kleinian Thought*. London: Routledge.

Stapley, E., Target, M., & Midgley, N. (2016). Experience of being the parent of an adolescent with a diagnosis of depression. *Journal of Child and Family Studies, 25*(2): 618–630.

Steiner, J. (1993). *Psychic Retreats: Pathological Organizations in Psychotic, Neurotic, and Borderline Patients*. London: Routledge.

Stern, D. (1985). *The Interpersonal World of the Infant*. New York: Basic Books [reprinted London: Karnac, 1998].

Stern, D. (1995). *The Motherhood Constellation*. New York: Basic Books.

Sussman, D. (2001). Finding a safe place: a four-year-old child's recovery from sexual abuse. In: M. Rustin, M. Rhode, A. Dubinsky, & H. Dubinsky (Eds.), *Psychotic States in Children* (pp. 39–55). London: Karnac.

Szapocznik, J., Murray, E., Scopetta, M., Hervis, O., Rio, A., Cohen, R., Rivas-Vazquez, A., Posada, V., & Kurtines, W. (1989). Structural family versus psychodynamic child therapy for problematic Hispanic boys. *Journal of Consulting and Clinical Psychology, 57*(5): 571–578.

Target, M., & Fonagy, P. (2002). Anna Freud Centre studies 3: the long-term follow-up of child analytic treatments (AFC3). In: P. Fonagy (Ed.), *An Open Door Review of Outcome Studies in Psychoanalysis* (2nd edn) (pp. 141–146). London: International Psychoanalytic Society.

Target, M., Fonagy, P., & Shmueli-Goetz, Y. (2003). Attachment representations in school age children: the development of the child attachment interview (CAD). *Journal of Child Psychotherapy, 29*(2): 171–186.

Terr, L. C. (1991). Childhood traumas: an outline and overview. *American Journal of Psychiatry, 148*(1): 10–20 [reprinted in: *Focus, 1*(3): 322–334].

Terr, L. C., McDermott, J. F., Benson, R. M., Blos, P. Jr., Deeney, J., Rogers, R. R., & Zrull, J. P. (2005). Moments in psychotherapy. *Journal of the American Academy of Child & Adolescent Psychiatry, 44*(2): 191–197.

Thomson-Salo, F. (2004). Walking in the lost child's tracks: revisiting the therapeutic nature of reclaiming. *Journal of Child Psychotherapy, 30*(2): 207–223.

Tonnesmann, M. (1980). Adolescent re-enactment, trauma and reconstruction. *Journal of Child Psychotherapy, 6*: 23–44.

Traux, C., & Wittmer, J. (1973). The degree of therapist's focus on defence mechanisms and the effect on therapeutic outcome with institutionalized juvenile delinquents. *Journal of Community Psychology, 1*: 201–203.

Trowell, J., Joffe, I., Campbell, J., Clemente, C., Almqvist, F., Soininen, M., Koskenranta-Aalto, U., Weintraub, S., Kolaitis, G., Tomaras, V., Anastasopoulos, D., Grayson, K., Barnews, J., & Tsiantis, J. (2007). Childhood depression: a place for psychotherapy. An outcome study comparing individual psychodynamic psychotherapy and family therapy. *European Child and Adolescent Psychiatry, 16*(3): 157–167.

Trowell, J., Kolvin, I., Weeramanthri, T., Sadowski, H. Berelowitz, M., Glasser, D., & Leitch, I. (2002). Psychotherapy for sexually abused girls: psychopathological outcome findings and patterns of change. *British Journal of Psychiatry, 180*: 234–247.

Trowell, J., Rhode, M., & Joffe, I. (2009). Childhood depression: an outcome research project. In: N. Midgley, J. Anderson, E. Grainger, T. Nesic-Vuckovic, & C. Urwin (Eds.), *Child Psychotherapy and Research* (pp. 129–143). London: Routledge.

Tsiantis, J. & Trowell, J. (Eds.) (2011). *Assessing Change in Psychoanalytic Psychotherapy of Children and Adolescents: Today's Challenge.* EFPP Monograph. London: Karnac.

Tsiantis, J., Boëthius, S. B., Hallerfors, B., Horne, A., & Tischler, L. (Eds.) (2000). *Work with Parents. Psychoanalytic Psychotherapy with Children and Adolescents.* London: Karnac.

Tustin, F. (1966). A significant element in the development of autism: a psycho-analytic approach. *Journal of Child Psychology and Psychiatry, 7*(1), 53–67 [reprinted as: A significant element in the development of psychogenic autism. In: K. Barrows (Ed.), *Autism in Childhood and Autistic Features in Adults. A Psychoanalytic Perspective* (pp. 39–62). London: Karnac, 2008].

Van Ee, E., Kleber, R. J., & Jongmans, M. J. (2016). Relational patterns between caregivers with PTSD and their nonexposed children: a review. *Trauma, Violence, & Abuse, 17*(2): 186–203.

Verheugt-Pleiter, A. J. E., Zevalkink, J., & Schmeets, M. G. J. (Eds.) (2008). *Mentalizing in Child Therapy. Guidelines for Clinical Practitioners.* London: Karnac.

Vilsvik, S. O., & Vaglum, P. (1990). Teenage anorexia nervosa: a 1–9-year follow-up after psychodynamic treatment. *Nordisk Psykatrisk Tidssskrift, 44*: 249–255.

Watson, A. (1990). The blossom tree and the number 4: some ideas about thought disorder in an adopted, diabetic boy. *Journal of Child Psychotherapy, 16*(2): 99–110.

Watzlawick, P., Beavin, J., & Jackson, D. (1967). *Pragmatics of Human Communication.* New York: W. W. Norton.

Windaus, E. (2006). The position and outcome of research in Europe in child and adolescence section. Paper presented at the research workshop at the 5th EFPP conference of the Child and Adolescent Section, Berlin, Germany, 10–12 November.

Winnicott, D. W. (1955). The depressive position in normal development. *British Journal of Medical Psychology, 28*(2-3): 89–100 [reprinted in: *Collected Papers: Through Paediatrics to Psycho-Analysis* (pp. 262–277). London: Hogarth, 1975].

Winnicott, D. W. (1968). Playing: its theoretical status in the clinical situation. *International Journal of Psychoanalysis, 49*: 591–599 [reprinted in: *Playing and Reality* (pp. 38–52). Harmondsworth: Penguin, 1971].

Winnicott, D. W. (1971a). *Playing and Reality.* London: Tavistock [reprinted London: Routledge, 2005].

Winnicott, D. W. (1971b). *Therapeutic Consultations in Child Psychiatry.* London: Hogarth.

Winnicott, D. W. (1977). *The Piggle: An account of the Psychoanalytic Treatment of a Little Girl*. London: Hogarth.

World Health Organization (1992). *The ICD-10 Classification of Mental and Behavioural Disorders. Clinical Descriptions and Diagnostic Guidelines*. Geneva: World Health Organization.

Wrangsjö, B., & Salomonsson, M. W. (2007). *Tonårstid. Utveckling, Problem och Psykoterapeutisk Behandling*. Stockholm: Natur & Kultur.

Young-Bruehl, E. (1989). *Anna Freud. A Biography*. London: Macmillan.

Yule, W., Bolton, D., Udwin, O., Boyle, S., O'Ryan, D., & Nurrish, J. (2000). The long-term psychological effects of a disaster experienced in adolescence: the incidence and course of PTSD. *Journal of Child Psychology and Psychiatry, 41*(4): 503–511.

Zeanah, C. H., & Boris, N. W. (2000). Disturbances and disorders of attachment in early childhood. In: C. H. Zeanah (Ed.), *Handbook of Infant Mental Health: Second Edition* (pp. 353–368). New York: Guilford Press.

Zeanah, C. H., & Gleason, M. M. (2010). *Reactive Attachment Disorder: A Review for DSM-V*. Report presented to the American Psychiatric Association.

ZERO TO THREE (2005). *Diagnostic Classification of Mental Health and Developmental Disorders of Infancy and Early Childhood, Revised (DC:0–3R)*. Washington, DC: ZERO TO THREE Press.

INDEX